Glory Days, they pass you by,
Glory Days, in the wink of a young man's eye,
Glory Days,
Glory Days,
Glory Days.

Bruce Springsteen

Glory Days

The Golden Age of Bishop Auckland

ALAN ADAMTHWAITE

**With a Foreword by Lawrie McMenemy
and an Introduction by Sir Bobby Robson**

The Parrs Wood Press
Manchester

First Published 2005

THE PARRS WOOD PRESS
St Wilfrid's Enterprise Centre
Royce Road, Manchester, M15 5BJ
www.parrswoodpress.com

© Alan Adamthwaite 2005

ISBN: 1 903158

Printed and bound by the Guttenberg Press in Malta

**This book is dedicated to the best friend that I ever had,
George William Adamthwaite, my dad.**

Oh, wherefore come ye forth in triumph from the north?

Macauley

5

COPYRIGHT

Every effort has been made to establish copyright ownership of photographs and other relevant material within this book. Unfortunately, because of the many company closures and mergers within the photographic and newspaper industries that have taken place over the last sixty years or so, it has proved impossible to trace the copyright owner in some cases. Where copyright has been ascertained, an appropriate acknowledgement has been posted.

The development of the World Wide Web and the Internet in recent years has resulted in many institutions updating records and forming databases, a consequence being that much unwanted material and information - text as well as photographic - has been destroyed.

If anyone believes that their copyright has been infringed, then the author will be pleased to rectify the matter at the earliest opportunity and in any future editions of this book.

Special thanks to: *The Northern Echo* newspaper, *The Newcastle Chronicle* and *Journal* newspapers, *The Middlesbrough Evening Gazette*, Scunthorpe United Football Club and, of course, Bishop Auckland Football Club.

CONTENTS

FOREWORD

by Lawrie McMenemy

Many things have changed, on and off the pitch, over the last fifty years… some for the better. The formation of the Premiership has divided the traditional ninety-two professional clubs into the 'haves' and 'have-nots'. Satellite TV not only brings the English game into living rooms all around the world, but massive amounts of money into the top clubs and the pockets of the elite players and their agents.

Footballers with unpronounceable names arrive from all parts of the globe, and even the referees are full-time professionals with sponsors' names on their shirts.

Some things, thankfully, never change… mainly the passionate support of the fans for their clubs, who go to great efforts to raise the funds to follow their heroes and have the hunger to know the results and read match reports if they cannot get to the game.

Alan Adamthwaite reflects all of this here as he relates his own story, following his beloved 'Bishops' - seeing them play in three Wembley Cup Finals before he was ten years old - and he also reminds us of some of the great professional players from days gone by.

He talks of times when we all went to the game on the bus and could be sitting next to one of the players, stars of Cup Finals at Wembley and watched by crowds of 100,000, who went to work on the Monday down the mine or in the steelworks alongside the fans.

Mainly, this is a detailed record of six of the eighteen Cup Finals which the 'Two Blues' took part in (they won a record ten Amateur Cup Finals in all). The highs and lows, which anyone who ever attended a match will appreciate, are re-lived - a look at football through the eyes of a typical supporter.

This is a labour of love from one who loves the beautiful game.

Congratulations, and thank you, Alan.

Lawrie McMenemy
(Another fan)

INTRODUCTION

by Sir Bobby Robson

In the 1950s, the name of Bishop Auckland Football Club was known by everyone in the land, mainly due to their regular Wembley appearances in the Amateur Cup Finals - a competition that, sadly, no longer exists. They did not always win, of course, but it seemed that they did.

Bishop Auckland was already a successful club, having won the Amateur Cup on several occasions previously, but during those post-World War II years their success seemed to be boundless. Between 1946 and 1957, the period that this book covers, the club appeared in seven Amateur Cup Finals, six of them at Wembley. Of the Wembley finals, they lost the first three but atoned to their fans by successfully winning the last three in successive years. They also managed to find time to win the Northern League Championship seven times, finishing runners-up three times and a disappointing third in season 1956-57.

Alan Adamthwaite has traced ex-players of the club whose personal anecdotes and reminiscences help cast a light on how the amateur game of football was played some fifty years ago. The names of Harry Sharratt, Corbett Cresswell and the legendary Bobby Hardisty frequent the pages, as well as profiles of other leading members of the club such as Warren Bradley, Jimmy Nimmins, Ray Oliver, Dave Marshall and Derek Lewin.

The club's achievements are told through the eyes of Alan as a young lad, brought up in the harsh reality of the Durham coalfields, who moved to the Midlands at the age of seven when his father sought employment as a result of the coal mining industry falling into decline in the North-East.

Having been born and bred in the North-East of England, I share his enthusiasm for the region's football and love of the amateur game. I remember well the enormous passion those games aroused and the attendances that they drew - each community following their local team in their thousands, hard as that is to imagine today.

I am proud and privileged to have been part of that scene and welcome the opportunity to write these few words of introduction to a book which gives the reader the opportunity to re-live, or perhaps experience for the first time, what it was like to follow The Bishops in those heady days; a time when amateur footballers played a much larger part in the game than they do today.

Glory Days

Written with a great degree of humour, the book includes all of the important football matches as well as such controversial issues as the Billy Russell Affair, Seamus O'Connell's omission from an important semi-final tie and a full account of what became known as the John Barnwell Affair.

Enjoy, and re-live the glory!

Sir Bobby Robson

PART ONE

Sunday 22nd April 1951

I stood on the middle rail of the three-bar wooden fence, my skinny knees pressed firm against the top rail to help give me balance. My arms waved wildly in the direction of the engine driver, and the hundreds of passengers, as the train billowed steam, straining to make the last mile of its journey, up past Greenhead, to the end of the line at Crook station.

Every so often I would climb down and run up the lane to the level-crossing, about two hundred yards from our rented cottage, to get a closer look at the passengers, to see if I could see him. Weary faces craned out of the sash-cord windows, eager to depart and relate their experiences.

All morning, trains had been arriving back in the North-East of England, bringing, once again, disappointed Bishop Auckland football supporters back home. They were returning from somewhere called Wembley.

I had probably been waiting about an hour, but it seemed like days. Time, as it always would in life, moved slowly for me.

The sun shone bright on this spring morning. Mum was in the kitchen, baking cakes and apple pie for tea.

I wish he would hurry up.

I was four years old and I was waiting for the man who forever would be my best friend... my dad.

WARM UP

In the pink

I have always loved football. Coming from the North-East of England that is hardly surprising. I was brought up listening to tales of George Camsell, George Hardwick, the Robledo brothers, Jackie Milburn, Hughie Gallacher, Raich Carter and Len Shackleton to name but a few. My only regret is that I never became good enough to play the game myself at a high level.

Every Saturday night, Dad and me would wait for the *Sports Despatch*, known to everyone as 'The Pink', getting on Mum's nerves with our impatience. That sports paper was like receiving news from Olympus. I can recall now how every match report was meticulously read and can still see in my mind's eye the distinctive font style in which the results were listed. We always looked for Bishop Auckland's result first and then we would catch up on the news from St James' Park to read how the Magpies had got on. Football League games involving local teams were covered, but it was mainly the Northern League matches that grabbed our attention. How had Bishop got on? Who scored? Who got injured? What about Crook? It was all in there. No other paper came close to 'The Pink'... *The Sunday Graphic*, *The Empire News*, *The Sunday Pictorial*, sadly all no longer with us, carried match reports, but looking back, nothing could compare to the intimacy of 'The Pink'.

Even after we had moved down to the Midlands, my granddad would send us his copy, so that the postman was always a welcome Wednesday morning visitor. It did not matter that we already knew the results, reading the match reports was the important thing, especially if there was news of injured players. Oh how I wish that we had kept those copies.

It was a bit of a shock moving to Stoke-on-Trent; after all, their football team was only in Division Two whereas Newcastle United and Sunderland were in the First Division. Even the Northern League was better than Division Two in my eyes. That is not to say that we didn't see some good games. I saw Tim Coleman score all seven goals for 'The Potters' against Lincoln City, and one foggy day Aston Villa went there for a cup match.

Then there was Port Vale. Try looking for it on the map... no chance. Port Vale does not exist, a bit like Total Network Solutions, there being no such place. Okay, let's make things a bit easier; try looking for Burslem. Still not there? Find Stoke-on-Trent. There, that's easy. Now look for Hanley, it's right in the middle of Stoke. Immediately above Hanley is Burslem and that is where The Vale play their games. They used to play right in the centre of Hanley, where the Potteries Shopping Centre is now, but they moved out to sunny Burslem in 1953. They had just gained promotion in the 1953-54 season having run away with the Third Division North title. They had also become only the third Third Division team (at that time) to reach the semi-finals of the FA Cup, losing out to a penalty 2-1 against West Bromwich Albion at Villa Park.

Dad and I would go to the football match on Saturday afternoons, Stoke one week Vale the other, whilst Mum went around Hanley shopping. After the game we would catch the football special bus into Hanley and meet mum outside Lewis's Arcade. We would have our teas in the Arcade or at Littlewoods and then go on to the Theatre Royal, depending who was on… The Beverley Sisters, Arthur Worsley (great ventriloquist), Hylda Baker and Sabrina, Ted Lune, Nat Jackley, Norman Evans, Jimmy James and Eli (Eli Woods was the funniest stooge man in the world)…we saw them all.

It was at Vale Park that I saw John Charles playing for Leeds United; I think that he played centre-half in the first half, but with the score 0-0, he went as centre-forward in the second. Despite his efforts, the score remained goalless. Other notable players I recall from that time were the two Middlesbrough 'foreigners', Ronaldo Ugolini (the goalie) and Walter Delapenha, the coloured forward. Wonderful names, wonderful players.

I remember Middlesbrough coming to Stoke for a Second Division match, probably about 1958, and playing for the Teesside team was a certain Brian Clough… he got a hat-trick in twelve minutes as Middlesbrough romped to a 5-2 win.

Wherever a ball was being kicked I wanted to be there. I've always been the same. I had my North-Eastern roots, of course, and Bishop Auckland and Newcastle United were my teams, but I always took an interest in local teams. In my teenage years I became more adventurous and would travel to other football grounds, if not with dad, then with a few of my mates. When I was about thirteen I remember going on my own on a football special to see Port Vale play away at Scunthorpe in an FA Cup game. Stoke station should have given me a discount, the hours that I spent waiting on the platform for trains to Derby, Wolverhampton, Blackburn, Manchester or wherever.

Manchester United was a particular good place to go to in the Sixties. The likes of Paddy Crerand, Nobby Stiles and Harry Gregg were wonderful players. But the Holy Trinity of Law, Best and Charlton were supreme (You are not going to get any of that imitation jealousy from me that seems so fashionable these days from the anti-Manchester United brigade).

In the pink

They were a fantastic side and played outstanding football. Bobby Charlton had an explosive shot and George Best was, for me, the best player in the world ever, but my favourite had to be Denis Law. Mercurial is an adjective that would best describe him. There was more meat on Lester Piggott's whip than there was on Denis Law but by God he could take the knocks and play some. His overhead kicks were his trademark and indeed he was the first player that I ever saw attempt them. More often than not he would actually connect with the ball and I was there when he scored from such an effort against Tottenham Hotspur. Sadly, the referee had spotted an infringement and the goal was disallowed. The referee ambled over to help Law to his feet and apologised for his decision. It is not recorded what Denis's response was.

I was also fortunate enough to be at Old Trafford on 7th December 1963, when, in his last game before serving a suspension, Denis Law entertained the crowd to an unbelievable one-man show. A couple of weeks earlier he had taken a bit of rough treatment throughout a game at Villa Park, most of it meted out by the Aston Villa defender Alan Deakin. It was inevitable that the fiery Scot would lose his rag at some stage and, of course, it happened. Deakin did a sliding tackle on Law - a two-footed tackle in the Scotsman's view - and he responded by gesturing to whack Deakin as he lay on the ground. Referee Jim Carr took this as violent conduct and sent him off for an early bath. Suspension was inevitable. Unfortunately for Stoke, Law took the frustration of his enforced 'holiday' out on them. He scored four and hit the crossbar twice in United's 5-2 win. He was absolutely brilliant that day and was probably playing the best football of his career all that season.

By now, of course, Stoke were in Division One and with the help of some astute signings of older players... Alex Elder, Eddie Clamp, Jimmy McIlroy, Dennis Viollett, Roy Vernon, George Eastham, Peter Dobing and, incredibly, Stanley Matthews... were serving up some decent football, for which a lot of praise should go to the manager Tony Waddington. He did a sterling job in keeping Stoke City in the First Division for as long as he did.

FA Cup semi-final disappointments against Arsenal (twice) in consecutive seasons, were tempered with the League Cup success over Chelsea at Wembley in 1972... the club's first ever cup success in over one hundred years. This was the era of probably Stoke's best team, but as I was getting older my employment ambitions were expanding and marriage, alongside newfound family responsibilities, resulted in football taking a back seat. Don't get me wrong, I still followed the game and each Sunday morning I would seek out the Northern League, and later the Drybrough League, results for my beloved Bishop Auckland, but work had, by necessity, become the major priority in my life, especially as I now had a wife and two children to support.

My employment as a Local Government Officer took me to Wrexham and sometimes I would go and watch them. International games were also frequently held at The Racecourse Ground and on one occasion Wales played Austria, I think it was a European qualifying game. It wasn't a particularly good match but it was full of interest, due mainly to the somewhat eccentric refereeing decisions by the official in charge. At one point he awarded Austria a corner when the ball had clearly gone out off an Austrian forward's boot for a throw-in! This brought a torrent of abuse - have you ever heard abuse in Welsh? - and a plastic cup was thrown to hit the unfortunate referee on the head. For a moment in time the world was devoid of all sound, there was absolute silence. You really could have heard the proverbial pin drop. The silence was broken by a booming Welsh voice; 'It should have been a fucking anvil.' The epithet was heard by all of the 20,000 crowd and picked up by the BBC outside broadcast team. Barry Davies must have been apoplectic.

Round about this time, a work colleague gave me the opportunity to go to Goodison Park to see Everton play Southampton in a Division One match. He and his wife held season tickets but for some reason she could not go so I went in her place. The rather officious gateman had the temerity to enquire if I really was Mrs Timmins! Before I could think of a suitable response, the fellow behind me, who had heard the inquisitor, shouted up, 'Of course he's Mrs Bloody Timmins… show him yer tits luv!' There really was no answer to that and not wishing to be embroiled in further discussion, the gateman let me through.

Everton scored eight that day against hapless Southampton. Eight! Yes, eight! But the incident I remember most from that game was not about any of the goals or scorers. It happened as Gordon West, the Everton goalkeeper - who, let's face it, wasn't having a particularly difficult match as all of the action was taking place at the other end of the pitch - was confronted with the sight of a home supporter offering him a cup of tea. West gratefully accepted the offering and spent the next few minutes sipping away and leaning against a goalpost as he watched the game continue as if with not a care in the world. I was instantly reminded of an incident that had taken place almost twenty years earlier when the best goalkeeper that ever put on a green jersey, Harry Sharratt, accepted a hot drink from an appreciative supporter in a Bishop Auckland game against Evenwood Town. Funny I should remember that and not the goals.

Even though such a scoreline belonged to the realms of fantasy and *Roy of the Rovers*, and obviously the game had been a joy to watch, the intimidating atmosphere that was pervading football matches at the time was marring my pleasure in actually attending games. This was the time of the skinheads and gang warfare at football grounds. Even at Wrexham, who only attracted crowds of about 3,000, you would see gangs of yobs waiting outside the railway station which is adjacent to the ground, ready to cause whatever mischief they could towards opposing fans. The hostile atmosphere and inherent problems drove many people away from football grounds, me included. My love for the game itself remained, but the enjoyment of attending was on the wane.

In 1975 my employment took me to Tamworth, about fifteen miles north of Birmingham, and I used to go and see them play, interspersed with visits to Villa Park and St. Andrew's. Surprisingly, I must have brought some good luck with me for the local team, as one year they got to Wembley and won the FA Vase Trophy, beating the East Anglian team Sutton United after a replay.

Wembley seemed to be the venue that I frequented most in the Seventies. The League Cup Final was a regular event that I attended, as tickets were easier to acquire than for the 'proper' cup final. One such encounter concerned Manchester City against Newcastle, so you can guess whom I wanted to win. The Magpies had a decent team then and I was sure that 'Supermac' Malcolm Macdonald would have a field day against the fragile City defence. How wrong can you be? I got more kicks from the bloke sitting next to me than he got. Tueart scored with an outrageously lucky - oh yes it was! - overhead kick and that was that.

It was about this time also that I was lucky enough to see Brazil for the first and only time. Joe Corrigan was in the England goal… nuff said. Brazil had Rivelino and Jairzinho in their line-up, but really they were a bit disappointing. The result was a 1-1 draw.

A constant companion with me to most of these games, at least after I had moved to Tamworth, was Keith Williscroft. Imagine that splendid actor James Robertson Justice or Keith Michelle as Henry VIII and you have the exact image of Keith. Now, to say that he enjoyed a laugh would be a gross understatement. If fun and joy did not exist then he would have invented them himself. One day I received a telephone call from my old boss in Wrexham saying that he was retiring and would I like to come over to attend his farewell party.

The day of the retirement party, which was scheduled for the afternoon, coincided with an international match at The Racecourse Ground, which would kick-off at 7:30pm. Keith came along for the ride and the opportunity of some free booze, as I would be doing the driving.

The farewell party went off very well and eventually we made our exits and walked up to the football ground. It wasn't a classic match, Wales and Scotland producing a 0-0 draw. As I started to drive out of Wrexham, Keith said that he fancied a drink. How could he? Hell's bells, he'd been drinking all afternoon. Anyway, I told him that I knew of a pub on the road back that we would stop at, only about five minutes away.

For some reason best known to himself, he then put on an act pretending to have a stammer. Now, I think that I should tell you that until I was about nineteen years old I had a stammer… a real one. It was therefore easy for me to talk back to him in similar fashion. This went on until we reached the pub.

'We can't go in talking like this,' I said.

'W-w-why n-n-n-not?'

'Don't be so bloody stupid. Stop it.'

'Come on, l-l-let's have a l-l-laugh, let's b-b-b-both d-d-do it.'

There was no persuading him otherwise; he wanted to continue in this mode.

I do not know why, but I relented and as we got to the bar I said to the barman, 'C-c-c-could w-w-we have two p-p-p-pints of b-b-b-bitter, p-p-please?'

To which the response was 'C-c-certainly s-s-sir, B-B-Brew XI or P-P-P-Pedigree?'

I stood there in horror at his misfortune and turned towards Williscroft. He wasn't there. All that I could see was the door to the gents' toilet swinging to close. I ran into the gents' and there was Williscroft bent double with tears streaming down his face as he laughed uncontrollably.

'Of all the pubs in Wales we had to pick this one. I think I'm going to piss myself,' he said.

'B-b-b-bloody good,' I replied mockingly.

Eventually, the hooligan element was diminished at football grounds and fans started to return. Family enclosures were set up at many stadiums and once more it was relatively safe to attend a football match. I would be one of the returning hordes. I had been fortunate over the years in as much that I had never been physically involved in any trouble. Not so my brother, who some years earlier had been set upon by some Manchester United fans for no bigger crime than wearing a different team's scarf.

Jacqueline and I moved to a beautiful part of Staffordshire in 1990, purchasing a bungalow on the edge of Cannock Chase, a delightful area of woodland with all varieties of wildlife, including deer. I took early retirement in 1992 and have been as busy as ever…how did I find the time to go to work?

As I said earlier, I have always taken an interest in local football clubs wherever I have lived and would occasionally go to see Hednesford Town. My interest in football, although never extinguished, rekindled and I decided to become a season ticket holder with Wolverhampton Wanderers, as I only live twenty-five minutes by car from the ground. I also wanted the opportunity of seeing David Beckham play. Getting tickets for Manchester United games is always difficult, nigh impossible, so I thought why not get a season ticket for a local team that is outside of the Premier League now, but has the potential of getting there? Hence, I chose Wolves. What happened? Three years later they got promotion to the Premiership... coinciding with Beckham's move to Real Madrid! C'est la vie.

Despite me holding a Wolverhampton Wanderers season ticket, nothing will ever erase my love for football 'North-Eastern' style, and the first results that I always seek out are those of Bishop Auckland, a task made much easier by the help of the internet - no more waiting for the Sunday papers - and the match report on the Bishop Auckland Football Club website, compiled by John Cowey. It was whilst browsing the web site one Sunday that I decided to contact John and, following a brief discussion, agreed to buy some old Amateur Cup Final football programmes from him. Rather than have the items posted, we agreed to meet up at Witton Albion in a couple of weeks' time, where Bishop were due to play their last game of the season.

It was whilst John and I were talking in the car park, when a rather elderly gentleman, clearly a Witton Albion supporter, came up to us and enquired 'Have you brought Bobby Hardisty with you?', a reference to the greatest player ever to don a Bishop Auckland shirt.

In that brief moment, from a statement made in jest by a complete stranger, memories flooded back and has resulted in them being recorded, as accurately as I am able, in the following pages.

I hope that you do not find my writing too distractive and I apologise from the outset if, at times, my ramblings veer off at a tangent...it is just my style, and I hope that you are not disappointed.

By the way: if any of you have additional information or comments that you would like to pass on to me, please feel free to contact me at: 'Kailua-Kona', 21 Coley Grove, Little Haywood, Stafford, ST18 0UW. Telephone: 0789 001 0292.

CHAPTER ONE

Willington: Blue is the colour

Sir Stanley Rous leaned over and commiserated, 'Well played, Bob. That was a most creditable game of football. Both teams put on a super show.' Language and phraseology that belonged to a dying age.

The recipient of those words reflected. It was scant consolation to him that the FA Amateur Cup Final that had just taken place between Bishop Auckland and Willington had produced a feast of quality football, the standard of which had been well above that usually associated with amateur clubs. He was now the holder of a losing finalist's medal. For John Roderick Elliott Hardisty - Bob or Bobby to everyone that knew him - right half-back of the beaten Bishop Auckland side, he would have much preferred to have a winner's medal in his hands, and no fine platitudes from the Secretary of the Football Association were going to ease the disappointment that he felt just now.

It was Saturday April 22nd 1950, and for those few weeks since the finalists were known, there had only been one subject on everyone's lips in the little corner of North-East England where the two clubs were situated, little less than four miles apart, and that subject was the FA Amateur Cup Final. Newcastle United might be doing good business further up the road, but just now, for this part of the world, the Wear Valley held sway over anything that Tyneside had to offer. Butchers, bakers, ironmongers, shops of every description, factories and even one or two schools, decked their walls and windows in the colours of their teams. The forthcoming match captured the imagination of everyone, young and old.

The week leading up to the final saw supporters of both camps setting out for Wembley, not all of whom had had the foresight to book a room in advance at any of the hotels and guest houses that filled north and central London. They would make do as best they could. At first it was just a trickle, but the exodus slowly gathered momentum and by Friday every bus, car and train seemed to have only one destination in mind…Wembley. The private bus companies were on to a winner right from the start with whole fleets being used to cater for the demand, and the LNER laid on hundreds more carriages for their special trains that had been commandeered for the big day. Not many people could afford a car in those days, but those fortunate to have one were carrying friends and families down the A1, so the result was that on that April Saturday, the streets were almost completely devoid of traffic around that part of County Durham.

Supporters were in full voice and almost everyone was seen to be wearing something blue (Willington's usual colours were blue and white striped shirts, navy shorts, whilst those of Bishop were light and dark blue quartered shirts, dark blue shorts).

Wembley seemed like the Promised Land; after all, only teams from the Football League and England internationals got to play there, and getting tickets for those games was never easy. Added to that, of course, was the little matter of a six hundred mile round trip, so it was little wonder that for the vast majority of the 88,000 crowd, this game provided their first opportunity to visit the giant stadium.

It had been a bold decision by the Football Association to allow the Amateur Cup Final to be played at Wembley, and not all members of the committee that constituted the meetings that had taken place had been in favour of the final being staged in such a venerable amphitheatre.

Controversy and innovation, however, was nothing new to the Football Association. Between 1888 and 1890 amateur football remained as popular as ever. However, many of the older amateur players were retiring from the game and the standard of football went into decline, as did public interest. The FA was concerned and many new suggestions were proposed to restore enthusiasm into the amateur game. None met with any success until someone hit upon the idea of the Amateur Cup competition, to be played for nationally.

The then Secretary of the Football Association, Sir Frederick Wall, wholeheartedly approved of the proposal and channelled all of his efforts in bringing the idea to fruition, convinced that the public would restore interest in amateur football. The idea was to prove successful, and yet, when the Amateur Cup was inaugurated in 1893, it did not meet with whole-hearted support, many of the leading amateur clubs of the day resenting the fact that such a competition should come under the control of the Football Association at all. Over the years, rules were changed and the competition came to be governed by an all-amateur committee. One of the basic principles that had been controversial in those early days had been the practice of former professionals being allowed to be reinstated as amateur players. This rule was tightened up and as a result anyone that had played as a professional was ineligible for amateur competitions. Historians may therefore cite the Old Carthusians who were the only team to win the FA Cup and the FA Amateur Cup. They defeated Old Etonians 3-0 in 1881 to win the FA Cup and won the Amateur Cup on two occasions, in 1894, defeating Casuals 2-1, and then three years later they beat Stockton 4-1, after a 1-1 draw, in 1897.

Just another little aside to this subject: R Chatt was the only former professional to secure an FA Amateur Cup medal after gaining a winners' medal in the FA Cup competition. He was a member of the Aston Villa team that beat West Bromwich Albion in the 1895 FA Cup Final and then four years later represented Stockton, gaining a winners' medal in the 1899 final against Harwich and Parkeston.

One of the arguments put forward by the doubters was the fear that few people would attend a final at Wembley in sufficient numbers. League games involving amateur clubs attracted crowds of anywhere between 'three men and a dog' and a few thousand, but cup games, especially those of the Amateur Cup competition, would see crowds increase markedly, with grounds full to capacity on many occasions. The likes of Bromley and Romford could record crowds well in excess of 10,000 or more and Amateur Cup semi-finals frequently drew attendance figures of well over 25,000. But what of Wembley, with its large open spaces and a capacity of 100,000? A crowd of 'only' 25,000 would be lost in it. Some members of the Football Association made their thoughts known... they did not wish to witness a final played in a barely half-full stadium, and wanted to continue with the practice of playing the final on neutral football league grounds as they were always full on Amateur Cup Final days. Their mantra could have been 'What has proven satisfactory in the past is satisfactory for the present and will be satisfactory for the future'.

Incredibly, just one year after the Olympic Games had been held in London with a major portion of events taking place at Wembley, there were some members of the committee who believed that Wembley was no place for amateurs.

Thankfully, the decision to hold the final at Wembley was taken and the men with vision were proved right. The first Wembley Amateur Cup Final took place in 1949 and featured two leading southern rivals in Bromley and Romford, attracting a crowd of over 70,000. Bromley won 1-0. Despite such a large crowd, there were still some sceptics pointing out that the game had been played between two 'local teams' and therefore a large crowd was guaranteed. They needed a little more convincing. Nevertheless, the South had led the way, now it was the North's turn.

Bishop Auckland and Willington were leading lights in the Northern League and although Bishop had the more glamorous history and was a bigger club, Willington had earned the right to be rubbing shoulders with their more illustrious neighbours.

Originally formed in 1890 as Willington Rovers and playing their games in the Auckland and District League, they changed title in 1899 to Willington Rangers. This was short-lived and in 1900 the name of Willington Town

Willington: Blue is the colour

Wednesday was chosen (I haven't a clue why!) until 1903 when they became Brancepeth Colliery Rangers. Then in 1906 they became Willington Temperance, a name that undoubtedly rivals that of Billingham Synthonia in uniqueness and romance. What a name! If ever the naming of a football club evokes visions of men in cloth caps drinking communion wine and reciting John 3:16 after every game, surely it is Willington Temperance. Regrettably, Temperance was dropped when the club was admitted to the Northern League in 1911 and the much less romantic moniker of Willington was adopted. It was also at this time that the club moved to their current premises at Hall Lane.

The club has not been without success and the team of the 1920s must have been a formidable one. The Northern League title was won in 1914, 1926 and 1930, and in addition the Northern League Cup was won in 1925, 1926 (thereby winning the double), 1928, 1931 and 1949.

Willington is classed as a town yet really is just a rather large village, stretching from Lane Ends on the Crook side to Low Willington on the Durham side, and straddles the main arterial route, the A690, from the county capital to Weardale. The River Wear is only a few hundred yards to the south. Old photographs showing the main street were generally taken from the railway bridge, but that bridge has now gone, together with Willington station, a casualty of Dr. Beeching's economy cuts carried out in the 1960s.

Until the 1840s, Willington was just a handful of farm settlements and smallholding cottages with a population of not much more than 250, but once coal was discovered in the area the population grew and over the next sixty years had risen to about 6,000. There were plenty of churches to choose from to look after the righteous and sinful. By 1905 the town could boast a Methodist New Connexion Chapel, a Wesleyan Chapel, a Presbyterian Chapel, a Primitive Methodist Chapel, St. Thomas's Catholic Church and St. Stephen's Church of England... no wonder they called themselves Temperance.

Coalmining became the leading industry with pits, owned by Messrs. Stoker and Love, running throughout the area at Sunnybrow, Oakenshaw and Brancepeth, as well as Willington itself, until the seams became uneconomical in the 1950s - 60s. The Willington Colliery finally closed in 1967. There are no pits there now, and the majority of old pit heaps have been transformed into country parks, but in April 1950, men were working harder and faster than ever to complete their quotas so that they could be quick off the mark to catch the excursions to the final.

One such miner was my dad, although he wasn't employed at any of the Willington pits, the Pease's West pit being situated at Crook. He worked his shift as usual that Friday and after calling home to wash and change, hurried back out again to get the bus to Durham where he caught the train to London. He was a keen Bishop supporter and he was not going to miss their first outing at Wembley.

The teams were used to meeting each other in cup football. In the first season after World War Two they had been drawn together in the first round of the FA Cup. For that season it had been decided to stage each round over two legs, the aggregate score deciding the outcome. Bishop had won 5-0 in the first leg at Hall Lane, then bizarrely lost only seven days later in the second leg at home 2-0, making the aggregate score 5-2. It just goes to show what a funny old game this football can be.

Only three weeks before the final the clubs had fought out a 0-0 draw when contesting the semi-final of the Durham Benevolent Bowl.

Just eleven years previously, the two teams had met each other in the Amateur Cup Final of 1939. Then, like now, Bishop had been firm favourites to win. That match was held at Roker Park, Sunderland and my dad, a lanky lad of thirteen at the time, was among the 25,000 crowd. Only three weeks before, he had travelled alone by bus to Darlington to watch Bishop beat Leytonstone 2-1 in a replayed semi-final, Bishop winning after extra-time. You could do that then. Nowadays you wouldn't let your children go half a mile without worrying yourself sick about them getting back all right. He used to tell me that the 1939 final was the first game that he had ever seen anyone score a hat-trick, Laurie Wensley netting three times in extra-time for Bishop to record a 3-0 win.

In that successful Bishop Auckland side was a certain Bob Paisley, who in later years would go down as one of the greatest football managers of all time with his numerous successes managing Liverpool.

Another member of that 1939 winning team was Harry Young, who played outside-left. He had joined the 'Two-Blues' in 1936. I met up with Harry in May 2004 and a more sprightly 86-year-old you have never met. He gives a fascinating insight to the way things were in that period:

'With two Northern teams in the final, it was arranged for the final to be held at Sunderland. I think it was the third Saturday in April. We got there by Rolls-Royce, laid on by the club...not a Rolls-Royce each mind, just the one for all of us that needed it. There was about seven of us in it...ample room. It was the type that the Royal Family had. There weren't many cars about in those days, let alone Rolls-Royces. At the time, my hometown club, Newcastle United, signed me as an amateur. So long as you had only signed amateur forms then it was all right to play for another club. Newcastle had three clubs going at the time - the first team, the reserves and the 'A' team. Any professional that had been injured invariably came

back through playing in the reserves or 'A' team first. As I was only on amateur forms it was me who would have to make way for the professional to make his comeback. Training for us 'A' team players was held on Tuesday and Thursday nights. It used to happen quite often that I would be selected for Saturday's game on the Tuesday night, only for a professional to return and take my place. Still, never mind, that's the way it was.

'Andy McCrombie of Newcastle recommended me to Bishop Auckland and I played my first game for them at the age of eighteen. It was against Ferryhill Athletic. I never dreamt that just three years later I would be appearing in an Amateur Cup Final and gain a winners' medal. My brother has the medal now. You had to qualify to play in the cup, which meant that you had to be registered with the club for seven days and you had to have played at least one league game before being eligible for the cup tie. The Ferryhill game was my qualifying match.

'Mind you, we didn't travel by Rolls-Royce then. I had to go by bus from Newcastle to Bishop or whatever game was taking place. Bus fare was 3/3d (17p). It was a bind for a young lad like me, eighteen years old, as it would be gone half-past eight at night before I got home, and I liked to knock about with my mates on a Saturday night. After every home match some of the players would walk over to Gregory's Café in Newgate Street and have pie and chips and a cup of tea and then I would catch the bus from the market square to Newcastle.

'We used to travel sometimes to away games in the Rolls-Royce - just the one, remember - and as I said, it could fit seven or eight of us in comfortably. We used to play Whitby away on the opening game of the season, and many is the time when we would be held up by the volume of traffic and have to strip off in the car and be ready to run off straight on to the pitch. The Rolls would pick me up in Newcastle then go on to Sunderland train station where we would pick up Jack Washington, the goalkeeper, and Billy Evans, the inside-left - he was an insurance man - at the end of the taxi rank.

'I worked as a printer for the newspapers and of course there was no such thing as a five-day week then. We had to work on a Saturday morning and then I would have to make it to the pick-up point, or if it was a home game, run for the bus to get to Bishop on time for the three o'clock kick-off. The Kingsway ground at Bishop might have a slope but the playing surface was the best anywhere. It was like a bowling green and was wonderful to play football on.

'As I said, we travelled by Rolls-Royce to the 1939 final, picking up players on the way. Laurie Wensley got the goals in extra-time. One of

the goals was scored after a Willington player thought that there had been a foul and handled the ball. The referee gave a free kick that was taken quickly and Lawrie scored. Three or four minutes later he hit the bar with a header and followed up to score with the rebound. Near the end, when everybody had run themselves into the ground, Lawrie went on a run and scored his third. We won 3-0. After that we still had about seven or eight league matches to play as the cup run had taken all of the time up. It seemed like everyday we had a game. Anyway, we won the title when we beat Stockton. A few days later we won the County Cup beating South Shields, who were a professional outfit mind, 2-1, again at Sunderland.'

(The war years curtailed Harry's career, as it did many others, and he gallantly served his country in North Africa, Palestine and was at Anzio. A leg injury meant that his football days were over and he resumed his employment in the printing trade, working for *The Northern Echo* in Darlington until he retired. He lives in Bishop Auckland).

Now, eleven years later, these two Northern League rivals were to grace the hallowed turf of Wembley Stadium.

Bishop had reached the final by beating fellow Northern League opponents South Bank 2-0 away from home in Round One. In a fast and lively game, only a brilliant display of goalkeeping by the home team's McDonnell prevented further goals to those by Davison (a first-half penalty) and Hardisty.

Ilford were visitors for the second round tie at Kingsway. The Isthmian League outfit had suffered a scare in the opening round, only defeating minor league Tilbury away after a drawn encounter on Ilford's home pitch. It was well known that the Isthmian League was a strong one, housing such leading clubs as Leytonstone, Walthamstow Avenue, Dulwich Hamlet and Romford as well as today's visitors. Ilford were fourth from bottom in their league and had won only four games of the sixteen played: they had drawn three but it would be unwise for Bishop to underestimate them.

Bishop Auckland supporters were hoping to have another view of Harry McIlvenny, who had made his impressive debut for the club the previous week. He was on the books of Football League club Bradford and was a bulldozer of a centre-forward, the type of player that could terrorise defenders with his aggression alone. However, he was in fact ineligible for selection as he had not been on the club's books for the qualifying period that the competition demanded.

Things were going well in the opening stages and Bishop were leading 2-0 after thirty-four minutes but were rather fortunate to win in the end. Ground conditions were not good but John Taylor revelled in them and scored both goals, the second with a brilliant left foot shot. Ilford fought back to level the scores with a couple from inside-right Heckman, but in extra-time Jimmy Nimmins popped up with the winner.

Moor Green of the Birmingham Combination League had surprisingly made it to the third round. The two clubs had been drawn together in the 1936-37 season, Bishop winning 2-0, and also in the 1945-46 season when Bishop were again winners by 4-1. Would it be a case of 'third time lucky'? Not bloody likely. Despite putting up a spirited performance the Midland outfit went down 3-1. Goals from Jacky Major, Bobby Hardisty (playing at inside-right) and a penalty from centre-half Bobby Davison were sufficient to beat the lone reply from Moor Green's outside-right Davies.

On February 25th, the 'Two-Blues' were faced with a tricky looking tie in the quarter-final away to Southern outfit Finchley. The North Londoners had never been beyond the second round of the competition and were looking forward to meeting the 'great' Bishop Auckland and such was the interest in the game that the BBC made provision to televise the second half! Television was on the march.

Bishop won 3-1 with goals from the left-flank combination of Palmer and the outstanding Alan Gilholme (two) with a late consolation response from Finchley's lively inside-right, Wingate. The Bishop defenders played particularly well in this game as goalkeeper Storey injured his hand and had to be protected from action as much as possible.

Wycombe Wanderers (conquerors of Crook Town 1-0 in Round Two), were the semi-final opponents with the game taking place at Griffin Park, Brentford. Both teams changed strips for the match, Bishop playing in white shirts, black shorts and red socks, whilst Wycombe adopted black and amber shirts with white shorts and red, white and blue socks.

The game attracted a crowd of over 30,000 and resulted in a 2-1 win for Bishop. Way scored for Wanderers but outside-right Riley and a penalty from coalminer Bobby Davison gave Bishop the lead. Wycombe piled on the pressure for an equalizer, amply bayed on by the mainly Southern contingent of supporters. Wycombe's outside-left Birdseye was ably frozen out by Auckland full-back Coxon... sorry, but I could not resist that line.

Willington's progress to Wembley had begun with a 2-0 away success at Penrith which was followed by a 3-1 home win over Northern League neighbours Ferryhill Athletic. The Isthmian League team Wimbledon provided quality opposition in Round Three, but they were beaten at Hall Lane in an entertaining game 4-2. Further Isthmian League rivals were met in the fourth round, away from home, this time Leytonstone the opposition. Leytonstone were a very useful outfit and had won the cup in 1946-47 and

1947-48. It was no mean feat for Willington to overcome them on their own soil 3-2. Trevor Bailey, the England cricketer, scored one of Leytonstone's goals. In the semi-final, held at Ayresome Park, Middlesbrough, Willington beat Barking 2-1, with a performance that some of their players admitted was the worst of the season. Fortunately, Barking were unable to capitalise on Willington's failings.

The sun beat down as the crowds made their way along Wembley Way and then up the steps that led in to the stadium. My dad would often say that you never forgot your first visit to Wembley, with its massed terraces, and that it must stay within anyone's memory.

Only three weeks previously, the clubs had fought out a 0-0 draw in the semi-final of the Durham Benevolent Bowl (Willington had defeated Bishop at the same stage in the competition twelve months earlier). Future events would see Bishop gaining revenge in the match at Kingsway by a solitary goal scored by Harry McIlvenny. The 'Two Blues' would then go on to defeat Ushaw Moor 3-1 in the final at Spennymoor United's Brewery Ground. Left-winger Riley would score two with McIlvenny again getting his customary goal, with Finlay getting on the scoresheet for Ushaw. A Northern League title would be the product of some consistent displays with only four losses in the season: results such as the 11-0 win over Heaton Stannington and a 6-0 win over Penrith did nothing to dull the confidence in a successful league campaign. But that was in the future... for the present, a far more important game was about to take place.

At ten minutes to three the teams strode out from the dark tunnel into the sunlight and were met with a cacophony of sound - rattles, bells, corncrakes, horns and anything else that could be gotten hold of to extract a sound.

The teams were:

Bishop Auckland (Red shirts, White shorts)
Washington - Coxon, Farrer (captain) - Taylor, Davison, Nimmins - Major, Hardisty, McIlvenny, Gilholme, Palmer

Willington (White shirts, Navy Blue shorts)
Snowdon - Craggs, Howe - Lewthwaite, Yeardley, Dodd - Robinson, Taylor, Larmouth, Armstrong, Rutherford

Referee: A. Murdoch of Sheffield

The teams were presented to the Earl of Athlone and Sir Stanley Rous, Secretary of the organisers of the competition, before the game got under way.

Willington: Blue is the colour

Stan Rutherford, the Willington outside-left, had played for Bishop Auckland in the 1947 semi-final against Wimbledon, transferring to Willington shortly afterwards. Similarly, John Dodd, who had scored twice in the fourth round tie against Leytonstone, had played in a losing semi-final when playing for Crook Colliery Welfare (later renamed Crook Town) in 1949, but no-one in the Willington team had cup final experience.

Jack Washington, not a particularly tall goalkeeper, being only five foot six inches, was the only member remaining of the 1939 Bishop Auckland side. Both he and captain Tommy Farrer had collected losers' medals when Barnet had beaten Bishop 3-2 in the final held at Stamford Bridge, Chelsea. He had played in five semi-finals in the past six years, and it was soon apparent that his experience would be tested.

Both teams strung passes together to create chances but Bishop were finding Jackie Snowdon particularly difficult to beat, especially the wingers of the Auckland attack, Major and Palmer, as they found their crosses being competently handled by the tall goal minder. At six foot two inches, Snowdon was well built for his position, being very agile and athletic as well as having a long arm reach. He wasn't called 'The Spider' for nothing.

Willington's wingers were also using the ball well, with intelligent crosses of the ball, switching play from one wing to the other. The underdogs had done their homework at the Hall Lane ground and such planning was about to reap dividends. With quick, incisive passing the Willington forwards began to weave patterns to spreadeagle the Bishop defence. Surely they would be rewarded for their efforts?

Then, after twelve minutes, Eddie Taylor opened the scoring to put Willington ahead. A shot by Armstrong went wide to Joe Robinson who sent over a lovely cross from the right wing, which was met by the little inside-right standing to the middle of the goal, midway between the six-yard line and the penalty spot, with a strong header. Jack Washington dived instantly to his left but the ball was already nestling in the net.

Nine minutes later Stan Rutherford scored Willington's second with a stunning left-foot shot into Jack Washington's top right-hand corner. Unbelievably, a third was added just ten minutes later when Willington centre-forward Bill Larmouth lashed the ball in through a crowded penalty area after good work by Rutherford. The Bishop Auckland supporters could not believe it. Neither could the Willington supporters. The quality of the football never dropped, from Bishop in particular; even though they were three goals down and had every right to be dispirited, they adhered to their reputation of good sportsmanship and trying to play 'proper' football. Jackie Snowdon kept the Bishop attack at bay and made at least four superb saves, one in particular when stopping a Bobby Hardisty piledriver.

At half-time Willington still held a 3-0 lead and when the second half got under way, Bishop tried to pile on the pressure. Jacky Major was full of trickery on the right wing but the Willington defence continued to hold. John Taylor at half-back tried to give assistance to the Bishop attack and was always looking to put the speedy Major away, but try as they might, Bishop could not get a breakthrough. Just one goal and they would stand a chance of getting back into the game. But Willington were having none of it. Snowdon was diving around like an Olympic Champion, aided and abetted by his erstwhile defenders, plumber Stewart Howe - who had curtailed his honeymoon to play in the semi-final - Bill Craggs, employed as a railway clerk, and Edgar 'Keg' Yeardley, only twenty years old and the youngest player on the pitch, proving a man-mountain at centre-half in his individual battle against the experienced Bishop centre-forward Harry McIlvenny.

McIlvenny was a typical centre-forward; big, strong and athletic. He could hustle and bustle defenders but had skill. He had league experience with Bradford and had representative honours with the Olympic squad and had been Bishop's leader for some seasons. There weren't many that could best him but on this day, young Edgar Yeardley was playing a blinder.

The Bishop Auckland forward line were unable to penetrate Willington's defence, but surprisingly Willington had not found their task as difficult and in the seventy-fifth minute Matty Armstrong added a fourth, firing in from twelve yards, he drove the ball into the corner of the net past a flat-footed Washington and that was the end of the scoring. A 4-0 win over the cup favourites had resulted in Willington winning the trophy for the first time in their history. Eddie Taylor was a proud man when he led his team up the staircase to collect the cup. His better-known brother, Ernie, might be playing for Newcastle United's first team (and would have his day three years later, playing for Blackpool in the 'Matthews Final'), but right now there was no prouder man in the land.

Jackie Snowdon, who signed for Bishop Auckland the following year but broke his kneecap in his first game and subsequently retired, recalls:

'We went down by Pullman Coach from Darlington railway station on the Friday afternoon. We stayed at The Imperial Hotel. Wives, girlfriends, mothers and fathers went down on the ordinary supporters' trains and they stayed in different hotels, but after the match they all came round to see us. When we arrived at King's Cross, a waiting bus took us straight to the stadium for a pre-match look. It was vast and I just thought 'Blimey!'

'I remember everything about the match but what struck me was the quietness - we walked out from the tunnel and it was just one great grey mass. It was impossible for me to pick out anyone because we were so far

away from the crowd and I swear I didn't hear a thing. We were more used to playing in front of much smaller crowds, of course. We would get five or six thousand at Willington but this was 88,000 at Wembley. With the much smaller crowds you could hear every spectator's comments, good or bad, throughout a game. I remember one incident when I had played for Wolsingham against Howden-le-Wear in front of about eighty people. Standing in my goal area, I was about to collect a high ball when I heard a woman say, 'I bet that long bugger misses it.' You hear things like that but you don't let them bother you. You just get on with it.

'In the Cup Final I managed to make a few saves, one from Bob Hardisty, and when the referee blew for full-time, I went over to shake his hand. He was in tears. I said to him 'Bob, you'll play worse than that in a Cup Final and win' and I was right. He was a superb player: the best; a master.

'We didn't experience the thrill of the victory until afterwards, when we were sat down in the dressing room. Then it dawned on us what we had achieved. All of us were delighted, of course, but we were just, well, flabbergasted. We were underdogs, you see. They had seven internationals in their side. Before the game some people had enquired, 'What are you bothering going all the way to Wembley for?' hey just expected us to get beat.

'In the evening we went out to Finnegan's Bar, which is where the Bishop Auckland players went to whenever they had a game in London. They were there then and Bob and I had a good natter. We knew each other, of course, not only through football, but also through our jobs. I was working in the County Planning Department, the Physical Education Department employed Bob, and so we would quite often bump into each other. After the celebrations we all went along to King's Cross station to see the trains off, packed with supporters of both clubs. We travelled back the next day and received a tremendous reception, being feted up and down the town.

'A few days later, I broke my collarbone playing in our next game. As a result I had to give up my international call-up and Bennett, the Southall goalkeeper, took my place.'

As Bobby Hardisty gazed out of the coach, taking the team back to the hotel, he looked on to the sea of blue that the supporters had created with their scarves, hats, coats, rosettes and banners. Blue was how he felt. Blue was the colour all right.

CHAPTER TWO

Pegasus: 'Hello World'

The road turning off from the A690 at Low Willington will take you to Todhills and Byers Green, and is a tricky one to drive at the best of times. On leaving the main road at Whitehouse Bank, you go down a steep hill and then level off for about four hundred yards, where gusty winds can take a good blow at high-sided vehicles. The Queen Victoria Jubilee Bridge, made of steel and dating back to 1897, spanned the River Wear at this point but was replaced in 1990 by the New Jubilee Bridge; after crossing this, the road takes a sharp right turn up Straker's Bank (named after the mine owner). About two hundred yards up the hill is a hairpin bend to the left, whereupon the road continues climbing towards Todhills. It's difficult enough to negotiate now, but it must have been more so back in 1942, before synchromesh gears became standard.

It was on this road one summer's day in that year that a certain George William Adamthwaite was driving his Bedford lorry laden with sand and gravel. On the incline, the lorry developed clutch trouble, right on the hairpin bend. The clutch plates seized, the engine stalled and the lorry began to roll back as the brakes began to fail. Fortunately, although only sixteen years old and weighing ten stone wet-through, George was able to bring the lorry to a halt next to the roadside by pulling the handbrake with both hands. All further attempts to restart the engine failed, and so he walked to the nearest telephone box to notify his company of the problem. The manager at Bailey's Transport, Crook, told him that a mechanic would be sent out as soon as possible.

Whilst sat by his lorry, waiting for the mechanic to arrive, a pretty fourteen-year-old girl came by and a conversation developed. That dalliance was to result in a friendship and marriage that would last the best part of the next fifty years. Margaret Gelson and George - my future mum and dad - would meet each other as often as possible. After this meeting, what is remarkable is the lack of navigational skills this young driver seemed to have. He seemed to be devoid of all sense of direction, as every journey thereafter would take him through Todhills and Byers Green. It mattered not if coal had to be taken to Penrith, Hexham or Timbuktu - the delivery was made by travelling through Todhills and Byers Green, even though those two villages lay in the opposite direction of his intended destination!

Courtship, Northern-style, followed i.e. forget dance halls: St James' Park, Hexham, Catterick and Sedgefield were the order of the day. Come to think of it, I probably had my first embryonic start in life on Sedgefield racecourse.

Mum's father, John Robert, worked at the local brickyard and in the evenings was an Air Raid Patrol warden. He had been employed as a chimney sweep and bricklayer in his early years and frequently carried out work at Binchester Hall, now a luxury hotel.

In his capacity as ARP warden, he used to go out at night and make sure that Jerry wasn't parachuting into the Wear Valley and plodging up towards Todhills. He also had to go around making sure that all the houses had curtains closed and that no lights were showing that could give German aircraft a target at which to aim.

One night he noticed a chink of light coming from one of the farmhouse cottages and dutifully marched up the path to admonish the recalcitrant occupiers. After giving the unfortunate couple a stern lecture on the consequences that could ensue if the Germans did attack, he insisted that all lights were extinguished before he left. Every light was put out and all curtains fully closed. Mr Gelson turned to go and wished the couple a pleasant evening. The door closed behind him and he heard the bolt being applied. He took two steps forward in the darkness and promptly fell arse over tip down the steps.

A minute later, the couple heard a knock on their door. Not wishing to put on a light or open up, they conversed with the visitor through the door. They were somewhat taken aback to hear the rather sheepish voice of Mr Gelson suggesting that it would be all right for them to turn on the lights and open the curtains until he had reached the roadway. Shades of Captain Mainwaring and *Dad's Army*.

Sometimes Mum and Dad would listen to the wireless (radio to the uninitiated) in the evening and tune in to Lord Haw-Haw (William Joyce), the Irish-born German propagandist. He would make outrageous statements that certain areas of military importance had been destroyed by the Luftwaffe and major cities like Tow Law and Willington had been razed to the ground. Such rantings no doubt brought the typically appropriate response from English listeners. In reality, of course, no such events had taken place.

In April 1945, on his nineteenth birthday, Dad received his call-up papers. It was always going to be doubtful that he would be accepted into the armed forces - Stevie Wonder had better eyesight. As an alternative he became what is known as a Bevin Boy. Please indulge me whilst I explain how the Bevin Boys came about (those of you not interested in this little history, or already know, can skip the following few paragraphs).

In the nineteenth century England was the major power producer of coal. Although coal was cheap in financial terms, it was costly in human terms. Miners' lives were always at risk and any degree of job satisfaction lay over a hundred years away in the future. As a commodity, coal was taken for granted. But in years of depression, with too few miners and lesser markets, those left in the industry suffered untold deprivation. Families would go for days without food, and not only those connected to the mining industry, but in Northumberland and County Durham, coalmining was a major factor in local industry. The situation reached a climax with the Jarrow March of 1936, when miners walked from Jarrow to 10 Downing Street to air their grievances. They earned little for their efforts, save the sympathy and respect of a grateful nation.

The Second World War made more demands on the coal industry and it was a shock for the government to be informed, by Ernest Bevin, the Minister of Labour and National Service, that coal stocks were dwindling to an unacceptable level. Not to put too fine a point on it, the coal industry was in crisis. Able-bodied men were being called up to join the forces, but fewer and fewer men were going in to the coal industry to replace those that had left, either through retirement or injury.

Drastic measures were needed and in May 1941 the Essential Work Order came into force which prohibited men leaving the coal industry and employers from dismissing them. An appeal to ex-miners to return to work to help swell the workforce fell on deaf ears. Not to be beaten, Bevin then drew up an order for the compulsory return to work of all miners that had left the industry since 1935. This resulted in over 60,000 men returning to the coal trade within the next two years.

It shows, to some degree, the fear of coalmining as a job, insofar that although the industry had the status of a voluntary alternative to the armed forces, very few opted for it. Don't forget, the National Coal Board was still years away and therefore mines were run by private owners who had one thing in mind only - profit. Working conditions and safety issues were not to the fore in their reckoning, and wages were not high. The average mine worker in 1941 earned a little over £4.00 a week, whereas an aircraft factory worker would receive nearly twice that amount. No wonder the workforce wanted aircraft factories in their area. It was not untypical therefore for a miner to slog his guts out all week and yet have less to put on the table than his wife or children who worked at a factory. Sweat, labour and danger never did equate to money received!

Bevin's measures, however, were only limited in success, and in 1943 he laid further proposals to the House of Commons. He informed the packed House that if the war was to be brought to a satisfactory conclusion - in other words, nothing less than victory would be acceptable - then further manpower and productive output was required in the coal industry. He announced later that year compulsory conscription to the coalmines was to be introduced.

All males, upon reaching age seventeen years six months, would register for National Service as normal, and they would be allocated a number ending with a digit 0 to 9. A number was drawn out of a hat and everyone whose number ended with that digit had to go down the mines. In addition, anyone who failed the acceptance medical for the armed forces would be required to apply to go down the mines. Of course, you could just as easily walk up to the colliery and make yourself available, in Durham, with very few alternatives, there was little choice. Mining was the only industry.

And so it was that Dad became a Bevin Boy. He gave up his job at Bailey's Transport, where he had worked since leaving school at fourteen. He had learnt to drive there and was taking lorry-loads of sand and gravel to such places as Peterlee, Consett, Penrith and all points of the compass well before his sixteenth birthday. I am not sure even now if he ever passed a driving test. He did his training at the Morrison Busty Pit at Annfield Plain and then went to work at Pease's West Colliery (sometimes referred to as Roddymoor Pit), near his home at Crook. Upon returning from his first shift he vowed that if he ever had sons then they would never work down a mine.

Mum and Dad were married in 1946, the same year that Bishop Auckland met Barnet in the Amateur Cup Final in the first season of football following cessation of hostilities. The game was held on Saturday 20th April at Stamford Bridge, Chelsea, the ground where Bishop had claimed the trophy in 1935 when they beat Wimbledon 2-1 after drawing 0-0 at Ayresome Park, Middlesbrough.

Barnet had made it to the final by beating Wood Green away 4-3 in the first round and then had a convincing 4-0 victory over Walton and Hersham. In the third round they beat a good Hitchin Town side 5-2 and in the quarter-final defeated Southall by the odd goal in seven. They won their semi-final 1-0 against Marine, of Southport.

Bishop's progress had begun with a stomping 7-0 win over Ferguson Pailin, from Manchester, and they progressed to the third round by beating Stanley United at home 3-0 in front of 8,000 spectators (Just a word for the unknowing: this Stanley United play at Stanley Crook just by Billy Row; it is not the Stanley that is prominently shown on all road maps close to Annfield Plain). South Bank were beaten 3-0 on their home soil and in the next round the Bishops were victorious 4-1 against the Midland outfit Moor Green. Bishop were now in the semi-final and met Walthamstow Avenue at Feethams, Darlington. The match attracted a crowd of over 17,000 and resulted in a 2-1 win for Bishop.

The teams for the final were:

Barnet (Black and Amber hooped shirts, White shorts)
H. Powell - G. Wheeler, E. Bunker - J. C. Gerrans, L. Tullen,
W. Weightman - A. J. Jordan, D. Kelleher, R. W. Phipps,
L. Finch (Captain), P. Reilly

Bishop Auckland (Dark and Light Blue halved shirts, Black shorts)
J. Washington - K. Humble, L.T. Farrer - J. W. Longstaff, A. T. Hadfield,
J. D. Fairs - W. R. Shergold, F. Richardson, H. Teasdale,
J. Tait, R. Anderson

Referee: Mr. C. J. Barrick of Northampton

The teams treated the 53,832 crowd to a football bonanza.

This was Barnet's first appearance in the final compared to Bishop's twelfth, but that statistic counted for nothing as the team from North London went a goal up for a 1-0 half-time lead. Teasdale equalized for Bishop with their first attack in the second half but Barnet went two goals clear before Teasdale obtained his second of the afternoon. Try as they might, Bishop could not score again, so Barnet won the cup for the first time in their history. It was a particularly poignant moment for Barnet stalwart and captain Lester Finch, who now held every major honour in the amateur game, having secured a winners' medal.

Mum and Dad lived with his parents at 4 Arthur Street, Crook, ostensibly until they could obtain accommodation of their own. Arthur Street was one of many of its type, typical of terraced housing built in the late nineteenth century. The street extended at least a hundred yards, intermittently broken by archways leading to the rear of the premises. The gasworks and allotments were at the top end by the high numbers.

The houses were originally built for mainly mineworkers and the occasional agricultural worker and were probably all rented. It is unlikely that the internal layout taxed the mind of the original architect, as all of the houses in this and the accompanying streets were exactly the same. The front door led straight in to the living room, a step down from street level. A cold-water tap and lead pipe were affixed to the wall immediately behind the door, and opposite this wall was the open range coal fireplace. That range could produce enough heat to get a rocket to the moon and back. A double sash window allowed light into this front room.

Beyond the front room was a scullery, again with a cold-water tap and further beyond lay a pantry where flour, meat, butter and milk could be stored. All shelves in the pantry were made of stone or marble in order to keep items cold. A staircase - sounds grand, doesn't it? - led upstairs to the two bedrooms.

A rear door gave entrance to a courtyard where there were coalstore sheds and a brick set of toilets, one for every two households. Number 4 Arthur Street therefore shared theirs with number 3. When I was older I always marvelled at the toilet walls as they were covered in coloured chalk drawings of Stanley Matthews, Jackie Milburn and Len Shackleton that had been there for years. I often wonder who the artist was. The toilets were fitted with proper flushing water closets, but I think we must have been posh as ours had a chain with a handle and the water pipe was actually connected.

At the back of the toilet block my granddad had a little patch of garden where he would grow chrysanthemums (why didn't he grow roses? Easier to spell), and from where there was a lovely view up Church Hill, forever known as Catholic Bank to the locals.

Grandma and Granddad kept a tidy house, as did many other families along there; they didn't have a lot of money but Grandma knew how to keep a house clean. She was a lovely person and a smashing cook, able to skin a rabbit as quick as you could blink, and her stew and dumplings were gorgeous. And let's not forget the homemade pease pudding with ham.

Granddad was the spitting image of James Cagney whilst Grandma was like Joan Hickson, the actress who played Miss Marple in the BBC adaptations. He was a miner and had been for most of his working life. He had seen some rough times, especially when mine-owners would regularly place the more experienced colliers on reduced wages or short time, giving work to men on a lesser rate of pay, but in the Twenties and Thirties times could be particularly difficult. Even surviving to the next day could be an achievement. But somehow there are always survivors, and a few of the out-of-work men would get together and play cowboys. No, I don't mean getting a toy gun and pretending to have a shoot-out. This type of cowboy became involved with animals. Rustling.

There was always someone who knew someone who had a van. The van needed a driver who could keep his mouth shut for a price, say a leg of lamb. Most of the miners could not drive. They would meet up at the bottom of Hope Street in Crook and then disperse in ones and twos to the waiting van. A casual leisurely drive up to Weardale resulted in the sighting of sheep, cows or a few pigs. They would scan the area making a list of potential targets and then return the next evening, waiting until nightfall to select their 'victims'. Funny how some pantries always seemed to have a leg of lamb lying in the pantry. Illegal? Probably. Survival? No doubt about it. Well done, Granddad.

It was into this household, on Tuesday 25th February 1947, at approximately 10:57 a.m. that I popped out onto this unsuspecting planet to be confronted with the worst winter since the second Ice Age. I weighed 6lbs 12oz. The nurse slapped my mum instead of me, for producing such an ugly child. When Dad returned from work to see his offspring he looked at mum and enquired 'What's that?' I ask you. Apparently I cried a lot. What did they expect, a comedian? I was to be named George Alan… if I had been a girl it would have been Virginia!!!

Mum and Dad continued to live-in but they wanted their own place. Unfortunately, so did hundreds of others, especially those returning from the war. Properties were at a premium and house building was curtailed with many constrictions and regulations. They put their name down for a council house of course but there was little hope. Mum or Dad made numerous visits, almost a daily process, to the housing office at Glenholme, but the answer was always the same; 'Nothing doing today.'

Then, completely out of the blue, a friend informed them that a farm cottage had become available at Greenhead, about a mile from Crook. Looking back, it must have sounded idyllic to Mum and Dad. A modern day estate agent would have been in his element with such a property: Number 2, Greenhead Cottages. A farmyard cottage, the second of a terrace of five cottages, looking out over fields front and rear. Wonderful aspect, bijou, full of charm, rustic appeal, lots of potential.

Bollocks. It was four walls and little else.

The front door opened straight out onto the lane. Inwards, the front door accessed the living room (a little more use of estate agent speak there) which had a coal fireplace and iron range. A scullery with a couple of wooden shelves lay behind this room and a pantry was annexed. There was no such thing as a staircase to the upstairs, just a ladder near the front door to the upper bedroom, which surprisingly had a fire grate.

The downstairs floors consisted of quarry tiles which were constantly lifting, due to water seeping through the floors or the fields flooding. Consequently the legs of our table and chairs were more often than not placed in empty jam jars to protect them from the water.

The rear door led onto a small communal yard where there were the toilets. In one respect this was upmarket from Arthur Street, as each cottage had its very own toilet building, except that they were a bit different from most. They did not flush using water; these were earth closets. Yes folks, earth closets… refuse was mixed with cinders, waste ashes and earth and then every Wednesday a nice man from the council, smelling of roses, would drive up in his dust cart and empty the chamber. Ah, sweet memories! I understand that some of these earth closets were still in use in outlying areas as late as the 1970s.

Despite these drawbacks, it was home. No, it was much more than that…
it was our home.

Dad continued to work at Pease's West Colliery and would come home with
his back covered in cuts and bruises. He had started as a hewer, cutting out the
coal from the seams, but often he would be asked to push the 15cwt tubs on his
seven-hour shift. It was exhausting work, especially when conditions were wet.
His physique didn't help him either, as he was six foot tall and had to stoop
down all the time to work in the three foot six inch high tunnel. His back was a
mass of sores from the constant rubbing against the tunnel roof.

Of course, there were no showers or bathing facilities at the colliery and
the sight of black-faced miners making their way home was a common one.

Without a bathroom, it was necessary for Mum and Dad to have a tin bath,
the type that can still be bought from some ironmongery shops today. After
every shift, when Dad returned home, Mum would have the kettle and pots
filled with water boiling away on the range, ready to fill the bathtub. In the
summer the tub would be placed in the scullery, but when it got colder it
would be placed in front of the fire. Mum and I would then get to work to
clean his back to get him ready for the next day's shift.

But life wasn't all bad. After all, they had me, and what is more, I had
them, the best parents in the world.

Dad continued his interest in football and the fortunes of Bishop Auckland
resulted in him making a return trip to Wembley in 1951, when they once
again reached the final of the Amateur Cup. One of the games he had seen
earlier that season was when Bishop had played league opposition in the form
of York City in the first round proper of the FA Cup. After taking the lead with
a Davison penalty, the amateurs allowed the league side to fight back and go
into a 2-1 lead. Then with only seven minutes left, Benny Edwards stuck
home the equaliser. York won the replay 2-1 in front of over 6,500 spectators
on a quagmire of a pitch. Right up to kick-off, water pumps were in use
getting the muddy liquid from the pitch. Bishop had as much of the play as
their league counterparts but tried to play out of defence with short passes to
wingers Major and Edwards, a ploy not suited to the conditions. York
penetrated the Auckland defence with long balls and got both goals that way,
despite the heroic efforts in goal of Bill White, who had a splendid game.
Bishop learnt their lesson all too late when, with two minutes left, Major
whipped over a long ball to find Nimmins whose prompt return caught the
City defence out of position and enabled McIlvenny to score.

A reproduction of the FA Cup and league form would surely see the
Bishops winning the Amateur Cup. Confidence was high, but a shock lay in
store as the favourites tasted defeat again.

Bishop 1 Pegasus 2!!!!!

No one could believe it. How on earth could a team that had only been in existence three years humble the mighty Bishops who had a history of winning league championships and cup finals over more than sixty years? Blimey, they were only twelve months younger than me.

At four years of age I wasn't really capable of understanding the magnitude of this event at the time, but as I grew up, when my Dad and other family members would sit around the table and talk football, I easily developed a love and interest in everything associated with the game.

Dad never grew tired of relating the games that he had attended, mostly involving local teams such as Bishop Auckland, Newcastle United and Crook Town. He sometimes went to see Arsenal; his sister lived in Hendon, North London and was well in with Denis Compton, the Arsenal and England international and cricketer who would kindly supply complimentary tickets when Dad visited her. But Bishop Auckland was my favourite team and I have always followed their fortunes. At this particularly early stage of my life, Pegasus would have been Public Enemy Number One and I hated them as much as someone of my age could hate anything.

Often, Dad used to tell me about football teams and these became my 'history' lessons. I can remember him telling me of how Pegasus had been formed in 1948 by a combination of Oxford and Cambridge University students - another reason for me to dislike them as they were simply copying Bishop in this respect, who had similar origins sixty years ago. Apparently, their first game had been against an Arsenal side. I do not know the score but I hoped that Arsenal thumped them.

Pegasus did not even play in a proper league at first and only played friendly matches and occasional cup games. The Football Association, in a display of favouritism (in my view), had then given them special treatment in their inaugural year when they were allowed to be exempt from the Amateur Cup competition until the fourth qualifying round because their players had university commitments. Bromley, the eventual winners of the competition that year, beat them 1-0 in the quarter-finals. Good!

Bishop had had a relatively straightforward run to the final. In the first round they were drawn away to local rivals Evenwood Town, who they defeated 2-0. The official programme for this game carries a photograph of father and son Warney and Corbett Cresswell. Warney had captained Everton and played for Sunderland as well as gaining international honours for England. Corbett was playing at centre-half for Evenwood that day and had to mark the experienced Harry McIlvenny. He did not do too badly but the wily Bishop centre-forward scored his usual goal accompanied by another from the penalty spot converted by Davison. Little did Corbett Cresswell know then that his future would be indelibly marked out with that day's opponents.

Round Two saw them drawn at home to Shildon and produced a 3-1 win: Anderson scored twice for Bishop with Hogg adding the third. Poor Whitby Town were the next opponents and they must have wished that they had stayed at home as they were sent packing 7-2. The goals came from Davison (two penalties), Anderson, Hogg, Edwards and McIlvenny (two). Kemp and Underwood replied for Whitby.

The useful Walton and Hersham, lying second in the strong Athenian League, were Bishop's next opponents. They were a useful side and had knocked holders Willington out of the competition. Coincidentally, Bishop were also lying second in their league, although they had played four games less than leaders Billingham Synthonia. However, they couldn't afford to take things lightly. They didn't. But in a tough game, watched by 12,000 spectators, the Walton and Hersham players proved every bit as equal to the Bishop team. Four goals were shared with Johnson and Sentence scoring for the visitors whilst Davison (penalty) and Hogg scored for the 'Two Blues'.

The replay seven days later was something of an anti-climax. Much had been expected of the Walton and Hersham lads but the 9,000 crowd saw them fail to perform on the day and were brushed aside 1-4 by an impressive Bishop team.

The semi-final was to be held at Elland Road, Leeds - the first time that an amateur cup-tie had been held at the ground - and Bishops' opponents would be Bromley. Previous Amateur Cup encounters between the clubs had seen a 1-0 win for the Southerners in the 1910-11 final and in 1946-47 Bishop had been the victors in a third round game 5-1. A repetition of that score would do very nicely, thank you. Bromley, however, were a tough nut to crack and had been winners of the Amateur Cup only two seasons previously in the first Wembley final. They were in good current form and had amassed an impressive thirty-four points out of a possible forty from their league games. They would go on to win the Athenian League title this season. An impressive forward line was ably assisted by an obdurate defence as only one goal had been scored against them in the Amateur Cup so far this season.

That semi-final was a full-blooded affair. The two teams put on a terrific display of football that day and it was the Bishops' centre-forward and captain, Harry McIlvenny, who secured the winner for them to win 3-2. Bromley had taken the lead after twenty-three minutes when a right-wing attack penetrated the Bishop defence. Bill White collided with an opposing forward and Brown poked the ball in the net. Four minutes later Anderson equalised for Auckland after a Bromley player miskicked. Then, with the Bromley defence at sixes and sevens, they gave away a penalty for handball. Davison, an excellent penalty-taker, slotted the ball home to give the Bishops a 2-1 lead. Brown headed a second for Bromley to bring the scores level in the second half but then, with reporters starting to write that a replay at Chesterfield would take place, McIlvenny got the winning goal six minutes from time, following another defensive error. The game had attracted over 20,000 spectators and grossed the princely sum of £2,500.

The progress of Pegasus had been somewhat more hazardous because of their liability to give goals away and thereby have to chase the game. In the first round, they were drawn away to Gosport and only survived after going behind to win by the odd goal of seven. Slough Town provided the opposition in Round Two and they were beaten 3-1. Then it was the turn of little Brentwood and Warley. A surprise certainly looked on the cards as the minnows went in at half-time 2-0 up. The home team, however, could not sustain their efforts and the second half saw Pegasus raise the tempo and they recorded three goals without reply to scrape through 3-2. Oxford City away were next and they were beaten rather comfortably 3-0.

The semi-final against Hendon was played at Highbury. Reports suggest that if not for goalkeeper Brown's heroics, it would have been the green and white of Hendon that would have appeared in the final. He put up a superb display of goalkeeping that day and helped give the defence the confidence required to stem the Hendon forwards. He even saved a penalty making a miraculous save, diving full length to his left to fingertip the ball over the crossbar. That game ended all square at 1-1. A week later the replay was held at Crystal Palace and Pegasus were winners 3-2.

During their cup run, Pegasus had acquired the assistance of Tottenham Hotspur coach Vic Buckingham and he was instrumental in planning the downfall of their Wembley opponents.

Both teams had international players. For Pegasus there was Brown, Cowan, Tanner and Saunders and for Bishop there was Tommy Farrer, Bobby Hardisty and Harry McIlvenny.

The game was played on Saturday 21st April and the teams were:

Bishop Auckland (Dark Blue and Light Blue halved shirts, White shorts)
White - Marshall, Farrer - Hardisty, Davison, Nimmins - Taylor, Anderson, McIlvenny (captain), Williamson, Edwards

Pegasus (White shirts, Navy Blue Shorts)
Brown - Cowen, Maughan - Platt, Shearwood, Saunders (captain) - Pawson, Dutchman, Tanner, Carr, Potts

Arthur Ellis, who would go on to become a television personality and co-presenter of the hit BBC television programme of the 1960s-70s *It's A Knockout* was the referee.

Pegasus: 'Hello World'

Watched by a crowd of 100,000 (although Wembley Stadium never provided actual attendance figures), the two teams produced a humdinger of a match. Both teams missed early opportunities and Bishops' Benny Edwards in particular was twice guilty of missing the target in the first fifteen minutes, and then John Taylor tried scoring from an impossible angle instead of crossing the ball to an unmarked McIlvenny. Pegasus played a quick passing game, so much the style approved by their adopted manager. One reporter surmised that Pegasus worked to a plan but that Bishop Auckland did not appear to have one, claiming that Davison allowed the Pegasus centre-forward Tanner too much room and that full-backs Dave Marshall and Tommy Farrer played too far apart. My dad always thought that this criticism was too harsh, reflecting that the marauding Pegasus wingers were just too good on the day.

Bobby Hardisty was the best of the Bishop players but he was having to do all of his work shoring up the left side of defence as the Pegasus wingers, Pawson and Potts, repeatedly broke through to send over menacing crosses. The unfortunate Willy Anderson was injured before half-time and became a passenger (don't forget that it would be almost another twenty years before substitutes would be allowed). The 0-0 scoreline at half-time was an indication of the parity of the two teams but goals should have been scored.

The capacity crowd did not have long to wait in the second-half for the opening goal and it went to the side wearing the badge of the Winged Horse, Pegasus. In the fifty-third minute, a long ball from Dutchman was met firmly on the head by Potts who steered the ball past White. Bill White had replaced Jack Washington, who had moved on to pastures new at Whitley Bay Athletic. He was only twenty-three-years-old and was much taller than his predecessor, standing six foot three inches tall in his stockinged feet.

With only ten minutes to go, Pawson took on Hardisty and beat him comfortably before sending in a cross for Tanner to collect. He rounded Davison and sent an unstoppable shot past White. The Northern voices were silenced. Bishop were finding it difficult to penetrate the Pegasus defence and it was not until the later stages of the game that half-back Jimmy Nimmins, adding support to the attack, reduced the deficit when he back-heeled the ball past a surprised Brown in the Pegasus goal.

Although they put everything into attack, the Bishop Auckland forward line could not find an equaliser. Shortly afterwards, Arthur Ellis blew the final whistle and it was Pegasus who paraded around Wembley with the trophy, winning 2-1.

Bishop would go on to win the Northern League title for the second successive season. Resounding scores over Heaton Stannington (9-1) and Penrith (9-0), both away, and Shildon (7-0) and the luckless Penrith (8-3) at Kingsway, helped to relieve some supporters of their Cup Final woes.

Supporters of the 'Two Blues' left the stadium a dejected party, walking solemnly down Wembley Way, while delighted Pegasus supporters danced in the road. It would be a long trek up the Great North Road, at least a seven-hour journey. Some would return by train from King's Cross station. Some would stay overnight and no doubt drown their sorrows and would find their way back the next day.

One of those that would return to County Durham on the Sunday was my dad. He had finished work at Pease's West Colliery on the Friday and travelled down to London on an evening train. He stayed at his sister and brother-in-law's house (my Aunty Dora May and Uncle Dick) and caught the train back to Durham on Sunday morning. From Durham it was a simple matter of catching a United bus to Crook and then a walk of a mile or so to our cottage.

On that bright Sunday morning Mum gave me a boiled egg and soldiers for breakfast as usual and then I dashed out the front door, crossing the lane that ran right by, and went to stand on the wooden fence opposite to watch the trains across the field.

I waited and waited and made innumerable runs up to the level crossing as the trains rumbled by. They reminded me of monsters and dragons, the way that they spewed out steam, and their great size added to the illusion. Time dragged by and eventually I trudged back home where mum was cleaning, tidying up and doing all the other household chores, singing Doris Day songs (she always sang Doris Day songs), and later on she would do some baking. Mind you, she would not have been doing any washing… it would never do to hang out washing on a Sunday! Strictly taboo in those days.

Eventually, I think I must have fallen asleep because when I awoke Dad was there, talking to mum. I climbed on his knee and cradled my arms around his neck and listened to him telling about how his weekend had gone. I knew little about football and was far more interested in my bright orange bulldozer that puffed 'smoke' (a mix of baking powder and air) and my cars, but as his conversation continued I heard him talk of a place that sounded magical - Wembley - and I can remember me thinking that one day I hoped to go there.

Little did I know that by the age of ten I would have been there three times to see my beloved Bishop Auckland in three Amateur Cup Finals and they would win the cup on each occasion, albeit once after a replay.

CHAPTER THREE

Crook Town: Making goals

There has been a football team in Bishop Auckland since 1882, when Bishop Auckland Church Institute was formed, consisting mainly of students from Oxford and Cambridge attending the theological college. The colours of those two university cities were adopted and shirts were of dark and light blue halves. The team had its first success in 1886 when winning the Durham Cup. It is likely that further success would have followed but the next year six players were suspended *sine die* by the Durham Football Association for acting in a way to soil the name of that organisation. This was the start of the demise of 'The Stute' as that year saw the formation of a rival football team, Auckland Town, affiliated to the cricket club. Several of the suspended players would end up playing for the new club.

Although the town had two football clubs, it was the fledgling Auckland Town that were in the ascendancy and they had the foresight to become a founder member of the Northern League in 1889, just one year after the formation of the Football League, thus being the second oldest league in the world. The Church Institute club declined to join the new league and effectively folded in 1892, due, in part, to the success of the newer club, who won the Durham Cup that year, and the better competitive football that a league programme produced with regular fixtures.

Auckland Town's residency in the Northern League only lasted one year and they transferred to the Northern Alliance for the 1890-91 season. They returned to the Northern League in 1893-94 under the name of Bishop Auckland and wearing the 'Two Blues' colours, their games from then on being played at Kingsway, adjacent to the cricket pitch. It was this season that saw the inauguration of the Football Association Amateur Cup Competition, for which the club would compete every season until it was discontinued in 1974.

Supporters did not have long to wait for success in the new cup competition, winning it in 1896, defeating Royal Artillery Portsmouth 1-0 in the final at Leicester. It was another four years before the trophy was won for a second time when Lowestoft Town were defeated 5-1 in the 1899-1900 final played at Leicester. In the following season local rivals Crook Town defeated the Bishops in the semi-final before going on to win the trophy by defeating Kings Lynn 3-0 in a replay at Ipswich.

Bishop Auckland were losing finalists in 1902, being thumped 5-1 by Old Malvernians at Leeds.

The 1904-05 season saw the club reach the first round of the FA Cup for the first time, earning a home tie against Second Division Wolverhampton Wanderers. This was a game that my great-grandfather went to see, along with 7,121 others. It was a bitterly cold January day and a lot of people were put off attending owing to the bad weather. Goals from Baynham, Pedley and Smith saw the gold and black striped shirts of Wolves stroll through to the next round with a 3-0 win.

Another appearance in the Amateur Cup Final soon followed in season 1905-06, when Oxford City were victorious 3-0, in the final held at Stockton. It was about this time that 'Kit' Rudd played his first game for the club, an association that would extend well beyond his playing days and reach into secretaryship of the club in later years.

Yet another final defeat took place in 1911 when the Bishops were losing finalists to Bromley 1-0 at Herne Hill. It is recorded by W.T.D. Reed in his excellent booklet *Football: The Amateur Game*, that the game was played on a quagmire in front of 3,000 spectators. Bromley had a player sent off and Walton, the Bishop Auckland goalkeeper, had to leave the field injured in the first half, Sowerby, the outside-left, taking his place.

Success returned just before the outbreak of the Great War with a 1-0 win over Northern Nomads at Leeds, but the following season, 1914-15, the Bishops lost in the final, 1-0 to Clapton, missing a penalty in the process, the game held at New Cross.

The competition was suspended until the 1919-20 season as a result of the hostilities and although they reached no further than Round Three, the following year saw the trophy return to the trophy cabinet at Kingsway. Swindon Victoria, who had played right through the competition from the initial qualifying round, were beaten 4-2 at Middlesbrough in the final. Bishop had been drawn away from home in every round, and it must have been a remarkable game in the fourth round where Esh Winning were only defeated in extra-time 5-4.

Bishop Auckland became the first team to retain the trophy by beating fellow Northern League founders South Bank in 1922, the final once again being held at Middlesbrough.

The score line of 5-2 is misleading. 'The Bankers' were leading 2-0 at one stage but Bishop managed to level the score. Then with only three minutes to go South Bank were awarded a penalty. Jack Thompson must have thought that his name would be written up in lights as he strode up to take the kick but Benny Potts in the Bishop goal had other ideas and pulled off a tremendous save, diving to his left to tumultuous applause. The game ended 2-2 after ninety minutes so extra-time had to be played for the first time in the history of the competition. That missed penalty must have played on the minds of the disheartened South Bank players as within eight minutes of play recommencing Bishop had rattled in three more goals. The crowd certainly had their money's worth that day.

Depression with a capital 'D' was looming, especially in the North-East where hard times was a way of life anyway for the majority. Many of the football clubs relied on local talent, but with little work, and mouths to feed, the economic situation of the country as a whole, and the locality in particular, took a toll. Some football clubs folded due to lack of players and money. Northern League clubs had regularly appeared in Amateur Cup Finals and numerous semi-finals but that was to change as Southern clubs, less affected than the North, became dominant for the next ten years or so. Stockton would make it to the Amateur Cup Final a couple of times without winning. And then there was little Cockfield.

Only the remarkable achievement of this two-street mining village football club brought any relief to the Northern League during this period, when in the 1927-28 season they reached the final of the Amateur Cup. They defeated Bishop Auckland after a replay in Round Four on their way to meet opponents Leyton in the final at Middlesbrough. Alas, there was to be no fairy tale as they lost the final, putting up a spirited performance, 3-2. Every member of the Cockfield playing team was out of work.

Following a barren spell of thirteen years, Bishop finally made it to the final once again in 1935. Their opponents this time were Southern club Wimbledon - now members of the Football League - and yet again the game was played at Ayresome Park, Middlesbrough. The match resulted in a 0-0 draw and a replay took place the following week at Stamford Bridge, Chelsea. This time the Bishops made no mistake and won the Cup with a 2-1 scoreline.

A four-year gap followed before the Bishops made their next final appearance a successful one, against Willington at Roker Park, Sunderland, referred to earlier in my interview with Harry Young. Laurie Wensley scored all three goals in extra-time for a 3-0 success.

Of course, during these sixty years or so, as well as making a total of seventeen semi-final appearances in the Amateur Cup, numerous other cups and trophies had been won by the Bishops. Prior to the eve of the Second World War, the Northern League Championship title had been won ten times, as well as eight appearances in the Durham County Championship Cup (winners twice), seven appearances in the Durham Benevolent Bowl Final (winners five times) and a host of miscellaneous minor competitions. In the early years one of these 'minor' competitions was for the Jean Dupuitch Cup, held in Belgium and successfully won in 1908 and 1909. Bishop were losing finalists in this competition in 1910. Another foreign venture to Hungary in 1912 resulted in the club winning the Hungarian Cup in Budapest.

Foreign visitors were always welcome and in their history Bishop have entertained such teams as Glasgow Rangers, Groningen (Holland) and Stade Francais. The Nigerian international team played at the Kingsway ground in 1949 and created a sensation. I wonder how the Bishop fans got their tongues around such names as Akioye, Onwudiwe, Anosike and Anieke, all rather more difficult to pronounce than others in the touring team with more common names such as Lawson, Henshaw and Ebenezer. My dad went to that Saturday afternoon game and, like 13,000 other spectators, marvelled at how some of their players could kick a football with only webbing on their feet...don't forget the footballs then were made of real leather, not the plasticised type that you get these days. Bishop won 5-2.

In addition, the club has been invited to attend tournaments abroad, visiting such places as Belgium, The Channel Islands, Rhodesia and Hungary.

Representative honours had come the way of many Bishop Auckland players throughout the years, players not only winning caps for their individual countries, but also as members of the Great Britain Olympic football team. Bobby Hardisty had captained the 1948 Great Britain Olympic team and would go on to further represent them again in 1952 (Helsinki) and 1956 (Melbourne). (It is a popular misconception that Bobby Hardisty captained the Bishop Auckland side. As a matter of fact, he declined the captaincy, always believing that he did not wish the responsibility of the post to interfere with his playing performances. When Jacky Major, and later Tommy Stewart, retired, the captaincy of the team was given to Seamus O'Connell, and then in O'Connell's absence, to Jimmy Nimmins).

The team of 1954 could count seven internationals in its squad. Bishop Auckland really were the Manchester United of the amateur football world.

By the start of the 1951-52 season, Bishop had reached at least the semi-final stage of the Amateur Cup five times since the end of the war, being beaten finalists three times. What followed in the following two seasons was, therefore, something of a mystery with two barren cup runs. Form in the Northern League, however, remained consistent. Having finished only fifth in a league comprised of fourteen members in the 1945-46 season, the league championship was regained the following year. Runners-up position was occupied the next two seasons, but normal service was resumed when the championship was won the following two seasons, as mentioned earlier.

A hat-trick of Northern League Championship wins was achieved in the 1951-52 season. The title was won by a comfortable eight points from second placed Billingham Synthonia, the only blemish being a 3-2 loss away to Evenwood Town. In addition, the club also won a basketful of cups, namely

Crook Town: Making goals

the Durham Benevolent Bowl, the Bishop Auckland Nursing Cup, the Durham Hospital Cup and the Durham County Challenge Cup. The latter was won for the sixth time when they defeated a West Stanley side 2-0 at Feethams, Darlington. It was the Bishops' fourth success over a North Eastern League side in that competition that season. The game was played in front of 3,560 spectators, well down on the anticipated figure due to the extremely cold weather, including snow showers. The conditions probably attributed to the performance of Clark in the West Stanley goal: although he pulled off some good saves in the first half, he was at fault for both goals scored after the resumption. For the first he allowed a centre from Cresswell to reach Edwards who scored from close range, and then he completely misjudged a Jacky Major lob, which went over his head into the net.

On the domestic front, a few changes were taking place in the Adamthwaite household.

Dad decided to transfer from the Pease's West Colliery to the Hole-in the-Wall Colliery, up Church Hill (Catholic Bank) at Crook. The work at this drift mine was still hard but he reasoned that the conditions and pay were slightly better, although there were still no pithead baths or showers there (Hole-in-the-Wall was popularly known as 'Craggses', after the original owner, Mr E. Craggs).

Mum and Dad still had their names down for a council house, despite us having our own rented accommodation. Unfortunately, the council were unsympathetic to mum's tales of woe regarding the state of our cottage. The staff who ran the housing waiting list did not seem to take any interest in her tales of flooding and constant water seepage into the dwelling. But Mum would not take no for answer and every day marched up to the Glenholme offices. They must have got sick of the sight of her, with me in tow. She always varied the time of our visit in order to try and catch the staff off guard.

Then Mum and Dad got a surprise. The Housing Department were prepared to offer them the tenancy of one of the new houses being built just down the road at Howden-le-Wear: 13 Hall View Gardens, a three bedroom house. They could not get out of the cottage quick enough. A few days later we moved... by horse and cart.

It was a lovely house, the end one of a block of four, on the edge of the development. It had everything that we wanted, including a garden and an inside toilet - no more trudging out to the earth closet in the dark.

We lived at Hall View Gardens for only a couple of years, during which time I remember starting school, and what a first day I had.

Howden-le-Wear Primary School was just down the road from the council houses (it is still there). I do not remember the date that I began school, but I do know that for a four-and-a-half-year-old I was quite tall for my age, though with not much meat on me at all. I went to school with all the other first-timers, being introduced to the teachers and headmaster, Mr Moore. We were allowed out of our class at playtime and then at dinnertime I went home until afternoon lessons started. We had a break again in the afternoon and we all went into the playground. And then I decided that I wanted a wee. Now, honestly, no-one had shown us where the toilets were… so I just flashed what I had and sprayed the playground.

No-one saw me. Or so I thought. In an instant this brute of a man had me collared and marched me into the hall where he told me to bend over in order that he could give me the slipper. His name was Mr Savage. Savage by name, savage by nature.

I cried all the way home.

Next day saw Mum accompanying me to the school. Savage was for it.

Before lessons started, Mr Savage was sought out and confronted by my Mum, with me cowering behind her. She tore into him and demanded to know what right he had to have punished me so shamefully on my first day at school.

'First day at school? But surely not? Your son looks much older.'

His face was ashen.

This day and age he would never get away with such action.

He didn't get away with it then, either. As he stood there, taking Mum's bombardment, I ran from behind her and took a good kick at him, catching him perfectly on the shin. It probably only hurt him slightly but I felt better.

He was full of apologies.

After that, Mr Savage was always nice to me. Thanks Mum.

The Coronation came and went in 1953. Everywhere was bedecked in red, white and blue. People collected old car tyres and placed them on their front gardens, painted in those three colours and decorated with flowers. Schoolchildren had the chance to purchase a Coronation mug, but if I had one I don't know what happened to it.

It was about this time that I went to my first football match. We went to Newcastle, and as Mum went around the shops, Dad took me to see Newcastle play Sheffield Wednesday. I remember very little of my first game, but I do remember a header from Jackie Milburn which nearly brought a goal. I think that Albert Quixall was playing for Wednesday.

From that day I accompanied Dad to most of the games that he went to involving Bishop Auckland.

That splendid actor/traveller Michael Palin created a television series a few years ago entitled *Ripping Yarns*, and one of the episodes was about a football club, namely Barnstoneworth United, that had fallen on hard times. A very young supporter was christened Barnstoneworth United by his fanatical father and taught the names of players past that had represented the once-great club. The poor soul had to recite the names of the players before breakfast, to a studious mother, every morning: *Haggarty F, Haggarty R, Tompkins, Noble, Carrick, Robson, Crapper, Dewhurst, McIntyre, Treadmore and Davitt.*

The lad in the story could have been me. Thankfully I wasn't named Bishop Auckland, but well before I was five years old I could recite the names of the Bishop Auckland football team and had been made fully aware of the relevant points of their history and other salient historical points of North-Eastern football, both amateur and professional. My favourite players were Jackie Milburn and Bobby Hardisty, or whoever was playing the best according to the reports in 'The Pink'.

If the mines had not become exhausted of coal I suppose that we would have stayed at Hall View Gardens until Mum and Dad could save enough to afford to buy a place. However, the pits in the Durham and Northumberland coalfields were antiquated and uneconomical to run, and the work was soul-destroying. A land of milk and honey was beckoning in the Midlands, and Dad had the foresight to realise that if he was not to go on the dole, then he must seek out employment away from his home county. Friends and relatives would have to take second place behind his immediate family. He and Mum discussed the idea of moving to the Midlands coalfields, where they had been told that all the collieries had modern machinery and facilities, especially pithead baths and showers. What was more, the National Coal Board had a house-building programme in operation and could provide new homes for any miner willing to make the move (In later years the NCB would also tempt miners to move with the carrot of a cash bonus). The idea was firmly planted in Mum and Dad's minds; it was only a matter of time.

Footballwise, Bishop Auckland had failed to live up to expectations. They had success in the Northern League, but every season the club's main priority was the Amateur Cup. Anything else was a bonus. The 1951-52 campaign in the competition had started off with a comfortable 5-1 away win in Round One, at Rotherham, against Rawmarsh. Round Two saw them pitched away against Hendon in the tie of the round. Hendon were riding high in the Athenian League, being in pole position. They had won thirteen and drawn five of their twenty league games, scoring fifty-two goals in the process with only twenty against. Hendon also boasted a smattering of internationals in their side, namely Avis (outside-right), Adams (centre-half), Topp (left-half), Evans (outside-left) and Stroud (centre-forward). Whoever won this match would probably be favourites, along with Pegasus, for the Cup.

The match was watched by a crowd of over 10,000 and resulted in a 1-1 draw, Hendon's goal coming in the first minute. Inside-right Armstrong got the equalizer for the Bishops. The referee for the game, Mr R. G. Southgate, commented afterwards: '...It has been one of the happiest games that I have ever handled, being entirely free from deliberate fouls.'

Seven days later Bishop won the replay, played in constant rainfall, 5-1 with a goal from Edwards and two each from Armstrong and Major. Round Three saw a home tie against a useful Walton and Hersham side, from the Corinthian League, but surely within the capability of this Bishop Auckland side.

Saturday, February 9th 1952 was a black day for all concerned with Bishop Auckland Football Club. Supporters' spirits were initially raised when the programme notes cited the return of Bobby Hardisty to replace young Barry Wilkinson. Not that Barry had let the side down in any way. On the contrary, he had proved himself an admirable understudy to the international star, who had been forced to miss the last two games through a nagging leg injury.

Notwithstanding Bobby Hardisty's selection, sadly, Bishop did not get going and were beaten 1-3, suffering their first home defeat in the Amateur Cup for eighteen years in front of 11,000 spectators. The Walton and Hersham defenders were always quicker to the ball and were able to pass directly to a positive forward line. And yet it was the Bishops that took the lead when Jacky Major scored after thirty-five minutes. Until then, the Bishop attack, missing the bustling McIlvenny, had been a distinct second best.

The lead was short-lived and four minutes later the Southerners equalized through Crooks. Three minutes later Johnson lobbed the ball over the frame of Bill White to put Walton ahead at the half-time break. A thirty-five-yard pile-driver from Martin after seventy minutes completed the scoring. Bobby Hardisty, Benny Edwards and the tireless Major channelled everything into attack but the opposition defence stood firm. Bishop had suffered their first home defeat in the competition for eighteen years and were out of the Cup... for the time being at least.

In an incident that brought nothing but shame to the name of Bishop Auckland Football Club, a protest was made to the Football Association that Walton and Hersham had played an ineligible player. At that time it was a rule of the competition *'...that every club playing in the competition after the second round of the qualifying competition shall, not less than five days before the match send...to the opposing club, a list of players from which the team for such match will be selected, and no objection to the qualification of any player mentioned in such list shall be entertained unless notice of objection...is given at least twenty-four hours before the commencement of the match.'*

After the game, Bishop contended that John Taylor (brother of Willington captain Eddie Taylor and Newcastle United's Ernie Taylor), one of the Walton and Hersham players, had signed professional forms for Consett, a North-Eastern League club in 1946, and therefore was not an eligible player. Their objection failed of course, on the grounds that it had been made outside the twenty-four-hour period prescribed by the rules of the competition.

Crook Town: Making goals

Supporters of the club let their feelings be known. The vast majority were of the opinion that it was sour grapes on Bishop's part and wrote letters of indignation to the club and local press. As far as they were concerned Walton and Hersham had proved themselves the better team on the day and should be allowed to keep the match. There was to be no reprieve for Bishop. The Football Association agreed and allowed the result to stand.

A trip to the Channel Islands followed at the end of the season, which resulted in yet another trophy being won, namely the Guernsey Victoria Cup.

No Amateur Cup to adorn the trophy room, but otherwise a successful season… and there was always next year.

Well, the 1952-53 season was not long in coming and of course Bishop made their customary fast start in the Northern League. They would not be relinquishing their title lightly, but relinquish it they did, finishing runners up to bitter rivals Crook Town.

One of the games that Dad and I went to that year was the FA Cup match against Coventry City. This second round tie at Kingsway attracted a record crowd of nearly 17,000.

Bishop had entered the competition at the Fourth Qualifying Round stage. Spennymoor United were beaten 2-1 at Kingsway, the teams having drawn 1-1 at the Brewery Ground. They then disposed of Selby 1-5 on the Yorkshire side's ground in Round One of the competition proper. Unfortunately, in this second round match, the league side proved their superiority, scoring four goals to Bishops' one.

It was no shame to be knocked out of the FA Cup by a Football League side but, alas, there was no significant cup run this year either in the Amateur Cup. The wheels soon fell off in that competition. Everything in the garden looked rosy when Shildon were thrashed 2-7 on their home soil in the opening round but in Round Two Southall inflicted a 2-0 defeat on the 'Two Blues'. Nothing went right for the visiting Bishops that day: captain Tommy Farrer, an England international, was diagnosed as suffering from jaundice on the morning of the match, but still decided to play, and to cap it all Bobby Hardisty missed a penalty. Some times you just know that things will not go right for you.

Successes in the Durham Benevolent Bowl and Bishop Auckland Hospital Cup failed to lighten the gloom of a disappointing season.

The players had a shorter time off than usual for the summer break as on 26th July they flew out to Rhodesia - now Zimbabwe - for an eight-game tour. Their first game took place on 1st August and resulted in a 4-0 win over Broken Hill. Bishop went on to win a further five games, losing the remaining two. Bishop were the first amateur club to visit Rhodesia.

After the disappointment of the previous season was put behind them, the Bishop Auckland players began the next campaign with renewed hope. Early season wins soon put them at the head of the division and players and supporters anticipated a more productive season The first real test arrived when Bishop were drawn away to near neighbours Spennymoor United in the Fourth Qualifying Round of the FA Cup.

Spennymoor were a doughty team who would be very difficult to overcome. They played the style of football that could kindly be described as 'getting stuck in'. A team like Bishop were quite capable of coming out on top, but it was no foregone conclusion, especially with the game being played on Spenny's pitch.

But let us add, or rather take away, another ingredient. Let us take four key players out of the Bishop Auckland side in order that they can play in a trial match, and still insist that the cup game take place. Ridiculous? Of course...but that is what happened. Imagine the Arsenal side of the Nineties being told to play without Seaman, Adams, Smith and Wright as they had to play in an England trial, and yet their league game against Chelsea at Stamford Bridge must go ahead as planned. There would be uproar from supporters, players and management alike. Back in the Fifties it was just accepted as one of those things. League and Cup games were not cancelled or re-arranged for international matches. Clubs had to make do with using other players from their squads; after all, what were reserve team players for?

Saturday November 7th 1953 was the designated date for the amateur football match between the selected Northern Counties against the Southern Counties at Bloomfield Road, Blackpool. It was also the date of the Fourth Qualifying Round of the FA Cup and despite Bishop's request to reschedule the match, the Football Association ruled that the game(s) must go ahead as planned.

The FA Cup game resulted in a 3-1 home win for Spennymoor, thereby allowing them to progress to the first round proper. It was the first time that season that Bishop had been defeated, and avenged Spennymoor's defeat from the competition by Bishop the previous season.

The 5,900 spectators saw Dixon give Bishop the lead, which they held until just after half-time, when Browntree equalised in the fifty-fifth minute. Spennymoor, as usual, were uncompromising but they started to show their aggression in repeated attacks on the Bishop goal. Makeshift centre-forward Doug Humble was a real handful and gave Dave Marshall the runaround in the second half, scoring twice in the seventy-third and seventy-eighth minutes. A considerably weakened Bishop Auckland side had given its best, but had been knocked out of the FA Cup nevertheless.

The trial game resulted in a 4-0 win for the Northern Counties. Representatives from Bishop Auckland in the side were Sharratt (goalkeeper), Cresswell (left half-back), Oliver (centre-forward) and O'Connell (inside-left).

The *Northern Echo* reporter of the day expressed surprise that the England amateur international selectors had seen the Northern Counties play much the better football in the match, and yet only saw fit to select one player from that side, namely Walton of Bury, to play for his country against France the following Saturday. He roared: '...*W J Slater, who preferred to play for his club Wolverhampton Wanderers at Middlesbrough on Saturday was, of course, an automatic choice, but the claims of the Northern League, and Bishop Auckland in particular, have once again been ignored.*

'*Bishop Auckland supplied no fewer than four members of the North eleven, and their supporters must feel very sore that, after having to watch a depleted side lose to Spennymoor United in the FA Cup, not one of the four has been given the honour of playing in the international. Cresswell, however, is one of the reserves.*'

Southern bias? Probably, but I agree entirely with the sentiment expressed by the newspaper correspondent.

There was no denying that the South had an adornment of good amateur clubs. There were six good standard recognised leagues around the London area: Corinthian League, Spartan League, Athenian League, Isthmian League, Delphian League and the London League. In those leagues could be found clubs such as Wycombe Wanderers, Kingstonian, Walthamstow Avenue, Leytonstone, Briggs Sports, Hounslow Town, Hayes, Finchley, Hendon, Barnet and many other strong teams. Good clubs, all of them, but the Northern Counties had just beaten their best comfortably, yet only one of its players was seen fit enough to play for his country.

That month, Keith Hopper of Shildon scored seven goals in a Northern League game, a post-war record that would undoubtedly stand for some time. It did... for fourteen days.

Saturday 12th December 1953 saw Bishop play at home to Penrith: and play they did. The score was 12-0 and Seamus O'Connell got eight of them. Not surprisingly with such a scoreline, Penrith were always on the defensive, and although centre-half Boyle kept Oliver off the scoresheet, he alone of the Penrith players came out of the game with any credit. First half goals from Dixon and O'Connell (2) put the home team three up at the interval. The floodgates opened in the second half when Penrith goalkeeper Hughes damaged his wrist in dealing with a shot from Nimmins and had to leave the field. Centre-forward Mattinson took over in goal and the Bishops showed no mercy, devouring the overwhelmed Penrith defence like a pack of wolves on an injured lamb. Second half goals were scored by O'Connell (6), Dixon, Major and Nimmins.

At this stage of the season Bishop were top of the league and had scored twenty-one goals in their last two games. They were five points ahead of closest rivals Crook Town with a game in hand. Their form figures were:

P	W	D	L	F	A	Pts
13	12	1	0	63	17	25

(Note that only two points were awarded for a win, the three
points system not coming in for another thirty years)

In another game, Bishop had been the visitors to Evenwood Town in a Northern League Challenge Cup tie. Evenwood were one of those run-of-the-mill sides that always seemed they should have produced more than they did. They had honest triers but more often than not came a cropper against the good teams…and this Bishop Auckland team was better than a good one.

There was no score in the game for the first twenty minutes, by which time Bishop should have been in front. Then, Cresswell was adjudged to have fouled Kilcran in the penalty area. Harry Sharratt was delighted. He had touched the ball twice until now, both of which had been back-passes from Dave Marshall and Tommy Stewart, and was over the moon that he would have something to do. He was completely unfazed about facing the penalty, which was taken by the Evenwood captain, Webb. The left-back placed the ball meticulously on the spot and turned his back, walking to the edge of the 'D'. He looked up and ran to smash the ball. In a blur, the Bishops' 'keeper flung himself to his left and clutched the ball on the goalline, with one hand. Webb was dumbstruck… he had hit the ball perfectly, hard and low and with precision.

In that moment of reflection, Sharratt had already made it to his feet and punted the ball downfield. Oliver, the predator that he was, was not at all surprised to see his athletic colleague pull off the save - Harry was a master at stopping penalties. The Bishop centre-forward stood on the edge of the centre-circle in splendid isolation, already anticipating the leather ball in flight coming his way. He watched eagerly as it by-passed his left shoulder and was already chasing it. The ball had bounced only once as the burly railway porter bore down on the Evenwood goal. Then, just outside the penalty area, Ray decided to take his chance. He drew back his right foot and with a crashing volley - 'Ah cowt the barl stottin,' says Ray, in the vernacular which translated means, 'I caught the ball on the bounce,' - sent a shot past a stunned Swainston in the home goal. Every one of the Evenwood players had gone up for the penalty, so eager were they to take the lead in the match, that not one of the outfield players was in the Evenwood half when the goal was scored. It had taken less than twenty seconds for Evenwood to have been awarded a penalty and Bishop to score. There were further goals. Evenwood got one through Geldart but Bishop were already in command by then and led 5-1. The final score was Evenwood 1 Bishop Auckland 9 and the goalscorers were Oliver (3), Dixon (4) and Blacklock (2).

The Amateur Cup campaign started in January with a comfortable away win against I. C. I., the Bishops scoring six without reply. Three weeks later the second round home tie took place at Kingsway, Ware Town providing the opposition. They were the reigning Spartan League champions but Bishop brushed them aside with contempt. Goals from O'Connell in the first and fourth minutes were quickly followed by a brace from Dixon in the eighth and ninth minutes. Game over.

The luckless Ware defender, Pedder, scored for Bishop with a thirty-seventh minute own goal but the deficit was reduced just after half time by Hibbert. The tireless Ray Oliver weighed in with a trademark diving header in the final minute to complete the rout and restore the five-goal advantage.

Ray Oliver only scored one goal in this match, but contributed so much to the game and had a hand in the build up of most of the goals. He was a superb centre-forward, and don't just take my word for it: nearly every club in the First Division wanted to sign him. Some people say he was like Malcolm Macdonald, but he was better than that, he was far more than a 'run-at-a-barn-door' type of player. Ray Oliver was skilful and could shoot with either foot as well as being a powerful header of the ball and, in my humble opinion, was more like Mark Hughes in his playing days for Manchester United. The 'Big Three' of the North-East, Newcastle, Sunderland and Middlesbrough, all made attempts to get his signature, in addition to Darlington, Luton Town and Manchester City, but Ray did not want to know. He was happy to play for Bishop Auckland and hoped to win an Amateur Cup winners' medal, that was his goal, and turning professional did not play a part in it.

Oliver had previously been with Whitley Bay Athletic of the North Alliance League. Originally a centre-half, he transferred to the forward line. It was a good move... he scored goals for fun and soon became known as the Trevor Ford of amateur football. It was not long before the league clubs started clamouring for his signature, but he wasn't interested.

He played for Bishop before he actually signed for them. Bishop's tour of Rhodesia was about to take place and he was invited to come along as a guest player; at the time he was technically still with Whitley Bay Athletic. Before he knew it he was on the plane and heading for a different continent. Those few games, where he was able to get to know the other players and their style of play, paid dividends in the following season. The other players liked him and vice versa. He was signed for the new season and never regretted it. His partnership with Seamus O'Connell was a marriage made in Heaven. The result was goals, goals and more goals.

At some time that season he was selected to play for a Football Association XI against Oxford University. The FA team comprised amateurs and professionals, one of whom was Bobby Robson, then of Fulham. Oliver had an outstanding game and scored two goals in the FA XI's 4-2 win. Ray Oliver had shown the selectors just what he was made of and staked an undeniable claim for the England number nine jersey.

Whatever the game, Ray gave nothing less than one hundred per cent. On one occasion he was selected to represent Northumberland at centre-forward: opposing him was teammate Corbett Cresswell. With an important Amateur Cup tie coming up the following week, Corbett suggested that they take things a bit easy in any personal duels. Within two minutes, Corbett was nearly sent over the barrier from an Oliver challenge - his friend and opponent had no notion of showing any favours in this contest. (Ray never stops chiding Corbett in friendly banter whenever they meet up, and repeatedly reminds the Bishop centre-half how he got a hat-trick in Northumberland's 3-2 win, despite the third goal of the 'hat trick' being disallowed. Corbett, quite rightly, reminds Ray that he was taking things easy!).

Ray Oliver was also a member of The Royal Life-Boat Institution and performed acts of bravery throughout his time. When he was only eighteen he was instrumental in saving the lives of three men who had been swept into the water in Cullercoats Bay. Without any thought of danger to himself, he dived into the heavy sea and helped in the rescue. His uncle also assisted in the rescue.

On behalf of all those members of the public who have benefited from such unselfish and heroic acts, I raise a glass to Ray Oliver and his lifeboatmen everywhere.

Hallam, the only remaining team from Yorkshire, were Bishops' opponents in Round Three. Ray Oliver (surprise, surprise) scored a couple, O'Connell, Major and Dixon getting the other three in a 5-0 win. The result meant that in the opening three rounds of the competition, Bishop had scored seventeen goals with only one in reply. Was there a team in the land capable of stopping them regaining the Cup this season?

Well, some people thought that if Bishop were to be beaten then it might be by near-neighbours Crook Town. They had beaten Shildon 3-0 away from home in Round One, and then demolished Romford 6-0 at the Millfield Ground after a 1-1 result at the Southern club's ground. On the day that Bishop were putting five past the Hallam defence, six miles up the road, the Crook team were scoring five without reply against Walton and Hersham... remember them? If that was a good performance from Crook, what about their next round tie against Hitchin Town? The crowd at the Millfield saw eleven goals in the tie, ten of them coming from Crook who won the match 10-1. Impressive.

For their fourth round opponents, Bishop had Hounslow Town of the Corinthian League. The Southern side, playing in their traditional strip of red and black halved shirts and white shorts, started brightly and were clearly going to give the home side a run for their money. They had done their homework and had decided that the best way of beating the favourites was to try to harry them into mistakes by quick passing and tackling.

The plan was obviously working as within ten minutes they went a goal up. Alan King, the England amateur centre-forward, obtained possession of the ball and whipped past Corbett Cresswell, and from twenty-five yards sent a shot past a diving Harry Sharratt. Fortunately, Bishop began to compose themselves and goals from O'Connell and Oliver put them ahead. But slackness in the Bishop defence, due in part to the pressure imposed on them by the Hounslow forwards, resulted in King grabbing his second goal.

Hounslow's cause was not helped by an injury to their centre-half Briggs, who became a passenger on the right wing for most of the second half. Bishop piled relentless pressure on an overworked Hounslow defence, but it was not until late in the game that the match was won with goals from Major and Oliver. Bishop had won, but they knew that they had been in a match.

Bishop and Crook were kept apart in the draw for the semi-final ties. Bishop would play Briggs Sports of Dagenham, who played their football in the Spartan League. The game would take place at St James' Park, Newcastle. Crook would have to travel to White Hart Lane to meet Walthamstow Avenue.

As semi-finals go, the encounter at Newcastle was a non-event as Bishop eased to a 5-1 success.

Harry Sharratt could never have had an easier game, certainly in the first half, as all he had to contend with were back-passes and goal-kicks. The Lancashire schoolteacher had taken over the mantle of goalkeeper from Bill White, having played his previous football for Wigan Athletic. Rather amusingly, the Cup Final notes in the official programme said that he used to play at centre-half but because he was always handling the ball and giving away penalties he was made to play in goal! His first game for Bishop had been against Evenwood, late in season 1952-53, the game ending in a 1-1 draw. He went on to command the Bishops' goalkeeping spot for the next twelve years, playing his last game for the 'Two Blues' in 1964. He had made his international debut for England the previous season, 1951-52, and soon established himself as the best of his trade within the amateur ranks. Before Wigan, he had been on Blackpool's books and appeared for them in 1952 against Tottenham Hotspur, thus becoming the first amateur goalkeeper to appear for the 'Tangerines' in a league game. He became my favourite player and for years I was convinced that he was the best 'keeper that I had ever seen, amateur or professional.

Harry was a joker. Ray Oliver tells the story that when the Bishops were touring Guernsey, the players found their shoes were missing from the hotel that they were staying in. All the players came down to breakfast in their stockinged feet... all except Harry, that is. When challenged, Harry denied all knowledge of the whereabouts of the missing shoes. Later that morning thirteen pairs of shoes were discovered on the garage roof of the hotel. Harry was forced to own up.

Five foot eleven inches tall, he had tremendous agility, was a wonderful shot stopper and could deal with the most awkward of crosses. In my (biased?) opinion, he should have collected more caps than the six that he was awarded. Perhaps his indifference to conservatism cost him votes from the selection panel. Do you remember Bruce Grobbelaar of Liverpool? Eccentric, wasn't he? Well, Harry could have wiped the floor with him. He was taking throw-ins for his team long before Grobbelaar was out of short trousers. During a match at Shildon he was having a quiet time and decided to build a snowman on the goalline to keep him company. The referee didn't like the idea of Bishop having an extra 'man' on the pitch and promptly booked Harry.

When Bishop were particularly dominant during a game, which happened quite a lot, he would attract the attention of a spectator behind the goal and send him to the dugout with a note to any other team member. The note would read, 'Come and talk to me, I'm lonely'. And, as I recorded in my 'Warm up', he was not averse to accepting cups of liquid refreshment from generous supporters. Full-back Dave Marshall recalls that if he was having very little to do, Harry would deliberately throw the ball to an opposing forward so that he could be involved in some action. Sometimes he would borrow a newspaper from a spectator and, leaning against a goalpost, proceed to read it smoking away at a cigarette that he had no doubt cadged from the crowd.

Ray Oliver played against Harry during a Lancashire v Northumberland game. *'The ball came across and I met it perfect with my head. The ball was travelling like lightning towards the top corner of the goal. Harry took off and somehow managed to fingertip the ball over the crossbar. Any other goalkeeper would not have bothered, but somehow he got to it. It was an amazing save.'*

Corbett Cresswell, who played many times in front of Harry in his centre-half berth, told me: *'Harry was a bloody idiot. He would pull off fantastic saves and then deliberately throw the ball to a marked Bishop player. Inevitably the ball would be returned to our penalty area, whereupon more*

September 3rd 1949, Kingsway. Tommy Farrer shakes hands with barefooted Nigerian F A XI captain, Henshaw, before the Bishops 5-2 victory over the tourists. *(The photograph was reproduced as the club's official Christmas card in 2003 hence the message).*

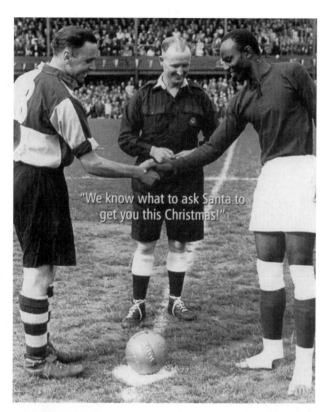

February 20th 1954 Amateur Cup 4th Round, Kingsway.
Ray Oliver scores against Hounslow in Bishop Auckland's 4-2 win.
(Copyright E. Johnson, Middlesbrough Evening Gazette).

**March 13th 1954 Amateur Cup Semi-Final, St James' Park, Newcastle.
Bustling centre-forward, Ray Oliver, worries the Briggs Sports full-back,
Bumstead, and goalkeeper Garrard. Bishop beat
their Spartan League opponents 5-1.**
(Copyright E. Johnson, Middlesbrough Evening Gazette).

April 10th 1954 Amateur Cup Final, Wembley.
Proud captains, Bobby Davison of Crook Town, and Jacky Major of Bishop
Auckland, lead the teams out on to the Wembley turf...the prelude to the
greatest and most dramatic Amateur Cup Final of all-time.
(Photograph courtesy of Newcastle Chronicle and Journal).

April 10th 1954 Amateur Cup Final, Wembley.
Crook Town full-back, Tom Riley, finds Ray Oliver a handful
as the centre-forward heads wide.
(Copyright E. Johnson, Middlesbrough Evening Gazette).

April 10th 1954 Amateur Cup Final, Wembley.
Twelve minutes gone and Les Dixon becomes the first forward
to score for Bishop Auckland in a Wembley final.
(Photograph courtesy of Newcastle Chronicle and Journal).

April 10th 1954 Amateur Cup Final, Wembley.
Ray Oliver and Seamus O'Connell (second from right) play
'Spot The Ball' with the Crook defenders.
(Photograph courtesy Newcastle Chronicle and Journal).

April 10th 1954 Amateur Cup Final, Wembley.
Crook Town goalkeeper, Fred Jarrie, pushes the ball away
to safety to thwart a Bishop attack.
(Photograph courtesy Newcastle Chronicle and Journal).

April 10th 1954 Amateur Cup Final, Wembley.
Jarrie is on his knees as Ray Oliver's brilliant effort finds
the back of the net to put Bishop 2-1 ahead.
(Photograph courtesy Newcastle Chronicle and Journal).

April 12th 1954 Bishop Auckland members, family and friends prepare to leave King's Cross Station for the journey home, following the 2-2 draw at Wembley against Crook Town. Sixth from left is Les Dixon with his girlfriend Helen. Next to Les is Jimmy Nimmins whose wife is behind, talking to Seamus O'Connell. In front of Jimmy is Bobby Watson (white shirt) then Ray Oliver, Ron Fryer and Corbett Cresswell. Dave Marshall is to the right (dark overcoat) linked by girlfriend Jane (holding newspaper). Chairman of the club, George Waine, is seated at the forefront.

April 22nd 1954 Amateur Cup Final 2nd Replay, Ayresome Park, Middlesbrough. Two views of Ray Oliver's disallowed goal. Oliver was adjudged to have pushed Crook centre-half, Bobby Davison, out of the way, before beating Jarrie. Crook went on to win this second replay 1-0.
(Copyright E. Johnson, Middlesbrough Evening Gazette).

April 22nd 1954 Amateur Cup Final 2nd Replay, Ayresome Park, Middlesbrough.
Same disallowed goal, different angle.
(Photograph courtesy of Newcastle Chronicle and Journal).

December 11th 1954 F A Cup 2nd Round, Selhurst Park.
Corbett Cresswell (left) watches apprehensively as colleague Ron Fryer tries to
head clear a Crystal Palace attack (goalkeeper Harry Sharratt hidden).
Bishop won 4-2.

January 12th 1955 F A Cup
3rd Round Replay, Kingsway.
Ray Oliver (number 9)
menaces the Ipswich defence,
as Derek Lewin waits to
pounce on any loose ball.
Bishop beat their Football
League opponents 3-0.
*(Copyright E. Johnson,
Middlesbrough Evening
Gazette).*

January 22nd 1955 Amateur Cup 2nd Round, Kingsway.
Derek Lewin's shot beats the Erith and Belvedere defence
for Bishop Auckland's second goal.
(Copyright E. Johnson, Middlesbrough Evening Gazette).

January 22nd 1955 Amateur Cup 2nd Round, Kingsway.
Seamus O'Connell's effort results in a third goal for Bishop Auckland
against Erith and Belvedere.
(Copyright E. Johnson, Middlesbrough Evening Gazette).

January 22nd 1955 Amateur Cup 2nd Round, Kingsway.
Ray Oliver (extreme right|) scores Bishop's fourth in a convincing
5-0 defeat of luckless Erith and Belvedere.
(Copyright Northern Echo).

February 5th 1955 Amateur Cup 3rd Round, Kingston.
The start of the demolition…Derek Lewin nets the first as a despairing Geoff
North looks on. The Kingstonian 'keeper would be beaten a further eleven
times as Bishop went on to record a 12-3 success away from home.

February 19th 1955 Amateur Cup 4th Round, Kingsway.
Finchley goalkeeper, Barham, competes for the ball with Bishop centre-
forward, Ray Oliver. The game ended 1-1.
(Copyright E. Johnson, Middlesbrough Evening Gazette).

February 19th 1955 Amateur Cup 4th Round, Kingsway.
In his inimitable style, Ray Oliver puts the pressure on the Finchley
defence during the drawn game at Kingsway.
(Copyright E. Johnson. Middlesbrough Evening Gazette).

March 12th 1955 Amateur Cup Semi-Final, Belle Vue, Doncaster
Ray Oliver refuses to give up in his attempt to score
against Wycombe Wanderers.
(Copyright E. Johnson, Middlesbrough Evening Gazette).

**March 12th 1955 Amateur Cup Semi-Final, Belle Vue, Doncaster.
Ray Oliver sticks out a right leg to score the goal against Wycombe Wanderers
that returned Bishop to Wembley.**
(Copyright E. Johnson, Middlesbrough Evening Gazette).

**April 15th 1955, Stamford Bridge, Chelsea Football legend, Ted Drake, gives
some eve of final advice to Derek Lewin (partially hidden),
Seamus O'Connell, Bobby Hardisty and Jacky Major**

April 16th 1955 Amateur Cup Final, Wembley.
Dexter Adams, captain of Hendon, and Tommy Stewart, captain of Bishop
Auckland, lead the teams into the sunlight of Wembley Stadium.
The author is in the crowd just above Ray Oliver's head (far right)
...next to the man eating an ice-cream! Bishop won 2-0.
(Photograph courtesy Newcastle Chronicle and Journal).

April 16th 1955 Amateur Cup Final, Wembley.
Field-Marshall Viscount Montgomery of Alamein, KG, GCB, DSO is presented
to the Bishop Auckland team prior to the kick-off of the final. Players in the
picture (from left to right) are Jimmy Nimmins (partially hidden), Ray Oliver,
Bobby Hardisty, Seamus O'Connell, Derek Lewin and Jacky Major.
Captain, Tommy Stewart, is hidden by 'Monty'.
(Photograph courtesy of Newcastle Chronicle and Journal).

**April 16th 1955 Amateur Cup
Final, Wembley.
Only three minutes gone and
Harry Sharratt has to produce a
brilliant save to foil Hendon
centre-forward, Erwin Bahler.**
*(Photograph courtesy of
Newcastle Chronicle and
Journal).*

**April 16th 1955 Amateur Cup Final, Wembley.
Hendon defender, Dexter Adams, is powerless to prevent Derek Lewin's
fine lob to put the Bishops in front, 1-0.**

April 16th 1955 Amateur Cup Final, Wembley.
Bobby Hardisty and Corbett Cresswell ensure that this Hendon attack
is repulsed, as Derek Lewin watches in typical style.

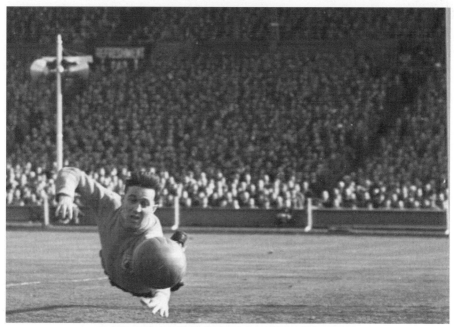

April 16th 1955 Amateur Cup Final, Wembley.
Harry Sharratt pulls off another fine save. Bishop Auckland
went on to win the match 2-0.

April 16th 1955 Amateur Cup Final, Wembley.
Derek Lewin is foiled in this raid on the Hendon goal.

April 16th 1955 Amateur Cup Final, Wembley.
Hendon goalkeeper, Reg Ivey, finds out what it is like to meet a determined
Ray Oliver, as fellow defender, Dexter Adams, looks pleased not to be involved.

often than not, Harry would produce another remarkable save. He would drive us defenders crazy at times, but without any shadow of a doubt he was the best goalkeeper, ever. He was an idiot, but we all loved the man.'

Eat your heart out, Bruce.

As usual, it was O'Connell who got the opening goal, as he had done in all of the previous cup ties. That goal was scored after fifteen minutes and then four minutes later, Ray Oliver got a second when Watson delivered a perfect pass to him. Watson himself scored the third, just three minutes later, after O'Connell had hit the woodwork.

Then, completely out of the blue, Briggs got a goal back, and what a good goal it was. Veteran Green, belying his thirty-three years, collected a crossfield pass from Smith, raced forward and sent a belter past Sharratt, just before the break.

Thirteen minutes after the restart, Bishop compounded their superiority with a fourth goal, Oliver tapping home from close range after an O'Connell effort had only been parried. The fifth and final goal was scored by Dixon.

The game ended with Briggs' goalkeeper Garrard pulling off good saves from the Bishop forwards, but a scoreline of 5-1 really flattered them, as they could have conceded more.

Crook, in the meantime, were drawing 1-1 in their semi-final and went on to reach the final after winning the replay at Roker Park, Sunderland, 3-2, Harrison scoring a hat-trick.

The North of England had got what it had wished for, namely, a final between the two best amateur clubs in the region, if not the country. For the second time in four years the Amateur Cup Final would be an all Northern League affair... not a National League as the printers had repeatedly stated in the official programme when Bishop had played Willington in the 1950 final.

As long as I could remember there had always been rivalry between Bishop Auckland and Crook Town, involving both players and supporters - rivalry almost bordering on the fanatical. As I mentioned earlier in this book, all of the Adamthwaite family had supported Crook - all except my dad, that is, and me. Thankfully, the allegiance to the main opposition by Dad had not resulted in any friction between him and other family members. To say that Crook Town Football Club had a somewhat chequered history would be an understatement. Formed in 1894, within seven years they had won the Amateur Cup, defeating King's Lynn 3-0 in the 1901 final. However, now was the first time in those intervening fifty-three years that they found themselves in a position to repeat the success, although technically this was a different club.

During their history, Northern League Championships had been won but the club's main claim to fame, or rather infamy, was a result of their being found guilty of making illegal payments to their amateur players during the 1927-28 season (although other clubs were perhaps not entirely blameless). The Durham Football Association banned the club and its players from the Northern League competitions (For a more detailed account see *Northern Goalfields Revisited* by Brian Hunt, pages 424-430). The club was allowed to return to the Northern League for the 1929-30 season, but after only this one season they took the rather adventurous step of turning semi-professional and played their football in the North-Eastern League. Two seasons later, in 1932, they reached the third round of the FA Cup and were drawn to play Leicester City at home. The directors of the club put financial expediency before the wishes of their supporters and transferred the match to Filbert Street. Crook lost 7-0 but, more importantly, lost the trust of their supporters - including my granddad - many of whom threatened to boycott the club thereafter.

1937 saw Crook returning to the amateur ranks and playing, yet again, in the Northern League. However, following the outbreak of hostilities in 1939, the Northern League was suspended and the club subsequently folded. Surprisingly, a new club was formed in 1942, adopting the name of Crook Colliery Welfare but still playing their fixtures at the Millfield. With the ending of the Second World War, the Northern League resumed, in which the club played its games under the Colliery Welfare banner until 1949, when it reverted to its original name of Crook Town. Northern League Championships, as well as a number of lesser trophies, had been won during the club's history but the Amateur Cup, as it was for all amateur clubs, remained the Holy Grail. Now, only their mighty neighbours stood in their path for Wembley glory.

In Round One, Crook had put aside fellow Northern League club Shildon, winning 3-0 away from home. A difficult tie at Romford in Round Two produced a 1-1 draw but, seven days later, the Essex club were soundly defeated 6-0 in the replay. A further thrashing was handed out, this time 5-0, in the home tie against Walton and Hersham, before another avalanche in the fourth round saw the 'Amber and Blank' produce a devastating show to humble Hitchin 10-1. The semi-final against classy Walthamstow Avenue at White Hart Lane, had been a tough encounter but a meritorious 1-1 draw was achieved thanks to a Jimmy McMillan goal. Now, as a result of that hat-trick by Ken Harrison in the replay at Roker Park, Crook found themselves Wembley-bound, about to meet their fiercest rivals from six miles down the road.

It was about this time that Mum and Dad had decided to bite the bullet and relocate to the Midlands. Work at Hole-in-the-Wall was depressing and conditions even worse. Mum gave Dad her full support and we looked forward to the move. But first of all Dad would have to live in a miners' hostel until a house was ready for us and in order that he could show his willingness to accept the new machinery and working conditions.

During Dad's upbringing in Crook he had made many friends, many of the friendships carrying on from when he left school at fourteen years of age. He had been a keen footballer and as a schoolboy had represented his county in a team that had included Jackie Snowdon (Willington goalkeeper). One of his close friends was Gordon Thompson, a Charlie Chaplin lookalike. Whereas dad was six feet two inches tall, Gordon was five foot nothing on his tiptoes so you can imagine they made a great pair together. They had worked together down the pit and when Mum and Dad went to live at Howden, Gordon and his wife Betty did likewise, taking over a council house just around the corner from us.

Mum and Dad were not alone, of course, in deciding to uproot and move. Many other mining families were facing the reality that the industry in the North-East was dying on its feet. The call of the National Coal Board for miners to move to the coalfields of the Midlands was not only addressed to the northern community. The call also went out to the Scottish miners and the Welsh, and those from the small Kentish collieries. The call became an international one as Latvians, Estonians, Poles, Slavs and probably every nationality under the sun was invited to become a miner in Staffordshire, Nottinghamshire, Leicestershire and Warwickshire.

Gordon and Betty were no doubt having similar conversations to those that Mum and Dad were having, for they too decided to move away. If George and Margaret are moving, then we will move too!

First, though, there was an Amateur Cup Final to see.

If the atmosphere prior to the Bishop Auckland-Willington game had been electric, then for the Bishop-Crook game it was mega electric. Once more, bus companies and the LNER would make handsome profits from the excursions laid on for everyone fortunate enough to possess a ticket for the big match. The area would once again resemble a ghost town. For both teams the message was the same: 'Best of luck lads. Don't come back without the cup.'

The match day edition of *The Evening News*, a London newspaper, highlighted once again that Bishop were favourites to win the cup. They had carried all before them so far in the competition, scoring at least four goals in each game that they had played. In their league campaign they had dropped only one point all season. If one included the Rhodesian tour, they had also taken part in more games than any other club that season. Victor Railton, sports reporter, pointed out that the club had a record second to none, having won the Amateur Cup seven times, been finalists fourteen times and had made twenty-two semi-final appearances in the fifty-one seasons of the competition.

Since the beginning of February, Bishop had had the assistance of George Ainsley, a former Sunderland, Leeds United and Bradford player. He was regarded as a first-class FA coach and had prepared Pegasus to win the trophy the previous season.

Crook Town were not going to be beaten easily, however, even though twice that season the league games had gone Bishops' way. They too had acquired coaching help, this time in the form of Joe Harvey, the Newcastle United coach, a respected figure in football. They were as confident as Bishop of winning the cup and why should they be afraid? They had good quality players, some with Wembley experience. The side included four who had played for Bishop Auckland previously.

Bobby Davison had turned out for Bishop Auckland in the 1950 and 1951 finals, so naturally he was hoping for a winners' medal this time. In addition to football, he played a decent game of cricket and had travelled to Holland as a reserve for England. Ken Williamson, an inside forward, had turned out for Bishop against Pegasus. Ronnie Thompson, another inside forward, had been Crook's top-scorer the previous season when they pipped Bishop for the Northern League title, but prior to that had been with the 'Two Blues'. Unable to gain a regular first-team spot, he had moved to Crook.

The fourth member of the ex-Bishop brigade was John Taylor. He had played for a number of clubs as an amateur, including Crystal Palace and Sunderland. Whilst at theological college he had even turned out for Leytonstone in their semi-final venture against Bromley in 1949. He had also played for Bishop Auckland in their losing semi-final against Leytonstone in 1948. He was the only one in the side with international experience, as recently as two weeks ago he had been capped against Scotland at Wembley. That was his second game for his country, as he had played against Holland earlier in the season. It is a tragedy that he did not gain more international honours, and the reason that he did not had nothing to do with his ability as a player.

John Taylor was a fine musician, being an accomplished pianist, trumpeter and choirmaster. He formed the Durham Youth Choir and was instrumental in many of the musical organisations in the area and was particularly fond of church music as he was a very religious man. In addition he had a fine baritone voice. He was employed as Music Master at Spennymoor Grammar School. He had become acquainted with Margaret Waterhouse, a lady who shared similar musical interests and in 1952 they were married. Their first son, John, was born in 1954 not long after John senior had won his first international cap.

His display in the game against Scotland, and his subsequent form in league games, once again attracted the attention of the international selectors and he was chosen to play for England in their forthcoming fixture. Unfortunately for John, that game was scheduled for the opening day of the school term, an occasion for which all masters had to attend. John asked his employers for permission to be excused the opening day ceremonies but the headmaster of the school was adamant: if he did not attend school as directed, then he must look for another job. He also knew that if he snubbed the England selectors, then that would be the end of his international career.

Stuck between a rock and a hard place, John was in a quandary.

In the end, the choice was inevitable. His wife and family had to come first, and he informed the Amateur Selection Committee of his decision not to make himself available for England's next game. This was something that you just did not do. You did not snub the Football Association selectors, amateur or professional.

John Taylor was not selected again to represent his country.

One other little fact. If you look at the team photograph of Bishop Auckland in the official programme for the final against Pegasus you will see that there is a caption stating, 'J.W.R. Taylor was not present when this photograph was taken'. John Taylor's employers would not allow him time away to have his picture taken.

(It goes to show what a small world it is, that during my research for this book, I discovered that John and Margaret moved to the Stafford area in 1969 to further their musical interests. Sadly, John died in 1982 and is buried in the local cemetery of the village where I live. Margaret has continued with her musical vocation and tours the country giving musical concerts).

Victor Railton surmised that whilst they had an outstanding attack, the Crook defence was slightly suspect, suggesting that deficiencies that had been exposed by Walthamstow in the semi-final, lay at the centre-back and full-back positions.

As usual on these occasions, Dad made his customary Friday night journey to London. I had been to some of the league games that season but, being responsible parents, they took the view that I was too young to go to the Cup Final. I went round Crook's shops with my Mum instead!

The game took place on Saturday 10th April.

The teams were:

Bishop Auckland (Dark and Light Blue Halved shirts, White shorts)
Sharratt - Marshall, Fryer - Hardisty, Cresswell, Nimmins - Major, Dixon, Oliver, O'Connell, Watson

Glory Days

Crook Town (Amber shirts, Black shorts)
Jarrie - Riley, Steward - Jeffs, Davison, Taylor - Appleby,
Thompson, Harrison, Coxon, McMillan

Referee: A. Bond of Middlesex

What was to follow was one of the finest spectacles of the year. The game would last five and a half hours and become a test of physical endurance as well as skill. It would have supporters of both camps chewing their fingernails and wishing/not wishing the game to end, depending upon which stage of the match was being played. It was a truly Titanic struggle.

Things had not gone well for Bishop in the build-up to the match, Tommy Stewart going down with an attack of jaundice. It was tough luck on Tommy who had joined the 'Two Blues' earlier in the season after spending nine years with the Scottish amateur club, Queen's Park. He had been a member of the Scottish team that had comfortably beaten the England team 4-1 at Wembley just two weeks earlier. Ron Fryer was drafted in as replacement for his first Amateur Cup game of the season. What a start. Ah, well, things could only get better.

The loyal Ron Fryer, who had not known that he would be drafted into the squad until only forty-eight hours ago, was determined not to let his teammates down. He was a versatile little player and although feeling sorry for Tommy Stewart, had no intention of letting sentiment rule his performance. He was confident of his own ability and knew that if he did make an error, then his colleagues around him would help him out. But he was focused on giving a performance to remember at full-back. Just seven months ago he was turning out for a Newcastle junior side. Jimmy Callaghan, who was running the club, decided that Ron had the potential to be a decent player. He sent a recommendation to 'Kit' Rudd at Bishop which resulted in young Fryer being asked to play for their reserve team, as a trialist at Frosterley. 'Frosterley? Where the hell is Frosterley?' enquired a surprised Ron. He performed well in his opening game, deep in the heart of Weardale, showing skill and control on the left side of the field, and became a regular in Bishops' reserve side. After only half a dozen games, he was elevated to travelling reserve for the first team. Today would be his first game in the Amateur Cup and it would be at Wembley... not a bad start! He had wanted to be a pilot, but was only offered a role as navigator when serving his time in the RAF. Well, he was flying today all right - flying without wings - the youngest player in the team.

Crook kicked off, but Cresswell gained possession of the ball and sent Bob Watson away down the left wing. The attack petered out and play became concentrated around the midfield area of the pitch.

Crook Town: Making goals

Only six minutes had been played when disaster struck for Bishop Auckland. Jimmy Nimmins lay prone in the centre-circle. He lay there getting attention from the trainer whilst a worried looking Ray Oliver and captain Jacky Major looked on concerned. He could not carry on. Jimmy would receive the best treatment possible, but would learn that he had suffered a broken fibula to his right leg and fractured ligaments to the knee and ankle. He would rejoin the players later that evening with his leg in plaster. Bishop were down to ten men with only five minutes gone, against one of the most prolific scoring teams in amateur football. If they were to win the cup, they had a mountain to climb, and not just any mountain… this one was Everest.

The remaining ten men put in a Herculean performance, and as play moved from one end of the pitch to the other, Bishop began to get on top. Then, with only twelve minutes gone, the blue-clad supporters had something to cheer. A long free-kick, from within the Bishop half was sent forward and cleared the Crook defenders, standing too square on the edge of the area. Inside-right Les Dixon controlled the ball with his right foot and in a flash crashed it past a despairing Jarrie for the opening goal. It was the first goal scored by a Bishop Auckland forward at Wembley in three Wembley appearances.

Les Dixon was one of those good utility inside-forwards who could create and score goals at will. Bishop had acquired his services during the previous season, when it was explained to him that the club needed someone who could get goals as well as serve the other forwards. Les did not let the club or his colleagues down. He was always buzzing around and was the type of forward that defenders hated with his nimble feet and constant movement. He had remarkable speed and had immediately formed a goalscoring partnership with Oliver and O'Connell. Ray Oliver thought him the best inside-forward that he had played with and had lost count of the number of goals that the inside-forward had provided for him. (Les told me recently that by the end of the season, the main participants of the forward line had scored an incredible 199 goals in all games and competitions, including the Rhodesian tour; Jacky Major 25, Les Dixon 48, Ray Oliver 50, Seamus O'Connell 65 and Bobby Watson 11).

Dad was standing on the packed terraces, right behind the shot, at the tunnel end of the ground, and always said that that goal brought the biggest roar that he had ever heard at a football match. I think that he had paid 2/6d (twelve and a half pence in modern day money) for his ticket. How times have changed.

Crook stormed back and put immediate pressure on the Bishop defence. They say that a team is most vulnerable after scoring a goal and Bishop did not want to give away the advantage. A failed attack by Bishop resulted in

Taylor collecting the ball and moving up the left-wing. A fine tackle from Hardisty gave away a throw-in which Taylor himself took. He found Ken Williamson who immediately passed it on to Ronnie Thompson, who collected the ball on the edge of the Auckland penalty area, facing the centre of goal. Thompson took two paces forward with the ball and before any of the Bishop defenders could get to him, fired an angled low drive to Harry Sharratt's left. The ball nestled in the goal. 1-1.

The game went to and fro, both sets of players giving their all. The extra man advantage was not showing up in Crook's play, but surely the stout Bishop defenders would be unable to keep up this level of defence and pace for ninety minutes? Then it was Crook's turn to suffer a casualty. All week there had been rumours relating to the fitness of Ken Williamson, and after only twenty minutes he was found out. He limped on and off the pitch from then onwards and became only nuisance value as the game progressed.

Bob Watson was having a fine game playing against his old club, and on the half hour mark played a big part in Bishop's second goal. Like Ray Oliver, he worked for British Railways. He was not very tall but was quick when in possession of the ball and was always willing to take on defenders. Collecting the ball in the centre-circle, he looked up and saw Oliver just outside the Crook penalty area. The pass was perfect, landing at the centre-forward's feet. Oliver instantly controlled the ball and dribbled around three Crook defenders. From two yards outside the penalty area he sent in a rasping shot to Fred Jarrie's right. The speed and accuracy of the shot matched the build-up to the play, the ball squeezing past the goalkeeper to put Bishop 2-1 ahead.

The amber and black players were stunned and fought back like alley cats. Sharratt brought off two good saves before producing another leap to tip Thompson's effort over the bar. Then with wave upon wave of attacking movement from the Crook half-backs, Harrison met a long ball from the right and the ball looped into Harry Sharratt's goal. 2-2. No. The referee disallowed the effort as he had seen a foul by the Crook attacker, a let off for the Bishops, who bounced back immediately and forced Jarrie to make another diving save.

Alf Bond blew the whistle for half-time and the crowd drew breath. The football had been tremendous, probably frenetic, at times, and although the quality of play had not reached the standard of the 1950 final, for sheer excitement there was nothing to compare.

Bishop started the second half having to go on the defensive. Constant Crook pressure was pushing the half-backs further to the rear in support of Dave Marshall and Ron Fryer. The pressure was bound to produce dividends.

Bishop were made of stern stuff and counter attacked with regularity. Ray Oliver met a Jacky Major cross only to see Fred Jarrie save comfortably. As

Jarrie bounced the ball in his area, Oliver gave him a good old-fashioned shoulder charge, (you could do that to goalkeepers then). Jarrie stood firm, continued to bounce the ball and kicked it up-field to set up another attack.

In the fifty-fifth minute Crook were rewarded with a second goal. Bill Jeffs had been signed in the close season from Whitby, mainly because of his ability to tackle quickly and effectively. He won the ball on the Crook right flank and passed it forward. Like a well-oiled machine, the Crook forward line moved up, and when the cross came over, there was Eddie Appleby to slam the ball past a despairing Harry Sharratt. The scores were level and all four goals had been beauties; modern day commentators would be eulogising about them still.

The remaining thirty-five minutes was very much more of the same with both teams pounding the other. The fact that there were no more goals was a result of tired limbs as much as poor finishing, although Crook had an effort that struck the crossbar before Harry Sharratt produced a first class save. Moving to his left, he suddenly had to change direction to save Williamson's shot and somehow got his right hand to send the ball clear. The end of normal time finished with Bishop attacking but without success. Extra-time was necessary, the first time for a Wembley Amateur Cup Final.

The momentum was with Bishop and the first period of extra-time saw the Crook defence being harassed by the incessant wing-play of Major and Watson. Until now, Seamus O'Connell had deputised for Jimmy Nimmins at left-half, but now he was released forward. The physical fitness and stamina of the Bishop Auckland team surprised the 100,000 spectators. Not only were they holding out against eleven men but they were actually beginning to take the initiative. O'Connell's presence upfront added a new dimension to the Bishop attack and they looked the more likely team to score.

The second half of extra-time began the same way as the first had ended, with Bishop dominating the play. Bobby Hardisty, or should that be 'Artistry', put everything in to gaining a winners' medal and his performance was exemplary. All through the match he had been encouraging and cajoling his playing companions to increase their efforts, seeking that one moment of inspiration that would produce the winning goal. He had played twice already in two Wembley finals and been on the losing side on both occasions - he had no desire to be a 'three time loser'.

In the dying moments Bishop applied more pressure and Crook defenders blocked two Bishop shots but the ball would not go in the net.

Then it was all over. For the very first time a major Wembley Cup Final would have to be replayed.

Kenneth Wolstenholme of the BBC told his radio listeners that he had just witnessed the finest two hours of entertainment that he had ever seen.

The teams had produced a memorable game but there was no winner. A replay would take place in ten days' time on Easter Monday at St James' Park, Newcastle. The majority of supporters looked forward to the next match, as after all it would be held on a Bank Holiday; Dad was already wondering if or how he would get there. The mines would be closed on Good Friday (the Durham and Northumberland miners never worked that day, considering it unlucky) but Monday would see workers back on the evening shift and he was scheduled to be one of them.

* * * * *

As things turned out, Dad was able to get to the replay without too much difficulty as one of his work colleagues, a Tow Law supporter, arranged to swap with him. However, the kick-off was set for six o'clock and he would have no time to waste if he were to catch the train back in time for work.

The crowds were buzzing all afternoon in Newcastle as the streets filled up with supporters of both teams. Many of the crowd arrived late inside the ground due to the congestion. Dad was one of the fortunate ones as he arrived in good time and was able to stand at his normal spot whenever he went to St James' Park, behind the goal at the Gallowgate End. Gordon would meet him there but for the moment was stuck in the crowd, trying to get in. The official attendance was given as 56,008 producing gate receipts of £10,500.

The teams were:

Bishop Auckland (Dark and Light Blue Halved shirts, White shorts)
Sharratt - Marshall, Stewart - Hardisty, Cresswell, Wilkinson - Major, Dixon, Oliver, O'Connell, Watson

Crook Town (Amber shirts, Black shorts)
Jarrie - Riley, Steward - Jeffs, Davison, Taylor - Appleby, Thompson, Harrison, Coxon, McMillan

Referee: A. Bond of Middlesex

A roar went up as the players took the field. This brought the usual surge forward at the turnstiles from those latecomers outside, anxious not to miss any of the action. As the players had their pre-match kickabout, Dad wondered where Gordon had got to. He had seen him earlier that day and had told him which part of the ground to head for. Now, with only seconds to go before kick-off, he scanned the faces around him... if he didn't hurry up, Gordon would miss the start.

Crook Town: Making goals

Dad looked around him and wondered how Gordon would manage to see through this crowd once he got in to the stadium. Then, before he could think any more, Harry Sharratt was picking the ball out of the net. Bishop had kicked off but had lost possession immediately. Ron Thompson gathered the ball and passed it to Ken Harrison, who had been guilty of missing some of Crook's best chances in the opening game, and the Annfield Plain schoolteacher netted with a looping drive to Harry Sharratt's right.

The setback stunned Bishop. It was a sloppy goal and should never have been given away. Bishop responded immediately as Jacky Major got possession of the ball close to the halfway line and fed it to Bobby Hardisty. A quick look up and the ball was passed swiftly to Ray Oliver who shot on the turn, but two defenders blocked his effort.

Things worsened for Bishop as with Crook's next sojourn forward their rearguard was breached again. The move that brought the goal began on the right and when the ball was sent in to the middle, there was Harrison standing on the penalty spot. He evaded his marker and sent a low shot to Sharratt's right, just inside the post.

The clock showed four minutes past six. Gordon puffed his way to the side of my Dad and squeezed into position. 'Bloody crowds! Any score, George?' He had an orange box under his arm. Somehow, in the crush he was able to drop it upright on the terrace and then stood on it, from five foot to six foot two in one easy lesson. Smart thinking Gordon.

'Two nowt to Crook.'

Gordon looked up and smiled; George was always joking. He craned his neck to look between the shoulders of those standing in front of him, moving his head from one side to the other like a metronome as he caught glimpses of the play. The mutterings of those around him sunk in as he realised the reality of what Dad had said.

'Fucking hell!' Perfectly put, Gordon…never before or since were those two words more apposite.

Crook settled down to play football. They had had the perfect start and with Bill Jeffs and John Taylor acquiring a lot of the ball, were able to set up chances for the forward line, brilliantly commanded by Appleby and Thompson. Eddie Appleby was a speedy winger/inside-right and had a clear advantage over the international full-back Tommy Stewart, now fit and returned to the Bishop Auckland line-up. Attacks down the Crook right wing were set up with constant rapidity. Ronnie Thompson had an opportunity to score a third for Crook when Sharratt came out to collect a centre and missed the ball in the ensuing melee but his lobbed effort cleared the crossbar when it looked easier to score. The Bishop defence held and managed to stave off further goals.

If the defence was getting to grips with the situation, the Auckland forward line was struggling and was not cohesive. Oliver and O'Connell were well held by the combination of Jeffs, Davison and Taylor. So in command was the Crook defence that Fred Jarrie had only two anxious moments in the remainder of the first half. The first came on the half hour when Les Dixon put Oliver through, but with only the goalkeeper to beat, the centre-forward's shot hit Jarrie's left leg and the ball rebounded to safety. Then, with half time beckoning, Major left Taylor in his wake but was unable to squeeze the ball past the Crook goalkeeper as Riley raced across to add extra cover.

Then it was Sharratt's turn to show off his agility once more. When Thompson shot from twenty yards it looked a certain goal, but the Bishop custodian was equal to the task and flung himself to his right to tip the ball around the post.

Despite allowing Harrison to bag a couple of goals, and carrying a head injury sustained in a collision with the Crook centre-forward, Corbett Cresswell was having a fine game and improved as each minute passed by, some observers venturing to comment that it was the best game that he had played in a Bishops' shirt, especially with his cool distribution of the ball and positional sense.

There was a tremendous buzz around the ground when the teams came out for the second half. The Bishop players knew that they had to up the performance in their game and could not allow Crook to dominate the second half like they had the first. From the outset, Bishop started to play the type of football for which they were renowned. Passes were strung together and tackles brought possession of the football. All that they had to do was continue in this mode and goals would come - but would they come in forty-five minutes?

Well, one came after sixty-nine minutes when Oliver scored from a well carved opening. Hardisty took a free-kick that was only partially cleared when Oliver was unable to control the ball. A centre from the left was headed down and there was the centre-forward making himself available to collect the ball and stroke it coolly past Jarrie, who was rooted to his goalline. Now the bit was between Bishop's teeth and Bobby Hardisty, in his customary way, began to influence the midfield play. The equaliser came after eighty-one minutes. Barry Wilkinson, only seventeen years old, deputising for the injured Jimmy Nimmins, played a through-ball to Seamus O'Connell who found Oliver. The lifeboatman from Cullercoats made no mistake with a powerful shot that left Fred Jarrie diving helplessly to his left.

There was no more scoring and once again the one-armed referee, Alf Bond, had to call for extra-time.

As in the first game, the thirty minutes of extra play turned into a power struggle. First one team, then the other, claimed the advantage, but neither could score a third and decisive goal. The best chance fell to O'Connell in the first minute but his header was a tame effort and the pressure was eased on the Crook defence.

Crook had played John Coxon (yet another ex-Bishop player) in place of the unlucky Ken Williamson for this replay. He initially started at inside-left but in extra-time switched positions with Tommy Riley, who it was thought could add extra punch to the Crook attack, but the ploy failed.

No more goals were added and so once again the match finished in a 2-2 draw. A second replay was scheduled for Thursday of the same week at Ayresome Park, Middlesbrough. The Bishop Auckland players had good reason to be pleased with this arrangement as they were unbeaten there in previous Amateur Cup Finals.

* * * * *

The third instalment of this enthralling encounter took place in front of 36,727 paying spectators (including Dad). (Les Dixon, inside-right for Bishop Auckland, lived close to Middlesbrough and was a frequent visitor to Ayresome Park when not playing. He questioned the official attendance figure, believing that it was more like 46,000 to his mind). It was decided beforehand that if the scores were level at the end of full-time there would be no extra-time and that the clubs would share the trophy. Each club would have possession of the trophy for six months, a spin of the coin to decide who held the trophy first. In the event of a draw there would be no separate winners' and runners'-up medals. New medals would be inscribed to indicate that the Cup was held jointly.

The BBC had once again come to an arrangement with the Football Association to broadcast the second half of the game on the radio (North Home Service 261 metres).

The teams were:

Bishop Auckland (Dark and Light Blue halved shirts, White shorts)
Sharratt - Marshall, Stewart - Hardisty, Cresswell, Wilkinson - Major, Dixon, Oliver, O'Connell, Watson

Crook Town (Amber shirts, Black shorts)
Jarrie - Riley, Steward - Jeffs, Davison, Taylor - Appleby, Thompson, Harrison, Coxon, McMillan

Referee: A. Bond of Middlesex

Bishop were able to field the same side that had performed at Newcastle, the RAF finally agreeing to release Barry Wilkinson to play for them. Crook's selection problems hinged around the troublesome position of inside-left. Ken Williamson was the normal player for that berth but he was injured. John Coxon had been a suitable replacement at Newcastle, but late in the game Tommy Riley had played that role. Coxon got the nod.

(A little aside relating to the knock-on effect that the replays were having: West Auckland were due to play a home match this evening against the 7th TR Royal Signs (Catterick). Not much interest there you might think, until you realise that the Catterick team was made up of First Division professional and international players. The match was cancelled).

Many of the supporters at the game were those that had received their heroes from Wembley and Newcastle. Various celebration plans, made pre-Wembley, had been thrown out of the window, although both clubs had been given a civic welcome - Crook after the Wembley draw when over 8,000 people assembled at the Millfield ground the following day, and Bishop Auckland on the Monday after the second draw. Bishop would only get an official reception at the Town Hall if they won the Cup. On the other hand, Crook players would be paraded through the town by a local band and received at the Millfield whatever the result, win, lose or draw, this night.

The Amateur Cup would be on display at either Willington the following night (where Bishop would meet Willington), or at West Auckland (where West Auckland were to play Crook)… no respite for the wicked.

The game kicked off at 6:00pm with Alf Bond once more in charge. Bobby Davison won the toss, as he had done at Newcastle, and in the windy conditions it was Bishop who set the ball rolling.

The swirling wind and a light ball made good football difficult, especially from two tired teams, who by now must have been fed up of the sight of each other. Bishop tried to play neat football but it was clear that Crook were producing the more effective game. O'Connell and Dixon's play was too intricate for the conditions and Oliver was being well policed by the able Davison, probably the man of the series so far. In truth, the standard of football was not as high as that produced in the two previous encounters. Both teams were guilty of playing the high ball too much and each set of forwards gained little from stubborn defences. But what was lacking in entertainment was more than made up for in tension. Both sets of supporters were shouting themselves hoarse, giving extra encouragement to their heroes.

With thirty minutes gone, Bishop were awarded a corner on the right. Major swung the ball into a crowded penalty area and there was Oliver, rising like a salmon to head a magnificent goal past a crowded area into Jarrie's left-hand post. The Bishop players were ecstatic and their supporters delirious. It was one of those goals that forever stays in the memory. And, oh, how it would stay in the memory!

As the jubilant Bishop players danced back to the centre-circle for the restart, their joy was turned to sorrow.

Just as Sol Campbell's goals had been disallowed in the 1998 World Cup for England against Argentina, and later in the 2004 European Championship against Portugal, so it was with Ray Oliver's effort. The referee had ruled that Oliver had pushed Bobby Davison in jumping for the ball. To this day, Oliver is convinced that no such foul took place: Davison, on the other hand, was always of the opinion that the referee made the correct decision. Having seen the *Gaumont News* report of the game, I am siding with Oliver on this argument.

The disallowed goal resulted in more pressure from the hardworking Wilkinson and Hardisty being applied to the Crook defence, but it was Crook who took the lead.

With half-time drawing near, Appleby centred the ball in to the Auckland defence. The ball was cleared, but as the Bishop defenders moved out, it was quickly returned. Harrison had remained just onside and was able to lob the ball over the advancing Sharratt, who had seen the danger all too late.

The second half began with Bishop throwing everything in to get an equaliser, but Crook were always able to repel the challenge. Even when Tommy Stewart was sent forward to give extra support to the frontmen, Crook always looked in control. The second half was an anti-climax for Bishop supporters, as at no stage did they look capable of drawing level. Bobby Davison, at the heart of the Crook defence, never put a foot wrong and his performance gave impetus to his fellow defenders.

When the final whistle went, it was almost like a sigh of relief. Crook Town had won the FA Amateur Cup and had only used twelve players throughout the campaign. The players shook hands and both sets of supporters congratulated or commiserated with each other as the case may be. Dad was one of the disconsolate Bishop supporters who remained behind to applaud both teams. He would have a lot to tell me when he saw me the next day.

The three games produced an official aggregate attendance figure of 192,735 spectators, grossing receipts of over £46,600. The two finalists collected 25% each, £11,650, with the same amounts going to the Football Association and the pool shared by each of the sixty-four clubs that had taken part in the competition proper. Club treasurers up and down the country were delighted. (Crook and Bishop Auckland football clubs each made £25 donations to other members of the Northern League from the money that they had accumulated from their cup run, a tidy sum in those days when admission to football matches was 6d, or two and a half pence).

Glory Days

Later that evening over 15,000 cheering fans greeted the victorious Crook team as they returned triumphant to the Millfield. As soon as the result was known, people left their homes in Crook and filled the market square and the streets leading up to the victorious club's ground. West Road traffic was brought to a standstill.

Half a mile away, a tall figure was one of many passengers who alighted from a special that had pulled up next to the platform and strode out of Crook's small railway station. He bade his farewell to his companion. In the distance behind him he could hear the cheering and celebrations that were taking place at the local football ground. A few 'Cheerio's' to other men that he knew, some of whom would be taking the road to the left, ready to get to work at Pease's West; a few braver souls were taking the short cut, walking alongside the railway track that was the service line and led directly into the colliery yard.

He walked halfway down High Hope Street and turned left. A few revellers were making there way up to the Millfield, oblivious of the cold wind. On he walked past the rows of terraced housing, raucous laughter and music coming from some, along Gladstone Street and on down Raglan Street and then Arthur Street, passing his parents' house. He did not have time for a social call and hurried on past, turning left into the dip and then taking the long sharp incline that was Catholic Bank.

He entered the colliery and found somewhere to change into his work clothes that had been stowed away, to prepare for the night shift. In the stables close by he heard the whinny of a pony, lazily munching on a carrot, left for him, no doubt, by his keeper. He tied the laces of his hobnail boots, checked that he had his bait tin and then double-checked that his lamp was secure. Sure in the knowledge that he had everything that he would need for the next eight hours, he clocked on and walked into the yawning drift mine. Hole-in-the-Wall beckoned. He thought 'it was a blessed good goal that Ray Oliver scored'. (Dad never swore, even when he was thinking).

He took two more steps forward. Then he was surrounded by total darkness.

* * * * *

That was not the end of the season for Bishop, or Crook come to that. The cup run had taken its toll and outstanding fixtures had to be met. Fixture congestion was nothing new for the Bishops; they had become accustomed to it. They would fulfil their fixtures and try to win the league title into the bargain.

80

As it turned out, results for the remaining matches were disappointing. The first eighteen games of the season had produced an incredible 35 points (two points for a win, remember) and an obvious place at the top of the table. The last eight games, however, only produced seven goals and seven points; fatigue had set in. And yet they still won the league championship, with Crook in second place.

The season's achievement was soured to a degree by the attitude of the Durham Football Association. In a fit of pique, they fined Bishop Auckland the quite large sum of £50 for fielding a reserve side against Spennymoor United in the final of the Durham County Challenge Cup. Spennymoor won the match 6-1. The decision to field a team of reserves was not taken lightly as four players had been selected for a representative game scheduled for the same date and others were injured. Fielding the reserves was seen as the best way to complete this fixture. The DFA took exception to this and fined the club. Bishop had requested that the match be postponed but this request was turned down by the DFA. (Given the number of games that they had to play in such a short period of time before the official end of season, you have to wonder what good a postponement would have been to the club).

W.T.D. Reed in his book, *The Bishops*, tells us that thereafter the DFA would be charged for the use of Kingsway. It had previously been granted free. How shortsighted can you get?

With the title won and once more winners of the Northern Football League Challenge Cup, Bishop Auckland's season came to an end. An oft-quoted statistic for the season is that from fifty-five games, including those played on the Rhodesian tour, they had scored the grand total of 214 goals…truly a wonderful achievement. But the big one, the Amateur Cup, had got away.

With all of the disappointments in the post-war Amateur Cup Finals that I have written about so far, some of you may be wondering why on earth this book is entitled *Glory Days*.

I would say to you: 'First the Pain, then the Glory.'

PART TWO

CHAPTER FOUR

Hendon: Moving out

'Get theeself away, son.'

Mum and Dad were talking to Grandma and Granddad, telling them of their decision to move to the Midlands. They had had similar conversations with Mum's dad and stepmother, and other family friends and relatives. Not one had disagreed with their decision to move.

'There's nee work around here. And don't forget; the trains travel in both directions. If things don't work out, you can always come back'.

I sat on the wooden rocking chair and continued to read how Dennis the Menace had managed to get paint over his next-door neighbour's cat and change it to blue.

It would be a new beginning for Mum and Dad, but leaving friends and relatives behind would not be easy. But they both knew that it was the correct decision. As far as work was concerned there was little that Dad would miss. The camaraderie amongst miners was universal and would continue where he was going. What he would miss most were the pit ponies. One of the least unpleasant tasks at the pithead was hosing these animals to rid them of the coal dust that accumulated on their bodies. The hosing-down process was one of those tasks that brought a welcome light relief to miners and ponies alike in the daily grind of coal-digging.

Pit ponies were treated well by the miners and I remember Dad telling me of an occasion he knew where a pony had helped rescue some workmen. A coal seam had collapsed in a tunnel and although no-one was injured directly, the fall had created a coaldust cloud blinding the men. All of the men groped around in the darkness, coughing and belching the acrid dust and eventually they were able to form a chain by holding hands. One of the team, luckily, reached out and grabbed on to a pony's tail. The pony led the chain of men to a ventilation shaft and onwards to the exit of the drift. No doubt there were a few extra carrots that night for the unlikely hero.

Round about August time, Dad left home and went to start work in the Midlands. He stayed in a hostel at Knutton, Newcastle-under-Lyme, just to the north of Stoke-on-Trent. It was here that Dad would do his training in preparation for starting a new job at one of the many local collieries. Originally, Mum and Dad had intended to move to Sutton Coldfield, just to the north of Birmingham, but somewhere along the line they must have changed their minds and opted for the Potteries instead.

Gordon was a surprise addition to the hut and no doubt his presence at the hostel helped relieve the time spent away from home. I don't know how it happened, but Gordon had managed to get himself transferred to the same hostel as Dad. I suppose it was a bit like 'Auf Wiedersehen, Pet - Old King Coal'.

Mum and I got on with life that summer and considering how much that I loved my dad, I must admit that I don't recall much about the time that he was away. I know that I was only seven years old, but there are other far more insignificant events from about that time that I can remember with total clarity. I am sure that he returned home for some of the weekends that he was away but I honestly cannot remember them.

It may come as a surprise to some, but officially rationing did not come to an end in this country until 1954. Up to that time it was not unusual for queues to form outside shops that had a supply of particular goods that had been in short supply for the duration of the war and thereafter. Neighbours would go knocking on doors informing the occupants of which shops had just had a delivery of jam, or rice pudding or bananas or anything. Mums would hurriedly get their hat and coat on, grab the youngsters from whatever they were doing and march up to the designated shop. I well recall those lines of waiting mums in their headscarves and ankle-covering booties, outside the large Co-op store that dominated the square (now converted into the new council offices). Kids these days don't know they're born.

Mum and I spent many days on our own that summer. We must have walked for miles. Naturally there were times when I had friends to play with, and of course I had my bike, a magnificent three-wheeler that took me all over the little estate where we lived. I knew every bump on those uneven footpaths.

It would be sad to leave Howden. It was, and still is, a pretty village. But the move had to be made. The house that we were leaving had been a wonderful home. It was obviously much better than the cottage that they had rented at Greenhead. Mum and Dad took a pride in the house and always looked after it. They had been grateful that they had been allocated such a nice place to live. I learned a lot from them in these early years and have inherited the same attitude as they have regarding home economics and husbandry. Their attitude was only to have what they could afford and to live within their means. Rent came first, because if you could not pay one week's rent, how could you expect to pay two weeks' next time? Unlike some others on the estate, they did not have a tallyman calling on a Friday night to collect payment for goods bought on credit. What they couldn't afford they went without.

Hendon: Moving out

Of course, not everyone was in a position to have Mum and Dad's virtues, and often we would see and hear money collectors calling for their payment. Some families developed a reputation for non-payment, no matter what the product was that they had obtained - milk, vacuum cleaner, catalogue goods - and thereby got a bad name. It was not unusual for these households to have a small mark etched on to the brickwork of their house by a disgruntled money collector. The sign was a code, known to the various tallymen, and would warn them of the danger of selling goods on credit to the occupants of the house. It was unfortunate that any future residents of the house would find themselves blacklisted from obtaining goods on credit. (I was unaware of this method of 'credit worthiness approval' until I became a local government officer in later life).

Eventually, the time arrived when it was time for us to move. Dad was already working in Stoke, of course. He had finished doing what he had to do and was working at Mossfield Colliery on the outskirts of Stoke-on-Trent. A new house was waiting for us.

The removal men turned up as planned and within three or four hours had dismantled the beds and anything else that needed doing and loaded the van. The last thing to be put away would have been the tea-pot and cups. Mum would never let anyone leave, no matter how long or short the visit, without offering them a drink. The removal gang were grateful for the tea and biscuits. They checked that everything was secure on the van and bade us farewell. The next time we would see our belongings would be in our new house.

Mum and I stood in the kitchen.

Emptiness.

Everywhere was bare. We went in to each room to make sure that every corner and window sill was clean. It would never do for the next tenant to find cause for complaint against Mum's housekeeping standards.

We went upstairs and slowly walked through the three bedrooms and toilet. Mum opened the airing cupboard door to ensure that nothing had slid down behind the tank. A slow walk down the stairs and a last look up.

Mum picked up a suitcase (which was full of nightclothes) and a shopping bag and slung her handbag over her shoulder, and with one final glance behind us we stepped out of the house. A few neighbours had come to wish us goodbye, but Mum had no desire to linger. It wasn't that she was hard, far from it; she just did not want a long goodbye.

We walked down the path that led out of the estate, on down past the school and *The Australian* public house and then crossed the road where the railway line - long since gone - ran under the bridge. Turning the corner we waited by the bus stop outside the newsagent's where we used to pick up 'The Pink' every Saturday night. The United bus was not long in coming and the pair of us struggled aboard with suitcase and bags. We weren't on the bus long, it only being less than two miles to Crook, before it was time to get off.

We went to the council offices at Glenholme and dropped the keys off, Mum taking the opportunity to thank the lady on the counter for granting us the house in the first place and telling her what a nice time we had had there. The lady wished us well.

After that we walked on to Arthur Street, where we would spend the night at Grandma and Granddad's.

* * * * *

Thursday, October 7, 1954 is indelibly written on my brain as the day that we moved from County Durham.

I had egg and toasted soldiers for breakfast and was munching away whilst Mum busied herself getting whatever we needed ready. When I had finished eating, she came over to me and with a wet hand tried to plaster down a piece of unruly hair on my head. She had checked her bags and suitcase and was satisfied that we had everything. Grandma had bought me a comic to read on the train and I had noticed a big bag of sweets as well in one of Mum's bags.

We said 'Goodbye' to Grandma and Granddad and hugged each other. We left them waving to us on the doorstep.

As we walked to the end of Arthur Street and crossed the road to the bus stop I wondered what awaited us. Was there a Woolworth's in Stoke? What kind of school would I go to? Would I ever see Bishop Auckland play again? These were really important questions that required answers.

A few minutes later the bus came that would take us to Durham. Before getting on board we gave one last wave and farewell to Grandma and Granddad who were still stood by their door. No-one else came to see us off. Mum had said her goodbyes already.

We had to walk up the steep winding hill from the bus terminus to the train station at Durham and it was there, whilst waiting for our connection, that Mum bought me another comic and herself a magazine. It was a pleasant surprise when my Aunty Ellen - Mum's sister-in-law - appeared. She had come to wish us well and witness our departure. There was only time for a few brief words and then the steam train chuffed and puffed its way out of the station, over the magnificent viaduct that is so much a feature of Durham City, carrying us south. Truth to tell, I don't remember a lot about that journey other than the engine must have been pulling about twenty carriages and that we had to change trains at Leeds and again at Manchester. At Manchester we had to transfer across the city from one station to another but we managed it all right without too much bother.

The final leg took us to Stoke station, by which time it was about 3:00pm, where Gordon had agreed to meet us. Dad would be at the house getting the furniture ready. When we walked out of the station, Mum's face dropped. We had been used to open fields and lush green countryside…Crook isn't known as the Jewel of Weardale for nothing. Here we were at Stoke and it was a grimy, smoke-filled… dump!

Gordon must have noticed the disappointment in Mum's face, for he immediately tried to put her mind at rest. 'The house that George has got for you is right on the edge of the estate, overlooking fields. You can see for miles, Margaret. Betty will be down in a few days' time.' Gordon had acquired a house in the next street to us.

Mum listened to Gordon explaining what had gone on and that everything was all right with regards the furniture, and that she would get to like the area and that the people were really friendly and that all of the miners' houses were new and that prospects down here were much better than up home and….

Home. Home? No. This was going to be home.

The remaining six miles or so of our travel was completed by bus, as neither Dad nor Gordon yet had a car. I looked out of the window of the bus and took in the scenery, mainly smoke-belching blocks of bottle shaped brick kilns. After a few miles, we had to change buses at Longton. This resulted in a thirty-minute wait and another journey of about twenty minutes. Finally, we arrived at Weston Coyney and the miners' estate. A short walk and we were there. At last.

'That's your house, pet. That one at the end.'

It was the end semi-detached house, pebbledash on the exterior, commonly called a Wates house and prevalent up and down the country on all mining and council estates. Further building work was being carried on in other parts of the development as we could hear dumper trucks and lorries carrying materials, but this part of the estate was almost completed. Gordon was right though; it did look on to open fields and was probably one of the best houses on the estate.

Mum crossed the threshold of the back door and entered the scullery and immediately nearly tripped over the gas-fitter, who was in the process of installing a brand new gas cooker. Dad was busily putting the finishing touches to the placement of the various bits of furniture in what would become the lounge and then they embraced.

Gordon said goodbye and we all thanked him for his help.

I gave Dad a hug and then we all had a look around the house.

* * * * *

We soon settled in and in no time at all I was attending the local school with all of the other 'immigrant' children, many of who had come from Durham (perhaps that explains why I still have a bit of a North Country accent).

Contact with the 'homeland' was on a regular basis with letters being exchanged by family and friends, but in the main I looked forward to the weekly delivery of 'The Pink', with all its sports reports. For at least one day of the week Bishop Auckland Football Club didn't seem too far away.

November arrived with anticipation the length and breadth of the country that only Cup football can bring - the first round of the FA Cup. Bishop had been drawn at home to non-league Kettering Town, a semi-professional club who played their football in the Southern League.

We didn't travel up to Bishop to watch the game, but from the subsequent reports in the press they had put up a clinical performance, winning 5-1. So far that season, Bishop had not been able to produce the kind of form that they usually showed in the Northern League. They were still capable of winning, but so far their performances had lacked lustre.

Against Kettering, though, the players found their true form with Bobby Hardisty and Ron Fryer showing up impressively in their wing-half positions. Harry Sharratt had pulled off two good saves when Kettering forwards only had him to beat, and Bishop were able to maintain the one-goal lead given to them by Major after ten minutes. A second goal was added by Dixon just before the interval.

The 6,200 crowd had more to appreciate when Oliver scored a third after fifty minutes, which resulted in Bishop taking their foot off the accelerator. This allowed Lamie to pull one back for the visitors. Any thoughts of a revival were extinguished when Dixon and Oliver scored additional goals.

In Round Two, Bishop were drawn out of the hat to meet Crystal Palace, then in the Third Division (South), away from home. As good as Bishop were, no-one seriously gave them a chance, but in front of 20,155 spectators they produced a wonderful performance.

It was a typical winter's day, drizzle, cloudy, cold and a good time to stay at home in front of a warm fire. Bishop Auckland supporters, though, only had one thing on their mind and that was to overcome their Football League opponents...and my, how they played.

According to reports of the game, Harry Sharratt gave one of those displays in goal that goalkeepers dream about. He was flinging himself all over the place to keep out the Crystal Palace attack. A few reporters merited his performance the equal of anything provided by any professional goalkeeper. His heroics fed the other players, in particular the full-backs Dave Marshall and Ron Fryer (deputising once again for the unwell Tommy Stewart). But the laurel must be placed on Jacky Major's head for this game.

Bishop had gone in at half-time trailing 2-1. Then 'The Galloping Major' came charging on to the scene. Within twenty minutes of the resumption Jacky Major had banged in a hat-trick - Bishop led 2-4. What a turnaround. Palace players were shocked and could find no way to respond. Bishop comfortably held them - even allowing the luxury of Ron Fryer missing a penalty - and saw out the remainder of the match. They had made it to the third round of the FA Cup and would be in the draw alongside the likes of Newcastle United, Arsenal and Blackpool. Roll on Monday for the draw.

Monday 15th December and Dad was sitting around the wireless. I was at school, but with Dad working nights, he did not have to start his weekly shift until tonight. He sat with his ear glued to the big brown Bakelite box that stood on a small table. It was a Philips and was as big as any modern day portable television. It was one of those wireless sets that had no correlation between size and performance. It was a big thing, but the sound output was weak, though it served its purpose in those days before we could afford a television.

And now the draw for the third round of the Football Association Cup. The home team will be drawn from the hat first, and the away team will be dr.....

All over the country there would be a unified, 'Bloody get on with it!'

...Sheffield Wednesday will play.... Hastings United. Derby County will play...Manchester City. Newcastle United will play...Plymouth Argyle. On it went, game after game. *Ipswich Town will play...Bishop Auckland.*

Ipswich Town. Away.

'Ipswich Town. Away from home. What division are they in, Dad?' I had dashed home from school in the afternoon rain and studied Dad's writing. He was a meticulous writer and for all he had had to write down quickly, the draw broadcast on the wireless, it was still neatly written.

'Second Division, son.'

I went to get a copy of the previous day's *Empire News* and looked up Ipswich Town in the sports pages. There was no match report of any of their games for that weekend but I discovered that they were indeed in the Second Division. What is more, they were rock-solid stone-bonking bottom of the pile...they lay currently at the foot of the division and had only obtained 14 points from over twenty games. Also in that division were clubs like Blackburn Rovers, Liverpool, Fulham, Stoke City and Port Vale. 'We stand a chance, Dad. Will we be going?'

Dad smiled. 'I don't think so, son...it's a long way and Christmas is coming.'

Dad was right. Christmas was coming and what is more it would be our first Christmas away from other family members. I do not intend to dwell on that first Christmas in our own home away from Durham, suffice to say that it was different but enjoyable. Mum and Dad had made new friends, as I had, and although we weren't a family for going into other people's houses, we had a real good time. I cannot remember what particular presents I had, but I do know that in the days leading up to Christmas we had acquired a new addition to the house; a television. It was a big cube-shaped KB 14-inch screen television that would be able to pick up not only BBC (only the one channel in those days) but also the new ITV channel, which Winston Churchill so vehemently opposed.

With the New Year came the traditional feast of football known as the third round of the FA Cup. Dad and I didn't go to any of the games. Port Vale were playing West Ham United away and Stoke had an away tie at Bury. Ipswich was simply too far away.

There was no such thing as *Saturday Grandstand* then and people had to rely on the wireless, or should that be radio now, for their news and entertainment. Sports coverage had not reached the saturated peak that is taken for granted nowadays and that is why, all over the nation, sports followers and football fans especially would tune in to *Sports Report*, that weekly, unmissable programme that kept everyone up-to-date with the day's football and racing results, and that has now been superseded by Radio Five Live.

The two of us sat by the wireless, waiting for the results. Dad had his coupon ready to mark off the scores as they were read out. Like the majority of players of the Football Pools, he won a bit and lost a bit. His forte was racing. Dad was the best reader of horse racing that I have known. He could read form and understand it readily, a skill that a lot of people believe that they have but have not. He never had sufficient money to win 'big-time', but he produced a tidy little profit each month from his selections. I am talking of an era when it was only possible to bet with a major bookmaker by sending selections on special slips provided by the betting company, such as William Hill. Selections had to be written on the slip and placed in an envelope accompanied with an appropriate postal order. The envelope had to have a post-office time-stamp on it to prevent after-time selections slipping through. Dad would make his selections first thing in the morning and would entrust me to post the envelope on my way to school. I always knew when he had won, because William Hill's envelopes were always the same. Thus I had an early introduction to horse racing and the gambling side of that great sport.

As we sat, the results started to be read out... *Bradford City 1 Brentford 1 ...Bristol Rovers 2 Portsmouth 1...*

Mum was making tea. She loved baking and Dad and I looked forward to munching her cakes and apple pie.

...Everton 3 Southend 1...Gateshead 0 Tottenham Hotspur 2...

'Do you know what I would do if I won the pools?' Mum said.

'No, Mum, what?' I replied mechanically.

The results continued in the background. Why talk now, Mum? Bishops' result will be on soon.

'I would buy a little bungalow, two up two down.'

Dad raised his eyebrows and I nodded.

.... Hartlepools United 1 Darlington 1...

'Here it comes.'

... Ipswich Town 2 Bishop Auckland 2...

Dad and I looked in amazement. Bishop had got a draw away from home against a team from the Second Division. 'The Pink' would be looked forward to with extra enthusiasm on Wednesday.

When it did come, the Bishop achievement was the first match report read. The report started by congratulating the Bishop team on a magnificent performance, and that how unlucky they were insofar as with only five minutes of play remaining, they had been leading 2-1. Then Corbett Cresswell scored an own-goal to give Ipswich an undeserved equaliser.

Ipswich had shown greater stamina as the game drew to its conclusion, but Bishop had defended stoutly. It was only in the final twenty minutes that the home side had shown any measure of superiority, but the Bishop defenders were truly magnificent.

Ipswich were never allowed any time on the ball with Bishop's defenders tackling with speed and persistence. The Ipswich forwards dallied on the ball and always gave a chance to the quick-tackling Auckland defenders.

As early as the second minute Ipswich had taken the lead. Many a team would have been disheartened to suffer such misfortune so early in the game, but the goal only acted as a spur for the red-shirted Northern League side. The lead only lasted seven minutes, as in the ninth minute the ever-reliable Ray Oliver headed home from Frank McKenna's corner. Just before half-time, the goalmaker turned goalscorer to put the visitors in the lead. This was Bishop Auckland's 100th goal of the season.

The black and white hooped shirted Ipswich players put the pressure on in the second half, in an attempt to salvage the game. But it was Bishop who had the best chance of scoring. With Ipswich defenders caught upfield, a long ball was sprayed to Oliver who raced for goal and only had Parry to beat. The centre-forward's effort lacked direction and was straight at the Ipswich goalkeeper. The ball rebounded to Lewin, who had raced up to give Oliver support, but his effort was saved again.

With the Ipswich forwards getting on top, it was time for Harry Sharratt to once more put in a sterling performance. He pulled off fine saves from

Garneys and Phillips before bringing off a superb diving save from outside-left McLuckie.

It was with only five minutes to go that Ipswich got a lucky break. Reed, the Ipswich outside-right, headed for goal. The ball was not travelling fast and it was not certain that a goal would have resulted. Cresswell stuck out a leg to hook the ball clear, but only succeeded in helping it on its way into the net.

The match report concluded that Bishop had fully deserved their draw and would start favourites for the replay. To Dad and me, ever the eternal pessimists, we were not so sure; Bishop had to try and obtain the services of McKenna who was scheduled to play in a Services inter-command tournament on Wednesday (today) the day of the replay.

Concerns regarding the availability of Frank McKenna were unwarranted as he was able to turn out for the 'Two Blues' in the replay, and how he repaid those that had made the effort to obtain his services. On a snowbound pitch and a bitterly cold afternoon, Bishop tore into the East Anglian side right from the outset. The rousing reception given to the home team from the 9,000 crowd stirred the Bishop players and they dominated the play. Save for two instances in the first half when goals may have been scored each time, all of the action was in the Ipswich half. The only surprise was that at half-time there was still no score.

The second half started how the majority of the first half had been played, with Bishop on top. It was just a case of when would a goal be scored, so in command were they. Then, after sixty-one minutes, McKenna paid his debt. He started a dribble down the right wing but was successfully dispossessed by full-back Feeney. However, in the collision, McKenna received a gash to the shin, an incident that resulted in the referee examining the studs to Feeney's boots. With the trainer giving attention to the injured leg it was thought that the Auckland player would have to leave the play. However, he decided to carry on without further ado.

Shortly after this, Bishop were awarded another free kick which was played into the penalty area by Bobby Hardisty. The ever-faithful Oliver went up for the high ball and although he missed it, in doing so he distracted goalkeeper Parry into mistiming his punched clearance. The ball looped to McKenna who headed the ball nonchalantly into the unguarded net. McKenna was swamped by delighted teammates giving their congratulations.

That opening goal was a long time coming, but it was no more than what Bishop deserved. Ipswich, despite their Football League membership, did not have the spirit to fight back and further goals from Major and another from McKenna saw the Bishops run out the winners 3-0.

Bishop Auckland had become the only amateur club since 1925, the year that the current day changes to the competition were adopted, to reach the fourth round of the FA Cup. They would entertain Third Division (North) side York City at the Kingsway ground, and on current form were well capable of reaching Round Five. In the meantime, there would be the little matter of the second round of the Amateur Cup. Erith and Belvedere would be visiting Kingsway and they probably were not looking forward to making the long journey from the south, to the Bishops' citadel.

* * * * *

Bishop had been drawn away in the first round of the competition, but had enjoyed a comfortable 3-1 success over Stork of the West Cheshire League, the game being played at Bromborough, Cheshire, the week before Christmas. The score could have been more emphatic had it not been for an outstanding performance from Leach in the home goal. In addition, both Hardisty and Dixon hit the crossbar with solid efforts. However, Hardisty did score twice, with Frank McKenna getting a third two minutes from time. McCallum had scored Stork's goal.

Now, it was Erith and Belvedere's turn to meet this impressive Bishop Auckland side. As things turned out, Erith's best chance of success appeared on the day to be the state of the pitch. It was unlikely that the Corinthian League side were ever capable of stretching this Bishop Auckland side, but with ground conditions negating stylish football, then the minnows may have been in with a chance. A light covering of snow that covered the pitch most of the week had been removed, thereby leaving a surface that was sodden, with even a few icy patches. It was impossible to play classic football and as is usual in such conditions, the team that plays to the conditions generally wins the game. Bishop did just that.

Now, it was Erith and Belvedere's turn to meet this impressive Bishop Auckland side. Erith proved not to be a test for Bishop and were swept aside. If the visitors had any predisposed plan to see off the 'Kings of Amateur Football' then it was not in evidence. With Bobby Hardisty and Jimmy Nimmins giving strong support to the forwards, the visiting defence was subjected to heavy pressure. At the other end of the field, Harry Sharratt was having one of those days when he could quite legitimately have read a newspaper. In the whole ninety minutes of the game he did not have one direct shot to save. Knowing Harry, he must have been bored to tears.

Within thirty-five minutes the game was all over. O'Connell had started the rout in the tenth minute, Lewin got a second and O'Connell added a third. Auckland were allowed the luxury of missing a penalty when Tommy Stewart's spot-kick crashed against the crossbar.

Ray Oliver and Jacky Major added goals four and five and the game was over. A 5-0 triumph in front of 8,500 spectators. Bishop were on the march to Wembley. Would it be for the FA Amateur Cup, or would it be for the FA Cup itself? York were coming to town next, and they must have had reservations as to what kind of welcome they would receive on the sloping green of Kingsway.

* * * * *

York City had proved Bishop's nemesis in the 1950-51 FA Cup competition winning after a replay, and now they were out to do it again.

A crowd of 16,000 crammed in to the tiny Kingsway ground; with Health and Safety regulations these days, a figure of only a fifth that would be allowed under current legislation.

Disappointment in the North-East and Adamthwaite household was in abundance when the result came through. York had won comfortably 1-3. Bishop Auckland Football Club had gained financially, with record receipts of £1,727 10.0d (£1,727.50p) so at least the Treasurer would be smiling. But it was all such an anti-climax. In previous rounds, Bishop had succeeded over clubs from the Football League, and York seemed of no greater danger than those clubs already vanquished. Such is football.

York proved themselves the better team and were deserved winners in the end. In the early stages of the game, Bishop gave as good as they got, but class told in the end. Sharratt gave his usual polished display of goalkeeping and Cresswell tried hard to buttress an overworked defence but the scoreline was probably a true reflection of the play and Bishop were out of the FA Cup.

We had not gone up to Durham to watch the game, although tickets were available for us. Mum had not been feeling too well. It seemed the best thing to do was stay in Stoke.

It was now February and I had settled in at my school. I was never the brightest light in the camp, but I tried my best and usually managed to be in the top ten of pupils. History and Art were my best subjects... and football of course. Like most children of my age, give me a ball and I was as happy as Larry. All the other lads from the estate joined in the Sunday afternoon game in a local field. You know the type of game; jumpers for goalposts, everyone from age five to fifty-five could join in, about twenty-a-side, and whatever the score, come dusk, next goal wins. We've all played that game, haven't we?

I said somewhere in the opening notes, that I would try to steer from merely producing a catalogue of Bishop Auckland's results and scorers. I have tried to remain true to that premise, but the period that I am describing now is one where an accumulation of reports is inevitable, and I ask the reader to acquiesce, as another match report follows.

Hendon: Moving out

One Saturday - I think it was Saturday 5th February - we were about to have tea. Naturally, at five o'clock, *Sports Report* came and Dad and me were crouched by the wireless to get the football results. It was the day of the Amateur Cup Third Round and Bishop were playing away to Kingstonian. The Football League results were read out first, then the Scottish results.

'George! Alan! Your tea's ready.'

'Yes, Margaret.'

'Yes, Mum.'

We carried on listening for the results, not moving. News reports continued but there was no sign of the Amateur Cup results.

'Come on, you pair. Tea's ready.'

'Yes, Margaret.'

'In a minute, Mum.'

The announcer coughed and began the scores for the Amateur Cup. He gave out a couple of scores; '...*Evenwood Town 2 Finchley 3...*'

'Tea. Now!' barked Mum.

'...*Hayes 0 Wimbledon 2...Hounslow 3 Bromley 0...*'

Our result was next.

'Will you pair come and get your tea. It's going cold!'

'...*Kingstonian 3...*'

Wait for it...

Dad and me looked at each other aghast. Three. Three goals scored against them.

'You pair. Now!!! For the umpteenth time. Your tea's going cold. Now come and get it.'

'...*Bishop Auckland 12...I repeat...Kingstonian 3 Bishop Auckland 12...Pegasus 4 West Auckland Town 1...*'

Dad and I laughed.

Mum glowered. 'Now will you sit down and eat your teas... it's cold.'

'But Mum...it's salad.'

'Don't be cheeky and eat it up.'

Mum went to lie down for a while after tea, but Dad and I could do nothing but repeat the score and wonder how it had come about.

Next day's Sunday papers gave little vignettes of the result, but as they concentrated on Divisions One and Two, there was not really a lot to read. 'The Pink' would put us right.

And of course it did. Every goal was recorded. Every scorer was named. And even Harry Sharratt had tried to get his name on the scoresheet.

The clubs had met twice before in the Amateur Cup competition. Way back in 1921, Bishop had made the long journey south to Kingstonian's Richmond Road ground and won a third round tie 1-0, going on to defeat

Swindon Victoria in the final. Kingstonian gained their revenge some twelve years later when they recorded a 1-0 success over Bishop in a fourth round game at Kingsway, the solitary goal coming deep into extra-time.

The 10,000 crowd at this year's encounter had been treated to thirty minutes Community Singing prior to the kick-off, conducted by regular Wembley orchestrator Sir Arthur Caiger, but it is hard to imagine any Kingstonian supporter having much of a singing voice at the end of the football match that was due to follow. In that incredible game, Bishop had been leading 12-0 with only five minutes to go. The poor goalkeeper for Kingstonian was Geoff North, a Bishop Auckland player on loan, whose father had also been a goalkeeper and had played and captained the Kingstonian side that had lost the 1921 game. Despite being beaten a dozen times, if it had not been for him pulling off some good saves, the result may well have been a cricket score. Bishops' goals came from Ray Oliver (5), Seamus O'Connell (3), Derek Lewin (3) and a final one from Corbett Cresswell. If Harry Sharratt had not decided to play outside his area for those final few minutes it is unlikely that Kingstonian would have found their way onto the scoresheet. But get on the sheet they did, with three goals from a very grateful Day (2) and Coates.

Ray Oliver remembers: *'Near the end of the game I recall the ball coming over from the wing. I was just steadying myself to shoot when I was pushed out of the way. It was Corbett. He said, "Give some bugger else a chance, you've got five already." We all felt so sorry for young Geoff, in the Kingstonian goal. Everything we tried just came off for us, that day.'*

Dave Marshall tells: *'In those final twenty minutes or so I was wandering around at the back like a lost soul. Everybody else was upfield, trying to score. Even Harry Sharratt was further forward than me!'*

Bishop really were showing everyone the way to Wembley now.

Mum was never really cross, of course. She just used to play along with the scenario as the best mums do. She always was beautiful - even now, in her seventies, she is stunning - and recently she had taken to wearing pretty flowered smock tops. She was a lookalike between Doris Day and Marion Ryan (remember her, from *Spot The Tune* television programme?).

The snows came in January and February, causing a lot of disruption to the football programme, but surprisingly we heard that there would be no problems in the north of England for Bishops' quarter-final tie with Finchley. We might have gone up to watch the game, if we had been a bit more certain as regards the weather, but with Mum not wanting to make the long and tiring train journey, Dad and I gave the game a miss.

The 9,000 crowd in attendance saw Bishop completely overwhelm the London club for ninety minutes…and all that they got out of it was a 1-1 draw. Finchley had even scored first on the snow-covered pitch, but thanks to a twenty-five-yard special ten minutes from time by Jacky Major, Bishop were saved any embarrassment. The natives had been getting restless, anxious for the equaliser and supporters worked themselves into a frenzy up to that point. They had been willing and praying for a goal and now it had arrived. It was the very least that they deserved and the Finchley rearguard rode their luck.

The Finchley goal was due to a rare error by Harry Sharratt. In the twenty-seventh minute he charged out of his goal and dived full length to collect a free kick but let the ball roll loose from his grasp. Head had a simple opportunity to tap the ball in to the net and the visitors were 1-0 up. That they held on to that slender lead for the best part of the match owed much to Dame Fortune and some powder-puff finishing from the Auckland forwards. Long high balls into the goal area were meat and drink for a goalkeeper of Barham's ability. However, the whole Finchley squad recognised that they may not be so lucky in the replay and knew that next time they could take a caning unless they improved to put some kind of pressure on the Auckland team.

Seven days later, the replay was held at Finchley's Summers Lane ground, and this time the Bishop Auckland players showed their true form, winning rather comfortably 3-1.

It was a nonchalant, bordering on arrogant, performance with Bobby Hardisty showing all his craft and majesty. Man for man, the Finchley squad were inferior to the Bishop Auckland team, but a treacherous playing surface of ice and mud may have given the Londoners a ray of hope before the game.

Dyke and Head brought saves from Sharratt before Benny Edwards scored direct from a free kick after twenty minutes. Finchley were instantly disheartened and Hardisty took over. Every ball in the midfield became his and he sprayed pass after pass, on a difficult surface, to his forwards with ease. Ray Oliver got a couple of goals to give the 'Two Blues' a three-goal lead, but Geddes scored a consolation goal for the home side. Bishop had made it to the semi-final again and in this form they would make it to Wembley again. It had been my eighth birthday a few days ago and I could not have had a better present.

* * * * *

It was a cold and damp March day when I set off for school that morning. Dad had made my breakfast (egg and toasted soldiers, naturally). Mum had not been too well, he told me. He had had to have the night off work and he would be here when I came home at dinnertime. He wished me well and I trundled off, catching up with some friends on the way. The morning lessons came and went and when the dinner bell rang, there was the usual melee to get out of school, for those of us who went home.

As I entered the house, Dad was in the kitchen with a worried look on his face.

'You had better go up and see your mum, son, she has something for you.'

Hooray, I thought... 'The Pink' has come a day early.

I ran up the stairs and stopped on the landing. The door to the bedroom was open. Mum was sat up in bed, a wan smile on her face.

'The Pink' had certainly come early. She was holding a beautiful pink baby.

'Where did you get that from, Mum?' (There; I told you I wasn't the brightest lamp in the camp, didn't I?).

I now had a brother and let me say that now, some fifty years later, no-one could have a better one.

I sat on the edge of the bed and held the bundle. He was going to be called William Barry, but as we tended to use our middle names (I am George Alan), he would be known as Barry. Alan, Barry...perhaps Mum and Dad intended to work their way through the alphabet, but it stopped there.

I went back to school for afternoon lessons. I liked Wednesdays as we always had football to finish the day off. If I played in goal I would be Harry Sharratt, if I played outside I would be Jackie Milburn. That afternoon I saved a penalty...just like Harry.

* * * * *

Saturday brought fine weather and the semi-final of the Amateur Cup. Bishop were due to play Wycombe Wanderers on neutral territory at Belle Vue, Doncaster. Because of Barry's arrival there was never any chance of us going to see the game, but from what we heard about it we did not miss much.

A paying audience of over 24,000 spectators saw Bishop win 1-0 in a dour game. Ray Oliver had scored the goal after sixteen minutes, but Tommy Stewart had missed a penalty, so the win could have been more convincing. But what did I care?

Bishop had made it to the final and Dad and me were going to see it. Next stop Wembley. In the meantime, it was a matter of Dad and I helping Mum as best as we could. Dad still had to go to work to bring the money in, but as usual at times like these, the neighbours were a great help. Looking back, I suppose I helped by not getting under Mum's feet. I was so pre-occupied with the impending trip to Wembley that I didn't dare get into trouble in case I was punished by not being allowed to go, but Mum and Dad were never like that and there was never much danger of it happening.

Arrangements were made for Dad and I to go to the final. I was told that Mum and Barry would stay at home and that Dad and I would travel by train on the Friday night to London. We would be staying at Uncle Dick and Aunty Dora May's place in Hendon, just a few miles from Wembley. I was as excited as any youngster could have been in my position. Time at school crawled by and each day seemed an eternity. It was a whole month between the semi-final match and the final itself, and not for the first time in my life, the Gods of Time were having a joke on me. They were making time stand still.

Eventually, the Friday evening came when the pair of us left the house to catch the bus to Stoke. Mum was on the doorstep, making sure that we had everything and giving last-minute instructions to Dad on how best to look after me. We said our farewells and walked to the bus stop. After a short wait the bus came and by six o'clock we were on platform one at Stoke station, waiting for the Manchester Piccadilly to London Euston express. Remarkably, it was on time, and after an uneventful journey, by about half past nine we had arrived at my uncle's house. I was given a nice hot drink and played a few games, despite the lateness, with my cousin Jeffrey, we always got on well together. Dad kept Dick and Dora May informed about Mum and Barry and all the other news.

It must have been midnight when I got to bed, but despite the lateness I was unable to get to sleep straight away as I was too excited about the game tomorrow. Uncle Dick and Aunty Dora May were going as they would be supporting Hendon, but because Dad had got all of the tickets from Bishop Auckland Football Club it meant that we could all be together - and that they would be with the Bishop supporters.

I must have managed some sleep, as Jeffrey had to wake me up. He had no interest whatsoever in football and would not be going to the game. He was staying at home with his much older brother and sister.

The morning dragged but finally it was time to leave for the stadium. I thought that we were going by tube but Uncle Dick surprised Dad and me when he said that we would go in his car and park right outside the ground. Imagine trying to do that now.

Somehow he was able get a parking space right up close to our entrance into the stadium. To this day I have no idea how he managed it; whenever I asked him he would just say, 'Know-how, son. Know-how.'

My first sighting of Wembley Stadium was at close quarters. As we went by car, it was not until we swept around a corner close by that I got my first look at it. It reminded me of some kind of wedding cake, due, I suppose, to the white masonry.

As Uncle Dick drove up Wembley Way in the procession of other cars it looked nothing like a football ground. The journey had not taken more than twenty minutes and the topic of conversation had mainly been about the probability of Bobby Hardisty finally getting a winners' medal. Aunty Dora May, who knows absolutely nothing about football, said that she hoped that he got a winners' medal but that Hendon won! Honestly!

Wembley Way was absolutely packed with people. I had been to football matches before but never had I seen so many different things going on before a game. I thought that people would just walk up to the ground as they usually did for a football match. No, this was different. Every kind of carnival act was going on to keep the supporters entertained; 'Have your photo taken with a monkey, sir…Oops, sorry madam'…fire eaters…jugglers…candy floss and toffee-apples…a man on stilts…it was all happening, not to mention the numerous rosette and programme sellers.

There was well over an hour to go before the kick-off but we made our way up the steps to the turnstiles. I stood in awe at the top of the steps and looked back beyond the throng streaming up Wembley Way, the green and white colours sported by Hendon supporters and the dark and light blue of Bishop supporters. It was a wonderful sight. Once through the gate, I was surprised to find that we still had to climb up even more steps, a stone staircase leading us to the terracing from where we would view the game.

Dad led me through on to the steps, and what a sight. The field of play looked so tiny compared to the whole stadium. It looked as if the game was about to be played in a shoebox, we were so high up. Dad, Uncle Dick and Aunty Dora May stood on the tier behind me, whilst I had a smashing view stood right against a restraining stanchion with an unimpeded view of the pitch, just above where the players would emerge from the tunnel. As I gazed around I thought of all the facts that I had stored in my empty head about Wembley.

Since the 1948 Olympic Games the dressing rooms had been moved from the opposite end of the stadium - not everyone knows that. Now they are on the left-hand side of the Royal Box. The dressing rooms are a lot nearer the pitch than most people imagine, only forty yards, and are each equipped with a plunge bath. The twin towers (no longer there following the rebuilding of the stadium) measured 126 feet high, whilst the bankings went to a height of 76 feet from the ground.

The area used to comprise a hilltop with magnificent views towards London. Originally there was a wood and before work could commence, in 1921, over 3,000 trees had to be felled and several miles of railway laid down to transport all the building materials on the spot. Then, to complete the work, the top of the hill had to be sliced off, just as you would a boiled egg. Over 150,000 tons of clay was dug out and deposited to form the foundation of the southern banking. The original playing surface was turf that had been used as a golf course at the Great Wembley exhibition, and it was King George VI who had cut the first sod to be laid at the stadium.

The stadium took 300 working days to complete at a cost of £750,000. 25,000 tons of concrete were used to create the terraces and in addition 1,500 tons of structural steel and 500,000 rivets were used on site. To test the soundness and stability of the terraces, a full battalion of infantry and hundreds of workmen were used as guinea pigs and marked time. There was no movement in the structure and the test was passed.

Now here was I about to see my favourite team come out on to this hallowed turf. But first there was the marching bands and the Community Singing, such a feature of Cup Finals, led by Master of Ceremonies, Sir Arthur Caiger. *The Daily Express* gave out the song sheets, for which there is now a collectors' market, and the repertoire included such songs like *Daisy*, *It's A Long Way To Tipperary* and *Abide With Me*. After one number, Mr Caiger, pointing with his finger, shouted from his podium in the centre-circle: 'There were two men at the Hendon end, and one guy at the Bishop Auckland end not singing. Now can you all join in this time.' Everyone laughed.

The singing ended and then it was time for the teams to come onto the pitch. They were greeted with a resounding roar that echoed all around the ground. The teams were presented to Lord Montgomery of Alamein and then they lined up for the kick-off.

Hendon's path to Wembley had been a difficult one. In the first round they had played Dartmouth United away and scrambled a 3-3 draw. They won the replay 2-1 and then in Round Two defeated fellow Athenian league rivals Cambridge City at home 2-1. A difficult away tie followed against Walthamstow Avenue, where they produced a good result in defeating one of the south's better teams by the only goal of the game. Round Four saw them pitched against another decent team, namely Wimbledon. The match produced a 1-1 draw but on home soil, at their Claremont Road ground, Hendon won the replay convincingly, 4-1. The semi-final against Hounslow was held at White Hart Lane and saw Hendon win 2-1.

In recent years, Hendon had produced some decent players, such as Denis and Leslie Compton (yes, the cricketer), Charlie Drinkwater and the evergreen Dexter Adams. The club held a close link with mighty neighbours Arsenal, who happened to use the Hendon pitch as a training ground. They had engaged Wally Barnes as coach but he had been forced to quit because of playing commitments. Nevertheless, they then procured the services of fellow ex-Arsenal player Laurie Scott as coach and he had guided the team to the final.

The Hendon side featured quite a few internationals from all over the place. In their squad were Hvidsten (Norway), Bahler (Switzerland),

Cunningham (Scotland) as well as England internationals Saffery, Topp and Adams. Also on their books were a Chinaman, a Costa Rican, an Irishman and a Jamaican. No wonder they were referred to as the 'United Nations' team.

The teams were:

Bishop Auckland (Dark Blue and Light Blue halved shirts, Black shorts)
H. Sharratt - D. Marshall, T. Stewart (Captain) - R. Hardisty, C. Cresswell, J. Nimmins - J. Major, D. Lewin, R. Oliver, S. O'Connell, B. Edwards

Hendon (Green shirts with White sleeves, White shorts)
R. Ivey - W. Fisher, E. Beardsley - L. Topp, D. Adams (Captain), P. Austin - G. Saffery, R. Hvidsten, E. Bahler, G. Cunningham, E. Parker

Referee: R. H. Mann of Worcestershire

100,000 voices roared in unison as the game got under way in glorious sunshine, Bishop attacking the goal where I was standing.

Bishop Auckland kicked off and set a furious pace trying to weave intricate passes together, but it was the Athenian League side that had the first goalscoring opportunity. Only three minutes had gone when Swiss international Erwin Bahler found himself in front of goal with only Harry Sharratt to beat. The goalkeeper pulled off an instinctive save diving to his left and pushed the ball out for a corner, which was cleared. The Bishop defence could have done without that scare to help clear their nerves but it proved to be Hendon's best chance.

Gradually, the 'Two Blues' began to get on top, but the game itself was proving much less of a spectacle than anticipated despite there being fifteen internationals on the pitch. The heights to which Bishop Auckland had ascended in previous finals, albeit unsuccessfully, were not attained and the game was turning into a scrappy affair. Bishop were having more of the ball than their southern rivals but the forward line was incohesive and many moves broke down as a result of bad play rather than Hendon's good defensive work. Benny Edwards produced a daisy-cutter to bring the best out of Reg Ivey, but that was all that Bishop could show in the opening twenty minutes. (Benny was a member of the losing 1951 team. Later that year he left Bishop to play for Horden Colliery Welfare, but had returned to the 'Two Blues' at the commencement of this season).

Midway through the opening half the deadlock was broken by Derek Lewin. The goal itself was worthy of the occasion, the inside-right perfectly lobbing the ball over Reg Ivey's head and, in a race to clear the ball, centre-half Dexter Adams could only bang the ball into the roof of the net. Adams was a fine player, having been selected seventeen times for his country and indeed had captained the England amateur team. It was unfortunate that his attempt to clear the ball was futile and to some eyes may have looked comical. It was the only bit of skill that the Auckland attack had shown thus far and had resulted in a fine goal. My arms were raised in delight and all around me ecstatic Auckland supporters cheered to the rafters.

Derek Lewin was a wonderful player. He had feet to match his brain and could conjure defence-splitting passes with apparent ease. This was his first season with the Bishops, making his debut for the club on Christmas Day. Previously, he had been on the books of Manchester City, his father's favourite club, but had been playing for Oldham Athletic, managed by George Hardwick, in the Second Division. He had made a dozen appearances for the Lancashire club and was already an England amateur international when Bishop Auckland made their approach. They had seen him, liked what they saw and they wanted him. In eighteen months' time he would be selected for the Great Britain Olympic squad when he would train with Manchester United and become friends with many of the Busby Babes. Roger Byrne, captain of England, would be his training partner. He had an uncanny knack of scoring goals in important matches - just look at his record in Amateur Cup games.

The goal gave confidence to the Auckland team, although the standard of play barely improved. Cresswell was a rock in defence, as was Dave Marshall who controlled Eric Parker, the prolific left-wing goalscorer who had scored a hat-trick in the replayed tie against Wimbledon. Parker switched to the right-wing for the second half but found Tommy Stewart just as uncompromising.

There was no further score until the second half when Lewin again popped up to score. I think it's fair to say that the goal would not be allowed in today's game. Ivey had possession of the ball and, as was the custom then, tried to advance in the penalty area by bouncing the ball every four paces. Lewin put Ivey under pressure and shoulder-charged him as he had the ball. To the dismay of the Hendon players and supporters, the ball ran loose and in a flash the Bishop inside-right completed a pirouette and tucked the ball into an empty net. To their credit, the Hendon players did not argue with the decision; in today's game there would be a full-scale riot if such a score was allowed to stand.

That second goal broke the heart of the Hendon squad and the game belonged to Bishop. In a stale second half, Harry Sharratt did not have one direct shot to save. Bishop were the better team but the brand of football for which they were now famous was missing.

The final whistle was blown and a delighted Tommy Stewart led his team up the steps to the Royal Box to collect the cup. Bishop Auckland had won the Amateur Cup for the eighth time. I had shouted myself hoarse and did not care that the game had been disappointing to some observers. My team had won at Wembley and I had been there to witness it. Nothing else mattered.

In a very poignant moment, Tommy Stewart handed the cup over to Bobby Hardisty who had finally won a winners' medal. The knowledgeable crowd saw the significance of the gesture and a great roar went up as a few moments later Hardisty was raised shoulder-high by his teammates, holding the trophy aloft. Hardisty would say that that moment was the greatest of his footballing career. Colleague Jimmy Nimmins, who now also held a winners' medal after four attempts, would no doubt echo the sentiment. Conversely, Tommy Stewart had now played at Wembley on three occasions (twice representing Scotland in amateur international matches) and had been on the winning side all three times.

I joined in the chorus of cheering around the stadium and looked out at my heroes, parading around the pitch with the cup. Supporters of both teams were applauding the victorious Bishop team, a very generous ovation rolling down from the Hendon ranks. Some supporters were leaving the ground and in the newly-created space around me I was able to sidle over towards where Dad was standing with my aunty and uncle. We held back to see the players finally make their way below us into the dressing rooms, and then it was time for us to leave the stadium.

I was the happiest lad in the world. I would be even happier a few weeks later when Bishop would wrap up the league title as well.

As we made our way down the steps and out of the giant amphitheatre, I turned to Dad and said what a great result it had been. He agreed but noted that Uncle Dick and Aunty Dora May were naturally disappointed.

I gave them a smile and then said, 'Dad.'

'Yes, son.'

'Do you know that man, in the white suit, who conducted the singing?'

'Yes, son.'

'Well, do you know, he must have brilliant eyesight because he said that there was one man not singing at our end?'

'Yes.'

'Well, guess what... he was standing right next to me.'

* * * * *

Hendon: Moving out

Some of the Bishop Auckland players were arriving back at their hotel with Club Chairman Councillor J. G. Waine in attendance. The doorman at the establishment complimented the Chairman on the club winning the Amateur Cup. 'Yes, we won it all right, and we'll be back next year to win it again,' he replied.

The remark was overheard by the players, one of whom turned to his fellow colleagues and said, 'We! We! What bloody position did he play?'

To this day the identity of that player has remained a secret, only a special few outsiders being aware of who spoke those words. I am honoured to have been told the name of the player but cannot divulge his name in these pages. I have been offered various incentives to reveal his name, including free drinks and money, but wild horses could not drag the information from me. I shall never reveal his name.

Don't worry, Ray, your secret is safe with me.

* * * * *

That year, Bishop Auckland also won the Northern League title by seven points from second-placed Crook Town. They had high-scoring wins over Shildon (7-0) and Durham City (7-3) at home as well as recording a 10-2 away win against Stanley United. Other notable away victories were recorded at Evenwood Town (7-3) and Tow Law Town (7-2), but a reverse was suffered when visiting Ferryhill Athletic, the home side winning 7-1.

The Northern League Challenge Cup was won for the second year running. The previous season a 4-1 win was achieved in the final over Shildon. This season the final opponents were Crook Town who were demolished 6-0 on their home ground.

With form like this, who could stop the Bishops' march?

CHAPTER FIVE

Corinthian Casuals: Not much change

The summer of 1955 was a pleasant one for me. The sun seemed to shine every day during the school holidays and my friends and me spent endless hours kicking hell out of whatever ball we could lay our hands - or should that be feet - on.

Although Dad did not yet own a car, it did not seem to handicap us getting about. There was a good bus service in the Potteries and whenever we felt the need to visit family in Durham there were always the trains, even if it did involve traipsing across Manchester to catch a connecting service.

It was coming up to a year since we had left Durham and we had made only one return visit, in the summer, during that time. We all enjoyed the time spent in the 'homeland', but equally it was nice to return to our new home.

We stayed at Mum's parents' house at Sunnybrow, a small hamlet on the Willington to Bishop Auckland road. They lived in a three-bedroom council house and had the room to put us up. Mum's brothers and sisters and their wives and husbands would frequently visit, especially on Sundays. There would be Uncle Joe and Aunty Margaret, Uncle Don and his wife Betty, Aunty Ruby and Uncle Fred with their children Sylvia and Thomas, and Aunty Ellen and Uncle John. Sometimes, Aunty Gladys and Uncle Jack would also come over from Spennymoor.

Uncle Fred was a character. He smoked like a chimney and never was seen without a cigarette in his hand. He liked a drink and was always the life and soul of any party. A more friendly man you could not wish to meet. Oh, but he could embarrass Aunty Ruby sometimes. Like when they went to Blackpool on holiday.

Uncle Fred still had the yellow Hillman Minx at the time and when they got close to their boarding house, he started to look round for a place to park. Thomas, bright lad that he was, spotted a car park right opposite where they were staying. The car park had an attendant and so there would be the extra benefit of added security when the car was left there.

Fred drove in to the car park and parked the car in a handy position close to a wall. As they began to unload the suitcases to take over to the boarding house, the attendant strode over and asked for the 2/6d (12.5p) daily charge.

'2/6d?' enquired Fred.

'That's right, sir. 2/6d for cars. Buses are 3/6d (17.5p) and three-wheeled vehicles 1/9d (8.5p).'

'Okay,' said Fred, and promptly went to the boot of the car.

Ruby, Sylvia and Thomas looked on, wondering what Fred would do next. To Ruby's embarrassment, Fred took the jack out of the car and proceeded to take one of the rear wheels from the car.

'There,' he said triumphantly, '1/9d you said for a three-wheeler,' and deposited the exact change into the astonished attendant's hand.

Apparently, all through the week the car remained in the car park, held up by the jack, until it was time for Uncle Fred and Aunty Ruby to return home. Every morning Thomas would go downstairs and cross the road to the car park attendant with a two-bob bit in his hand and would return with a threepenny piece.

That was Uncle Fred.

* * * * *

Unfortunately, that year, our holiday in Durham was in the close season as far as football was concerned so I never got to see Bishop play. Their FA Cup campaign got off to a winning start, however, when they beat Northern League rivals Durham City 3-1 at Kingsway.

The score was not a true reflection of Bishop's superiority over their near neighbours as Bishop forwards rained in goalbound shots from all angles. In particular good form for Auckland was sixteen-year-old schoolboy John Barnwell, striking at the heart of the Durham City defence like a blonde Lochinvar. The skill that he showed that day on a difficult pitch had to be seen to be believed: the local reporter recorded that 'he showed great promise'. Indeed it was Barnwell who opened the scoring after ten minutes when he gathered the ball and cut inside a defender before unleashing a fierce shot which thundered off the underside of the bar before crossing the line, but Durham fought back to gain an equaliser after half an hour through centre-forward Alf Smith. Ray Oliver then put Bishop in the lead again and in the second half Derek Lewin finished the scoring with a brilliant effort that left the Durham goalkeeper stranded.

(It was about this time that the football press made much of the decision that the replayed first round FA Cup game between Carlisle and Darlington had been replayed under floodlights. This was the first time that an FA Cup game had been played under lights).

The draw for Round Two saw Bishop Auckland drawn at home to League Division Three (North) side, Scunthorpe United. They were doing quite well in their division and were currently ninth in the table and in addition they had a strong reserve side. They owed much of their position in the table to good early season results. A dip in form had slowed down their progress but a couple of wins in the last two games had shown that they were a team to be respected. Bishop faced a tough task; but why should they worry? They had only suffered one defeat in nineteen games and that had been because of fielding a weakened side. Scunthorpe would know that they had been in a fight.

Scunthorpe had been drawn at home to defeat Northern League club Shildon in the first round 3-0, all the goals coming in the second half, but they knew that a stiffer task awaited them on Bishop Auckland's own pitch.

The match at Kingsway was a disappointment for Auckland fans. Despite incessant pressure, the Bishop forwards were unable to penetrate the packed Scunthorpe defence. The Lincolnshire side did not come with the intention to defend but right from the outset they were on the back foot. Derek Lewin and Benny Edwards worked particularly hard down the left flank but the uncompromising defenders, Lamb and McGill, ably supported their goalkeeper Norman Malan whenever danger threatened. The majority of the 13,500 crowd went home disappointed but at least the Bishops were still in the Cup. Only the Scunthorpe supporters went home smiling.

The following Thursday, the replay was held at The Old Show Ground and, sad to say, nothing went right for Bishop. Corbett Cresswell and Jimmy Nimmins were brilliant in defence, but the attack never got going. Scunthorpe on the other hand, playing on their own soil, were a different proposition to the team that had played only five days before. They showed a commitment to win every ball and a more positive attacking approach. Harry Sharratt had to be on top form and it was mainly due to his heroics that the score was held to only a 2-0 defeat.

There was one comical moment near the end of the game with Bishop desperately seeking a goal to get them back in the game, when Harry decided to take a throw-in on the halfway line. Unfortunately, Derek Lewin, for whom the throw was intended, failed to control the ball which was collected by a Scunthorpe player who, left with a clear shot at goal, promptly despatched it into an empty net. That goal sealed Bishop Auckland's fate and they lost the match 2-0. No-one could quite pick up the comments from the Bishop Auckland players directed at their wayward goalkeeper but no doubt they were unprintable.

The youngest member of the Bishop team for that match was John Barnwell. He had started his football career at Whitley Bay, playing in the Northern Alliance League at the age of fourteen against such clubs as Blyth and Newcastle United Reserves. His potential had been noticed by many clubs who would have given anything for his signature. His father defended

Corinthian Casuals: Not much change

John from making any rash decision about his future and clubs like Burnley, Sunderland and Newcastle United were shown the door. Arsenal, however, would show a greater degree of professionalism in their conversations with young John and his father, which would result in him signing amateur forms for The Gunners. In the meantime he was playing for The Bishops in their cup runs. He remembers the match at Scunthorpe well:

'I had to take time off school. Having drawn at Kingsway we had to travel to Scunthorpe. We stayed overnight in a hotel at Doncaster and that was a major experience for me.

'I think we were coming back by train and I remember 'Kit' Rudd sitting there issuing the players' "expenses". After a while he called for me and said, "Now young John, how much time have you had off work?"

'I just stood there and said, 'But Mr Rudd, I'm still at school.'

'"I'll ask you again, John... how much time have you had off work?"

'"But Mr Rudd, I'm still at school," I repeated.

'For the third time he asked, "How much time have you had off work?"

'Just then, Bobby Hardisty came along, having heard the conversation and said, "Don't worry, John, I'll handle this."

'A few minutes later I had more money in my pocket than my old fella probably earned in a week.'

The programme for that game carried an interesting article about the advent of floodlight football, a relatively new innovation, which I have referred to in an earlier paragraph. Entitled *Floodlighting Prospect Brighter?* the article read:

Clubs who have held cautious views on the issue of floodlit football (among them Scunthorpe United) because the economic aspect is so vital, may be having second thoughts before long. One or two recent events have provided emphasis on the possibilities of the installation paying for itself in more ways than one.

The Carlisle-Darlington cup replay at Carlisle at night attracted 19,000, and the second replay, at Newcastle, brought in a 35,000 attendance. The latter attendance, of course, was in a thickly populated centre.

But the fact remains that now the FA allow cup replays by floodlighting in an evening, there is a much better chance of getting a bigger crowd at night for a 7:30pm start than in an afternoon when you have to begin at 2pm or even 2:30pm - however large or small the town.

There is also the added advantage of less absenteeism from work, from school, office or anywhere else, which sometimes causes embarrassment and difficulty.

With the exit from the FA Cup, Bishops' attention was focussed on a repeat win of the Amateur Cup, and another title win of the Northern League.

111

The Amateur Cup campaign started against the toughest possible opponents, Crook Town. It did not matter that the southern clubs could boast an abundance of quality teams…Crook were the one team that Bishop did not wish to encounter, especially so early in the competition. The southern clubs must have been salivating at the prospect of the two best northern teams embroiled in a first round duel.

Customarily the game was scheduled to take place in mid-January and so our Christmas visitation to Durham was held back to coincide with the match. I looked forward to that game as much as I had done for the final itself only a few months before. Crook had beaten Bishop in the final less than two years ago and the memory still burned.

As usual we stayed at Sunnybrow, travelling up by train on a Thursday and arriving sometime in the afternoon. I had been allowed to have the day off school.

We were pleasantly surprised to find Aunty Ruby and Uncle Fred were there. I was particularly pleased as Uncle Fred made me laugh. The reason for their visit was a sad one, however. A close neighbour who occupied one of the nearby houses had recently died quite suddenly and his funeral was scheduled for tomorrow.

Mum and Dad had known the person concerned and after a brief conversation Fred left the room, only to return a few minutes later to say that if they wished to pay their respects, then they could go round to the house where the body was laid out. I had no intention of standing over a corpse and stayed where I was.

After about half an hour Uncle Fred returned with Mum and Dad. They were saying the usual things that make polite conversation in such circumstances. I cannot remember the exact words of course but at one point Mum enquired of the deceased if anyone had noticed any change in him.

Fred replied, in all seriousness, 'Aye, about fowr 'n' ten pence worth…there were two half-crowns over his eyes yesterday and now there's only two pennies.'

* * * * *

The crowds flocked to the quaint Kingsway ground. Local rivals Crook would inevitably bring their army of supporters with them, the two clubs being only six miles apart. Looking back, considering the importance of the occasion, it amazes me that such a game was not all-ticket. A big crowd was obviously expected, and yet it was never felt necessary to restrict admission to ticket-holders only. I suppose the clubs took the attitude that to queue up for tickets people would have to take time from work, and given the cold financial climate in the North-East, such a choice was impracticable.

Mum and ten-month-old Barry kept Nana and Granddad Gelson company whilst Dad and I caught one of Bond's buses outside St John's Gardens, Sunnybrow to Bishop. The bus was full of supporters going to the match and we managed to claim the last two seats, although a couple of stops down the road, as the bus called at Hunwick, we reverently gave them up to allow some elderly folk to sit down. It was now standing room only and the bus tootled on its way through Toronto and down towards Newton Cap bank, all the while the only topic of conversation being the probable outcome of the impending duel between arguably the two top northern amateur football teams. The bus descended towards the little stone bridge high above the River Wear and came to a halt. Traffic from the opposite bank, coming out of Bishop, had gained the advantage and had claimed the right of access across the one-lane bridge. The wait seemed interminable but eventually there was a break in the traffic and we were able to cross. The driver crunched through the gears and the bus inexorably climbed the ascent up towards High Bondgate. It never ceased to amaze me how such vehicles were able to negotiate that incline.

(Dad once told me that shortly after he had met Mum, he had been driving a fully-laden lorry up this hill. He had got halfway up when, to his horror, the lorry started to roll backwards. Not wishing to end up in the River Wear far below, he had been forced to take drastic action and jumped out of the cab. The lorry gathered momentum and just missed the buildings close to the bridge. Fortunately, the lorry came to rest overhanging the embankment… something like the bus scene at the end of the Michael Caine film *The Italian Job*).

We walked towards the ground and picked up a programme (long lost I'm afraid) and started to queue up at the Kingsway entrance, which would gain us admission to behind the goal at the 'top-end' of the ground. The queue seemed to move as slowly as the bus that had brought us, but eventually we got in. No sooner were we through the turnstile when a kindly man shouted out, 'Another one for the front,' and as quick as a flash I was taken to the side of the playing area, close to where the players came out, and seated on a bench right up close to the pitch. What a view I would have. I would not have to stand on tiptoe and crane my neck, but I could actually sit down and watch the game. Marvellous.

Then it dawned on me…where was Dad?

I need not have worried. I spotted his tall figure not far away behind the goal and we waved to each other, silently wishing us the best of luck and a Bishop win.

I used the adjective 'quaint' earlier on to describe Kingsway, but perhaps 'eccentric' would be a better word. For the uninitiated, Kingsway is a sloping pitch, as were most in the Northern League. Visitors were often surprised to find that the ground perimeter only covered two-and-a-half sides of the playing area; the cricket pitch making up half of one side and the viewing area at the Delwood end (the bottom side) having only very limited capacity to a depth of about three rows of spectators. Players emerged from the clubhouse close to the halfway line and were faced from the opposite touchline by a grandstand and traditional terraced area, although this terrace was idiosyncratic, insofar as the terracing in front of the grandstand only went down beyond pitch level, thereby giving spectators a worm's-eye view of the pitch. The viewing area behind the 'top goal', where my Dad was standing, was made up of terraced steps.

On important match days, a local brewery supplied beer crates and planks to help provide temporary terracing alongside the cricket pitch side and Delwood end; there was no such thing as Health and Safety Law then and nobody seemed to mind. Hundreds of these crates would be brought to the ground prior to the game and placed end to end to form the required stepping. Today was such an occasion that the crates and additional steel frames had been put to good use as over 13,000 spectators packed in to the ground.

The dressing rooms were in an old building that formed the clubhouse behind me to my right. Bishops' dressing room was upstairs and took up half of that floor, the other half being the Committee Room. Surprisingly, the lay-out of the floor meant that the only access to this Committee Room was via the dressing room. Committee members' wives must have been in a continual swoon on matchdays, having to witness the Bishop players getting changed. The visiting-team dressing room was downstairs as were the showers and recently-installed plunge bath.

At last, the teams made their entrance and the game got under way. It was a cold dank day and a fine mist hung in the air. The early stages of the game were frenetic with neither side showing any ability to take control. Long balls upfield from both sets of defenders failed to give either forward line a scoring opportunity, and it was generally felt that one goal may prove enough to win the tie.

The standard of play was poor with both teams frightened of adventure and content to play safe. By the end of the game over one hundred throw-ins would be amassed, fifty-four to Bishop and forty-seven to Crook, surely some kind of record. Perhaps the occasion was getting to both teams.

From my front row seat I had a good view of all that went on, and could almost touch the winger and full-back when play was on my side of the field. I remember one sliding tackle from Dave Marshall on Jimmy McMillan that happened right in front of me. I heard the 'thwack' of the crunching legs as the defender stormed in and the winger fell to the ground. It was a perfectly good tackle and typical of the Bishop full-back (According to Dave Marshall, Jimmy McMillan was the best player that he ever played against in a long and distinguished career).

At 6' 1" tall and weighing in at 13 stones, Dave Marshall was built to be a sportsman. It was Bishop Auckland's fortune that Benny Potts (he who had saved the late penalty in the 1922 final against South Bank), recommended him to them in 1948, after representing the army. Dave was a welcome acquisition to the defensive ranks and started playing in the reserve team. He soon showed his paces and played in the 1951 final against Pegasus, as well as those against Crook and Hendon. He had studied at Bede College, Durham and was a schoolteacher; woe betide any pupils that took him on. He was far removed from the archetypal full-back that swelled the ranks of amateur (and professional) football, insofar he was a clean tackler for the ball and used his brain as well as his feet to distribute passes - kick-and-rush was not his style. He would go on to win only three caps for England, a scant amount given his ability.

Then, after twenty minutes, just when it looked as if Bishop were getting on top, Crook were awarded a penalty when full-back Tommy Stewart was adjudged to have handled the ball. Davison, who had scored a few for the 'Two Blues' in the past from similar situations, made no mistake from the spot. The Crook supporters went barmy. Hats and scarves were thrown in the air and showered down on heads in a black and amber snowstorm. I just sat on the bench, resting my chin in my hand, looking a picture of misery.

The goal encouraged Crook and they started to control the game putting a few passes together. Bishop, on the other hand, were rattled, and their play continued to be punctured with the final pass often going astray.

Bad went to worse when play was held up for Lewin to get attention to a shoulder injury - he last thing we wanted was for Bishop to be down to ten men. Thankfully, he was able to restart and he resumed his usual inside-right berth, but it was likely that he would not be fit for any replay if the scores were level at ninety minutes. Ray Oliver, normally so productive, was getting little change from Davison, who seemed to know the bustling centre-forward's moves inside out, and altogether the Bishop forward line was failing as a unit. The half-time whistle went with Crook attacking but thankfully not adding to their tally.

Bishop came out for the second half hell-bent on getting the equalizer. Crook would have expected as much, but the ferocity of the Auckland forward line had the Crook defenders perplexed and forced into some rashful challenges.

The breakthrough was not long in coming and it was the tenacious Derek Lewin who levelled the scores, five minutes after the break, with a blistering shot that left Jarrie clawing at thin air. I will let Derek himself describe it:

'*Quite frankly, it was the best goal that I ever scored. I had collected the injury when I went for a high ball with the Crook defender, May. As we came down together his arm smashed on to my shoulder, quite accidental. I went off for a while but obviously came back on. I had not been on the pitch long when this ball came across from the right and I was loitering just outside the penalty area, probably twenty or twenty-five yards out. The ball came out to me and I hit it on the volley and it went straight in the goal. That was the equaliser. All the Bishop players came rushing towards me to congratulate me and jump on me and there I am with this, I thought, bloody broken shoulder. I shouted 'Get off. Get off.' I wasn't able to play in the replay because of the injury.*

'*I went to Blackpool General Hospital and the specialist had a good look at it. He said that the shoulder was not broken, although it might have been better if it had been. It was dislocated. He said that dislocations could take longer than breaks to mend. They could have treated a fracture but with a dislocation all they could recommend was leave it to put itself right.*

'*The following week a woman Bishop Auckland supporter came up to me and accused me of being a southern namby-pamby for not playing in the replay.*'

Misery went out of the window and Happiness returned. I jumped up in to the air, as did thousands of other Bishop supporters. We were level and now everything was to play for.

Play became more attractive after that, with both teams striving for the winning goal. Sharratt and Jarrie produced top class saves and all efforts proved in vain. Ken Harrison was well handled by the ever-dependable Cresswell but missed a golden chance in the closing minutes when his shot went inches wide. Even then, Auckland should have won the game but Seamus O'Connell missed a glorious chance in the last minute, but 1-1 was probably a fair result.

I stood up and sidled towards Dad who was waiting by the corner flag for me. We struggled successfully through the exit gate whereafter movement became a bit easier in the open streets. Dad and I exchanged views about the game as we walked down Newgate Street towards the bus stop in High Bondgate. Crook supporters went in the same direction as their bus stop was immediately ahead of ours at the small bus stand.

There would be much to tell Mum about the game, but really the main thought in my head concerned whether or not I would get to see the replay which was set for the following Saturday at Crook's Millfield ground.

* * * * *

Corinthian Casuals: Not much change

I need not have worried, as arrangements were made that evening for our immediate return next Friday. I would not be able to miss school, but with fine timing we should be able to make the five o'clock train from Stoke and with a bit of luck be in Durham for just after ten.

And that is just how it happened. The following Friday night, Uncle Fred met us at Durham station with his yellow and white Hillman Minx and transported us back to Sunnybrow, where a warm welcome awaited us from Nana and Granddad Gelson. There was just time for me to say a quick 'Hello' and then I went to bed...to pray for a successful outcome in tomorrow's replay.

* * * * *

Calamity.

Corbett Cresswell's back-pass was never going to reach Harry Sharratt on the snow covered surface, and Bishop supporters were silenced as Ken Harrison waltzed through to tuck the ball into the net. Only four minutes had been played and we were a goal down. Crook fans went mad.

For a few brief seconds only Crook fans could be heard, but suddenly the 'Two-Blues' supporters started a roar of encouragement... they didn't just shout when they were winning, but, unlike many of today's so-called fans, they actually shouted encouragement when their team was behind. And I shouted as loudly as any of them from the cinder embankment that formed the terracing at Crook's ground.

The noise was near deafening as the almost 12,000 crowd roared on their team. All except Dad, that is. He was one of those people who could watch a football match or a horse race and show the minimum of emotion. In later years, I would be like him, but for now I was screaming as loudly as I could for Bishop to sneak an equaliser.

Then they got it. Marvellous Bobby Hardisty got the ball in the Crook net and things looked brighter.

'Come on... let's have another one!'

Another goal did come along, and just like number nine buses, not one but two: but it was the black and amber brigade that were cheering as Harrison and McMillan gave Crook a comfortable-looking 3-1 lead.

My world was falling apart. Never being much of a religious person, I think it was at about this point that I did the kind of thing that any sane eight-year-old would do.

'Please, God, let Bishop win. If Bishop win I will go to church for ever and ever. Amen.'

Well, God made a start. Just before half-time, Frank McKenna, who was proving himself to be a capable replacement for Jacky Major who had departed to play for Hull City, pulled one back for the Bishops. 3-2.

The pace was fast and furious and a complete contrast to the fare that the teams had produced seven days earlier. Then the play had been dull and tiresome, whilst today's game was inventive and full of flowing moves. Nevertheless, Bishop were a goal behind when referee Rhodes blew the whistle for half-time.

Proceedings got under way with a flourish for the second half and both sets of forwards received rough treatment as uncompromising and obdurate defenders fought for every ball. Even though they were a goal down, Bishop started to control the game and an increase in passes out to the wings had Crook defenders running hither and thither. Stamina might prove to be important. Still, pretty play did not always have positive results, and for us Bishop Auckland supporters the clock was ticking away.

Bishop became more dominant as time marched on. The diminutive Warren Bradley, in for the injured Derek Lewin, tried showing his skills but came in for some rough treatment from the Crook defenders. Warren had played at outside-left for Bishop in the past but was now in the inside-right berth, and adapting to it like a duck to water. The tackles became fiercer and every player would carry some scar or other from this game.

Then the scores were level when Ray Oliver scored for Bishop with a trademark header. Dark and light blue hats, scarves and anything else were thrown in the air as Bishop supporters went crazy.

The Bishop half-back line was now in command, but no matter how hard they tried to create an opening for the forwards, chances went begging.

At the end of ninety minutes the score was 3-3. Thirty minutes extra-time would follow - surely stamina would prove the dominant factor now?

I was wrong: stamina was a factor in the game being won, but it was not the main factor. That accolade must go to Warren Bradley, who gave an extra-time display of ball control and incisiveness that broke the hearts of the Crook defenders. His skill and perceptiveness caused confusion in the black and amber ranks, and such was the magnitude of his performance that some eyewitnesses likened him to Raich Carter.

No goals were scored in the opening period but shortly after the restart, Warren slid a through-ball to Frank McKenna and the winger bore down on the Crook goal. Jarrie was superb and pulled off a fine save, but the ball rebounded straight back to McKenna who rammed the ball home for the winning goal. It would be Bradley who would take over the position of outside-right in the following season, as McKenna would have moved on to play for Leeds United.

Corinthian Casuals: Not much change

Warren Bradley had joined Bishop earlier that season. He had been on the books of Bolton Wanderers and had attended a trial at Manchester United.... note those words... 'attended a trial'. Yes, he was there all right, but he never got a kick. It was the usual practice at such trials for the 'game' to go on ad infinitum, each trialist playing for about thirty minutes then making way for someone else. Young Warren was there with his father and waited to be called on...and waited...and waited...and waited. To his dismay, and his father's annoyance, he was not called, his father uttering that his son would never play for Manchester United. He remained on Bolton's books until he was twenty-two but lack of playing opportunities due to attending college led to him joining the RAF upon graduating. During his time attending the Officer Training course, Northern Nomads referred his name to Bishop Auckland who promptly showed an interest in gaining his signature. Warren was asked to choose where he would like to be stationed and immediately requested the Middleton St George camp, just a few miles down the road from the Kingsway ground.

It was whilst at Officer Training that young Bradley failed a rigorous medical examination. It was discovered that his left nostril was narrower than his right one, thus rendering him susceptible to colds. This would mean that he would not be available as often as he should be and as a consequence was prevented from becoming a flyer. Instead he became a Flying Training Officer at Middleton St George.

Warren soon fitted into the Bishop style of play, and early games saw him at inside-forward. Future displays would see him as a flying winger, no pun intended, and it was at outside-right that he would make his mark in the years to come, with Bishop Auckland, Manchester United (despite what his father had threatened) and England. For pub quiz buffs, he is still the only player to have represented England at amateur and professional level in the same season (1958-59), a record unlikely to be broken.

Crook tried in vain to overcome the deficit, but gave the ball away too often and never raised a serious threat on Sharratt's goal, and when the final whistle went Bishop were deserved victors 4-3.

Three weeks later, Bishop would inflict another defeat on their rivals, this time 3-2 at Kingsway, in the Durham County Challenge Cup.

After calling in at Arthur Street, where Mum and Barry had spent the afternoon with Grandma and Granddad, we listened to the rest of the results on the radio. We stayed there most of the evening and eventually caught the last bus that went through Willington. From there we connected with the Bishop Auckland service bus and arrived back at Sunnybrow tired. All I wanted to do was get into bed. Tomorrow we would have to get the train back to Stoke, and I had school on Monday. All the lads would be talking about Stoke City and Port Vale. I would tell them of a *real* football team.

* * * * *

There was nothing of note to record on the domestic front before Round Two took place. Compared to the struggle that Bishop had endured against Crook, their next task should prove a cakewalk, whoever they were drawn to meet.

The Football Association had decided, in their wisdom, that Round Two of the competition should be made on a regional basis. The Northern League Management Committee spokesman, Bob Frankland, expressed concern at such an arrangement, supported by all of the remaining northern clubs, but the draw went ahead all the same.

Little Gedling Colliery, of Nottinghamshire, were next in line, and like everybody else, Dad and I did not foresee any problems for a team of Bishop's pedigree there. And so it proved, Bishop winning comfortably 4-1 without being at their best, on the compact Colliery Welfare club's ground at Mapperley.

We did not go to the game but heard the result on the wireless.

'The Pink' arrived a few days later and we caught up with the match report. The game had taken part on what the reporter described as 'treacherous ground conditions', thereby making turning difficult for all players. The light covering of snow, on a rock hard surface, called for nimble feet and a certain degree of self-preservation, players were excused for not taking risks. Probably, the weather conditions accounted for the poor attendance figure; a crowd limit of 10,000 had been imposed by the police but there were only 2,800 paying spectators to witness the match.

Ray Oliver scored after twenty minutes from close range and added further goals in quick succession in the seventy-second and seventy-third minutes to register his hat-trick. Frank McKenna, who seemed to be getting better with every game, also scored. He was due to make his international debut the following week.

Gedling had been holding the Bishops to 1-1 but were trailing 1-2 when they were awarded a penalty after sixty-six minutes. Outside-left Martin took the kick, but blasted it wide, much to the relief of the cup holders. That penalty miss knocked the stuffing out of Gedling and Ray Oliver went on to finish the scoring as Bishop piled on the pressure in the last twenty minutes.

* * * * *

Corinthian Casuals: Not much change

Freedom of a sort arrived about this time; Dad acquired a car.

It was a black - they were all black, weren't they? - Ford Prefect, registration number HRE 131, and it allowed us to get about. It was not a new one, of course, but it was perfectly okay. No more waiting for buses: if we all wanted to go anywhere, now Dad could take us to...wherever. As like all mining families, Mum and Dad did not have a lot of money, and every penny counted. It was only through prudent saving (which involved not going up to Durham as regularly as they would have liked), that they were able to take the plunge and buy the little second-hand car.

One of the first places that I remember him taking us to was Alton Towers, only a few miles from where we lived. Forget all images of the theme park that dominates the Staffordshire Moorlands and causes traffic chaos in the peaceful hamlet of Alton now. Back in 1956 it was beautiful landscaped parkland and not much else. The old ruins were there, of course, as were the beautiful gardens, just like they are today. The lake was also there and back then model boat enthusiasts would bring along their craft and control manoeuvres from the lakeside. It was fascinating just watching the boats and listening to their masters, especially when there happened to be a collision in the water. Many were the times that my tender ears heard language as never before!

Despite us having the means to get about a bit easier now, it was not possible for us to travel up to Durham again to watch Ferryhill or Shildon take on Bishop in the next round of the Amateur Cup, and although the game would take place on my ninth birthday, a trip to watch it was out of the question. Quite simply, finances would not allow, and anyway, it would not have been fair on Mum, who would have had the major responsibility of looking after baby Barry throughout the journey. Also, Mum and Dad did not wish to chance such a long trip with the new car - if anything went wrong on the way then we could have been in trouble. Cars were not as reliable then as they are now.

Once again we had to make do with catching the result of the match from the wireless and then had to wait for the postman to deliver 'The Pink' to us so that we could read the match report.

The report for the game was critical of Bishops' play. They had been firm favourites to win the game, indeed they were favourites to retain the trophy itself, but little Ferryhill Athletic, whose ground is only a few miles from Bishop Auckland, gave the 'Two Blues' one hell of a fright. Athletic had surprisingly overcome Shildon 4-2 in a game delayed because of the bad weather in the previous round.

Ferryhill could be quite a useful team on their day and had won the Northern League Championship in season 1947-48. In the current season they were the only side so far to have inflicted a 3-1 defeat on the Bishops. Bishop had fielded a weakened side that day, but Ferryhill supporters could point to the fact that for a period of play, their team was down to nine men as a result of injuries. Bishop had won the return game in a tight encounter at Kingsway 3-2. It was clear that Bishop Auckland would not have it all their own way in the cup-tie.

By all accounts, Ferryhill deserved a draw at the very least. At no stage of the game were they overawed by their esteemed neighbours, and gave as good as they got. Once again, ground conditions did not cater for elegant football, the type that Bishop liked to play, and the Ferryhill players took whatever advantage they could. The Ferryhill ground staff had worked hard to get the game played and had cleared the pitch of all snow, large mounds of which were piled behind both goal areas.

Dave Marshall, that fine stalwart of the Bishop defence, was injured early on in the game when he twisted his knee and was limping for the major part of the match. Unfortunately for Ferryhill, their forwards were unable to evince the skill required to breach the Bishop defence and were often caught offside. Mind you, the Bishop forwards were just as ineffective as the few chances that did come along went astray. Ray Oliver and Seamus O'Connell were particularly guilty of wasting chances and on another day may have been more successful. For some reason, however, the Bishop forward line was stuttering and, except for when Lewin saw his effort come back off the post, at no stage looked like getting the required breakthrough. Of the Bishop Auckland forwards, Benny Edwards was singled out for particular praise as he constantly teased the Ferryhill defence.

Bell, for Ferryhill, and Corbett Creswell for the Bishops, were considered the two best players on the pitch, in a game where defences were clearly on top.

The goal that settled the issue came as a surprise to the 8,364 crowd, some of whom had decided that they had seen enough and had left early. Auckland, noted for their stamina and recognised strong finishers, had started to get on top, but there were only three minutes remaining when O'Connell popped up to score the only goal of the game. Pundits may have argued that Ferryhill deserved a replay, but the result was in the bag. Ferryhill Athletic 0 Bishop Auckland 1. Bishop Auckland, like all good teams, were capable of winning, even when playing badly.

* * * * *

Only seven days after producing a lethargic performance against minnows Ferryhill, Bishop were on the Amateur Cup trail again, this time visiting Finchley, who they had successfully conquered twice before in seasons 1949-

Corinthian Casuals: Not much change

50 and 1954-55. Harold Wilson, in years to come, would utter the quote: 'A week is a long time in politics'. The quotation could have been paraphrased to 'A week is a long time in football', as Bishop supporters saw their idols produce a display of flowing football, the likes that had probably never been seen before on the Summers Lane ground. Finchley were played to a standstill. Bishop won the game by scoring four perfect goals, without reply, and in demolishing a good Finchley side so easily, let it be known that it was their intention to retain the Cup.

The white shirts of Finchley swept in to the attack during the opening stages of the game, but there was no direction in their play, and really, the Auckland defenders coped comfortably with any pressure, although at one point Corbett Creswell had to head off the line to prevent a shock opening goal, with Harry Sharratt beaten. Such scares were rare, however, and solid play from the Northern League side put them in the ascendancy. It was only a matter of time before the amount of possession produced a goal.

Almost twenty minutes had passed before Seamus O'Connell scored the opener. Finchley tried hard to get back into the game but too many times passes went astray and were lapped up by a grateful Bishop half-back line. Any plans that Finchley had had of wearing down those tireless wing-halves, Bobby Hardisty and Jimmy Nimmins, backfired as they continued to give a duet display that could not have been bettered by Flanagan and Allen. Hardisty's vision and ball distribution earned high praise and Nimmins was a tiger in every tackle for the ball. And in between this pair was Corbett Cresswell who gave a commanding performance at centre-half. Anything sent down the middle was swallowed up by him with monotonous regularity.

On forty minutes O'Connell netted a second and then with metronomic timing he added a third on sixty minutes to complete a wonderful hat-trick. This third goal led to some Finchley fans heading for the exit, fully thirty minutes before the final whistle was due.

The metronome must have been swinging as sweetly as ever, because on eighty minutes, left-winger Benny Edwards finished the scoring with a fourth goal. That was it. What was left of the Finchley supporters among the 5,462 crowd began moving for the doors, as Bishop calmly played out time. A 4-0 romp had been achieved and none of the remaining clubs in the competition would want to meet them in two weeks' time.

That dubious honour fell to Kingstonian, the very team that had been thrashed 12-3 by Bishop Auckland on their own soil twelve months ago. Despite that result, they were considered the best southern side around. Well, they would have to be good to beat the Bishop Auckland that had turned up at Finchley. If, on the other hand, the Bishop Auckland that had negotiated

Ferryhill turned up, then things might be interesting. Whatever, the general feeling was that whoever won the tie at St James' Park would win the Cup.

* * * * *

Team spirit at Bishop Auckland was always incredibly high, with players generally reluctant to leave the club. The likes of Ron Fryer, who was an able and versatile player, had the opportunity to join Willington, where he could have commanded a first team spot every week, but preferred instead to stay with the Bishops, telling 'Kit' Rudd, 'If you want me to stay I will; Bishop Auckland is the only Northern League club I want to play for.' Joe Robinson and Brian Arksey, members of the Reserve Team, held similar views, and although they could probably have walked in to most Northern League teams, were content to stay at Kingsway. It was not just the second string players that were sought by other clubs as such an established player as Seamus O'Connell was said to be the target of neighbours Crook Town. Seamus had made the situation perfectly clear, however, stating that he would play for no amateur team in England other than Bishop Auckland. The contents of the following paragraphs illustrate the extent to which this statement was put to the test.

Controversy reared its ugly head, prior to the forthcoming semi-final, when the Bishop Auckland committee responsible for team selection, decided that Seamus O'Connell would not be selected. Seamus had decided to play for Chelsea Reserves rather than turn out for Bishop Auckland in a recent Durham Challenge Cup match against Willington. The Committee took a dim view of this and at their team selection meeting on the Monday immediately dropped him from the team for the Saturday semi-final tie. Consequently, one of Bishop's finest players would be missing from the semi-final line-up. His place was to be taken by young Warren Bradley. O'Connell was so upset that he threatened never to have anything to do with the club again.

News of the incident had many Bishop supporters worried. Warren Bradley was a fine player but O'Connell was a prolific goalscorer, especially when alongside Ray Oliver.

Perhaps I should mention at this point an incident that took place at about this time, relating to the non-appearance in a Bishop shirt by O'Connell. Although I was only a child, I can certainly remember members of my family discussing the number of times that O'Connell was missing from the Bishop Auckland line-up. He had missed a number of games for the side that season and more than one supporter was of the view that he only wanted to play in the most important ones. He was on Chelsea's books and was a regular member of their squad, but whenever Amateur Cup ties were to be played he suddenly became available for Bishop Auckland, a fact that had not gone unnoticed by fans and players alike. Some fans resented this and, although not exactly hostile towards this very good player, would have preferred a more dedicated member of the team to be playing for them, even suggesting that youngster John Barnwell be given a playing opportunity.

Derek Lewin became an unfortunate target when these rumours were running around, as inevitably they came to the ears of O'Connell himself. For some reason he decided that the instigator of the rumour was Lewin.

Derek Lewin told me; '*I always travelled up to Bishop on a Friday from my Lancashire home for Saturday's game and stayed at the Queen's Hotel in Bishop Auckland. It was owned by one of the club Committee members whose daughter was the television star, June Laverick. I always stayed in room Number Eight. More often than not, Bobby Hardisty and I would meet up, go for a walk around the town and end up at a Gentleman's Snooker Club, playing until God knows when.*

'*One particular Friday I decided to go and see Seamus who was staying at The White House. Apparently he had heard it said that someone in our team had commented that he should make up his mind whether to play for Chelsea or to play for us…not just make himself available for us when the Amateur Cup games came around. He was taken aback by the stinging remarks but had decided that it was me that had made them. Why me, I do not know. I went round to where he was staying and tried to have it out with him. He was unbending. No words on my part could persuade him otherwise and for a while we had a fall out. I would like to think that it did not affect the team, but it was rather unpleasant for a while between us.*'

(I have been unable to make contact with Seamus, who now lives in Spain, to obtain his views on the matter.)

As it happened, Bishop supporters had no need for any apprehension. Once again they produced a first-class performance that ripped the southern pretenders to shreds.

Kingstonian had in their squad, although he did not play in the semi-final match, a certain 'Sandy' Busby, son of Manchester United manager Matt Busby. The First Division manager had been asked to provide a report to help plot the downfall of the Bishops and the Kingstonian players had attended a midweek meeting to discuss the report and plot tactics, as well as listen to former Bishop player Len Langford, now the Kingstonian centre-half, who was able to give a briefing about the Auckland players. The chairman of Bishop Auckland, Councillor George Waine, met all this with the dismissive comment, 'All of the southern teams have plans when they meet us. We let results speak for themselves.'

The remark could not have been more appropriate.

In the opening twenty minutes, Kingstonian goalkeeper Parsons had to collect the ball from his net four times. Ray Oliver gave a display of centre-forward play hard to imagine in the amateur game, as he rattled in three goals in the opening nineteen minutes, the first two before five minutes had been played. His first was a typical header from a glided pass from Hardisty. The second followed almost immediately and again Hardisty was the provider. His third was stroked in after Lewin, Edwards and Bradley combined to cut the Kingstonian defence to shreds to lay the ball on a plate for him. The fourth goal was a result of Nimmins moving forward and passing to Lewin, who coolly slotted the ball home.

Opposing Ray was Len Langford, playing centre-half for Kingstonian. In the early Fifties, Len had been with Bishop Auckland (prior to that he was on Manchester United's books), becoming a regular member of their squad in 1952 and 1953, when he suffered a serious leg injury. The injury resulted in Len quitting football and he and his family moved down south. He took up playing football again in this 1955-56 season and signed on for Kingstonian. He played a couple of openers for the reserves and was then chosen for the first team. Within four games here he was at Newcastle United's stadium, playing against his former colleagues…and getting hammered by Ray Oliver in the process!

Twenty minutes gone and four goals down and already the Kingstonian players were looking for the shelter of the dressing room. There was no respite for them and before the referee blew for half-time Langford hauled McKenna to the floor. Lewin converted the penalty, placing the ball to the goalkeeper's right and just inside the post. Game over.

Leading 5-0 at half-time in an FA Amateur Cup semi-final was beyond Bishops' supporters' wildest dreams. Everyone knew that the game was won, and the Kingstonian players knew it too. There may have been some who wanted to see a repeat of that 12-3 scoreline, but the Auckland players were content to let the scoring stand as it was. The Kingstonian players were a dejected band at the end but were commended for their sportsmanship and deserved their consolation goal, a twenty-five yarder from Peter Bessex, going down 5-1.

One of the first to congratulate the Bishop Auckland players upon reaching the dressing room was Seamus O'Connell, who relented his outburst of a few days earlier when he had claimed that he had played his last game for the Bishops. He had a meeting with club officials and after a head-to-head talk the 'misunderstanding' was cleared up and he continued to be available for selection. Seamus O'Connell's next outing for The Bishops was in a weakened side, due to international and county calls, when the 'Two Blues' defeated Penrith 5-1 away from home.

* * * * *

Corinthian Casuals: Not much change

We had had the car for a few weeks now, and Dad had promised that if Bishop got to the final, then we would go to see it. Now that they had got to the final I was anxious that he kept his promise. Those three weeks from the semi-final to the final itself seemed like ten years. I was the envy of my class, if not the school, as I was the only one who had been to Wembley before and was now going there again. I don't think that my friends were jealous... well, perhaps just a bit. Ah, well, serves them right... they should support a decent team!

I cannot remember very much about this period in our lives, so I presume that nothing major happened. Barry would have had his first birthday and I remember being selected to play for the school team as a goalkeeper. We played the next village down the road, Caverswall, and the score was 1-1. Guess who saved a penalty again? Harry would have been proud of me.

'Little Betsy', as the car had been christened, got us to Uncle Dick and Aunty Dora May's place without any trouble, although we had passed a crash at St Albans (this was in the pre-M1 days remember, so the A5 was the main route from the Midlands). We had travelled down on the Friday evening and traffic had been light: let's face it, not everyone had cars then, unlike today.

As we pulled up outside the house, it was getting on for 10:00pm. and a light glowed from the front room. We walked up the path, Mum carrying Barry, Dad carrying a suitcase and me carrying a comic. Before we had reached the door, Aunty Dora May opened the door and called out 'Where's my Dick?'

I struggled to prevent myself bursting out laughing, and I think Mum and Dad did as well.

'Where's my Dick?' Aunty Dot repeated, looking up and down the street.

Thankfully, further embarrassment was avoided when Uncle Dick came down the stairs and pronounced that all the beds were made up and ready to be occupied. I ran to the bathroom before I peed myself from laughing.

Next day I was up bright and early and passed the time playing games with cousin Jeffrey until we got bored, and then I read bits of the newspaper, picking up snippets about Bishop's opponents, Corinthian Casuals.

Corinthian Casuals were an amalgamation of two clubs, not surprisingly, Corinthians and Casuals. Corinthians had been one of football's most famous clubs in the early days of the game and many of their players of the 1880s and 1890s had represented England - on two occasions they had provided the full England squad against Wales. The club remained amateur but fortunes began to wane in the 1930s and it was only an amalgamation with Casuals that saved the club from probable extinction. The union of the two clubs, however, had not met with any material success, until now. Here they were on the brink of winning the most prestigious prize in amateur football. All that they had to do was defeat the best amateur football club in the land.

Corinthian Casuals were coached by ex-Fulham goalkeeper Douglas Flack, in his first season with the club. The road to Wembley for Corinthian Casuals had begun with a first round 4-1 home win over Sheppey United at their Kennington Oval ground. Doughty fighters Wimbledon were overcome 3-2 in the next round, once again at home, before they won an away game by a solitary goal at St Albans in Round Three. Hitchin Town provided the opposition in Round Four and the Kennington Oval crowd were treated to a six-goal thriller, the teams drawing 3-3. In the following week's replay, 'Cor-Cas' as they were known, surprised the opposition and routed a stunned Hitchin side 5-0. The semi-final against Dulwich Hamlet was held at Stamford Bridge, Chelsea, and the 3-1 win resulted in them being in today's final. Norman Kerruish had scored a hat-trick that day and clearly was a man to watch.

I read the sports page that carried a preview of the game and read out to Dad the names of the teams that Corinthian Casuals had played. He looked at the scores relating to the Hitchin game and recollected that Crook had beaten them 10-1 only two seasons previous. I thought to myself that it was unlikely that Bishop would have anything to fear from a side that had needed a replay to defeat Hitchin on the way to Wembley. Some columnists were predicting a Bishop Auckland win by as much as six clear goals. 'I am going to enjoy this game,' I thought.

Soon it was time to get ready. We had dinner at about twelve o'clock and then Dad and I set off in the car for Kilburn, where we would catch the tube to Wembley Park. This time, it was just the two of us going to the game, unlike last year, when Uncle Dick and Aunty Dora May had come along.

We parked the car in a sidestreet close to Kilburn underground station and walked back to climb the stairs onto the platform. There were, to my eyes, a surprisingly small number of people waiting for the next train, as I had expected a lot more to be going to the match.

A few minutes later the train pulled in. It was crowded with supporters, for both Bishop and Corinthian Casuals. It was immediately apparent that tube stations further down the line were the ones being used by fans to get on the train, and explained why Kilburn station was almost empty. Nevertheless, when the sliding doors of the train opened, Bishop supporters inched further into the carriage and Dad and I were able to squeeze in. We now knew how a sardine felt.

Not many people were able to get on after that and the train rattled along towards Wembley Park. Just short of the station someone pointed out the twin towers of Wembley Stadium on the skyline not far away. It looked marvellous, bedecked with flags of every colour. Even the threatening rain clouds could not darken their spectacle.

April 16th 1955 Amateur Cup Final, Wembley.
Harry Sharratt safely collects the ball to stop another Hendon attack.

April 16th 1955 Amateur Cup Final, Wembley.
Bobby Hardisty clears the ball to safety as Harry Sharratt
and Corbett Cresswell look on.

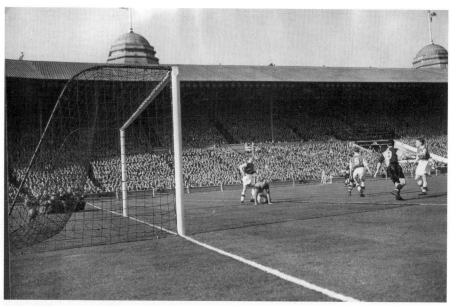

April 16th 1955 Amateur Cup Final, Wembley.
Hendon 'keeper, Reg Ivey, is on his knees as the ball nestles in the net. Scorer,
Derek Lewin, (hidden by Hendon number 5, Adams) turns away as colleague
Ray Oliver (number 9), runs over to congratulate. Safe to say that such a goal
would not be allowed to stand nowadays.

April 16th 1955 Amateur Cup Final, Wembley.
Seamus O'Connell fails to connect as the ball is cleared
to safety by anxious Hendon defenders.

April 16th 1955 Amateur Cup Final, Wembley.
Tommy Stewart smothers a Hendon attacking move.
(Photograph courtesy of Newcastle Chronicle and Journal).

April 16th 1955 Amateur Cup Final, Wembley.
Field-Marshall Montgomery of Alamein passes over the trophy to victorious
Bishop Auckland captain, Tommy Stewart (number 3). Also in picture are
Harry Sharratt, Jimmy Nimmins and Corbett Cresswell.

April 16th 1955 Amateur Cup Final, Wembley.
Everybody loves a winner.

April 16th 1955 Amateur Cup Final, Wembley.
The winners (left to right) Derek Lewin, Jacky Major, Bobby Hardisty (holding
the trophy), Corbett Cresswell, Harry Sharratt, Dave Marshall,
Tommy Stewart, Benny Edwards…(kneeling) Jimmy Nimmins,
Seamus O' Connell and Ray Oliver.

April 16th 1955 Amateur Cup Final, Wembley.
At last… a winners' medal for Bobby Hardisty, probably
the greatest ever amateur footballer.

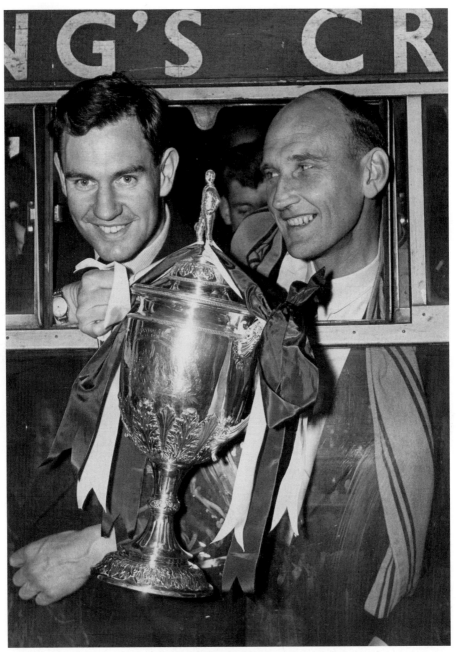

April 18th 1955, London.
Great friends, Derek Lewin and Bobby Hardisty about to leave
King's Cross Station with the Amateur Cup.
(This is Derek's favourite photograph).

April 18th 1955, Bishop Auckland.
No, the crowds aren't lined up for Doggarts sale. It appears that everyone in
the North-East wants to get a glimpse of the Amateur footballing heroes
on their triumphal return.

1955 F A Cup 1st Round, Kingsway.
Bishop Auckland's John Barnwell (3rd from left), sees his shot strike the
underside of the Durham City crossbar and go in to the net
to set the home side up for a 3-1 win.

1955 F A Cup 1st Round, Kingsway.
Derek Lewin is on hand should the Durham defence make any errors.

December 15th 1955 F A Cup 2nd Round Replay, Scunthorpe.
Ray Oliver sees Scunthorpe goalie, Norman Malan, bring an Auckland attack
to an end. Scunthorpe won this replay 2-0.

1956 Amateur Cup 3rd Round, Ferryhill.
This is the author's all-time favourite football photograph. Derek Lewin (2nd from left) slips the ball past Ferryhill goalkeeper, Robinson, only to see it hit the post and rebound to safety, as fellow teammates Ray Oliver and Seamus O'Connell look on. In the background, Jimmy Cain (Ferryhill number 4) looks as if he has other interests in hand, so to speak. Bishop Auckland won 1-0.

March 17th 1956 Amateur Cup Semi-Final, St James' Park, Newcastle.
Kingstonian defender, Len Langford, is unable to prevent Ray Oliver from opening the scoring for Bishop Auckland. The 'Two Blues' won 5-1.
(Photograph courtesy of Newcastle Chronicle and Journal).

March 17th 1956 Amateur Cup Semi-Final, St James' Park, Newcastle.
It's that man again…Ray Oliver sends a trademark header past Kingstonian
goalkeeper, Parsons, during the Bishops 5-1 demolition job. Len Langford
(Kingstonian number 2) can only look on in dismay.
(Photograph courtesy of Newcastle Chronicle and Journal).

March 17th 1956 Amateur Cup Semi-Final, St James' Park, Newcastle.
Derek Lewin slots home the perfect penalty against Kingstonian.

April 14th 1956 Amateur Cup Final Replay, Ayresome Park, Middlesbrough.
One for the scrapbook…Derek Lewin (Bishop number 8) scores with a header
as he outjumps Corinthian Casuals defender Gerry Alexander
and goalkeeper Paul Ahm to put the cup holders in the lead.
Bishop went on to win the match 4-1.

April 14th 1956 Amateur Cup Final Replay, Ayresome Park, Middlesbrough.
Derek Lewin pops up to put the ball past Ahm for
Bishop Auckland's third goal.

April 14th 1956 Amateur Cup Final Replay, Ayresome Park, Middlesbrough.
Cup-winners, again. (From left to right) Bobby Hardisty, Ray Oliver, Derek
Lewin, Tommy Stewart (aloft), Warren Bradley, Harry Sharratt,
Corbett Cresswell, Dave Marshall, Seamus O' Connell,
Frank McKenna and Benny Edwards.
(Photograph courtesy of Newcastle Chronicle and Journal).

November 17th 1956 F A Cup 1st Round, Kingsway.
Warren Bradley's effort is too good for Tranmere goalkeeper Payne as Bishop
record another notable Football League scalp, winning this game 2-1.

February 23rd 1957 Amateur Cup 4th Round, Millfield, Crook.
Crook goalie, Fred Jarrie, is left helpless by Derek Lewin's stunning goal,
the game ending 2-2. Seven days later, Bishop won the replay 2-0 at Kingsway
and booked a semi-final place against Hayes.

April 13th 1957 Amateur Cup Final, Wembley.
Ever dependable Derek Lewin scores yet again in an Amateur Cup Final,
sliding the ball past Wycombe goalkeeper, Syrett, for Auckland's second goal,
despite the attentions of burly centre-half, Wicks. New boy, Billy Russell, is in
close attendance to pick up any rebound.

April 13th 1957 Amateur Cup Final, Wembley.
Bobby Hardisty sends in a shot on the Wycombe goal but Syrett is equal
to the task. Bishop came out on top 3-1.

April 13th 1957 Amateur Cup Final, Wembley. Harry Sharratt clings on to the ball as Trott plays leap-frog with Bishop defender Bert Childs also wanting to join in. Full -back, Dave Marshall wonders what is going on.

April 13th 1957 Amateur Cup Final, Wembley.
Wycombe Wanderers full-back, Freddy Lawson, and goalkeeper Dennis Syrett, can only watch as Warren Bradley's splendid shot hits the back of the net for Bishop's third goal.

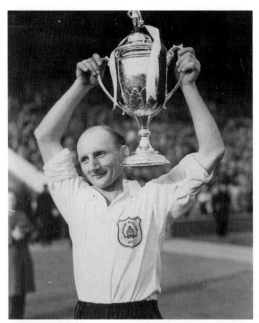

April 13th 1957 Amateur Cup Final, Wembley.
Jimmy Nimmins, captain of Bishop Auckland, holds the Amateur Cup aloft. The club had won the trophy for the third year in succession, and for a record-breaking ten times altogether, having played in eighteen finals.

The victorious 1957 Bishop Auckland Amateur Cup Final team, (back row, left to right) Dave Marshall, Bob Thursby, Corbett Cresswell, Harry Sharratt, Bert Childs, Jimmy Nimmins, (front row, left to right) Warren Bradley, Derek Lewin, Billy Russell, Bobby Hardisty and Benny Edwards.

Corinthian Casuals: Not much change

As is usual in such circumstances, there was bedlam trying to get off the train, with those closest to the doors being pushed and shoved by those behind. Like a cork from a bottle Dad and I emerged from the crush to join the slow moving column, exiting the station. Slugs and snails have moved faster.

As the station gave way to the approach to the stadium, I once again took in the proceedings, as I had done twelve months ago. This time the opposing fans were sporting blue and white scarves and rosettes. Dad and I delayed our entrance to the stadium to enjoy the atmosphere but in no time I was restless and anxious to get in to the stadium itself.

Once again I found myself standing in awe, marvelling at the giant amphitheatre, and surprisingly, in almost the exact spot where I had stood for last year's final against Hendon. The Community Singing was taking place, again conducted by Sir Arthur Caiger, but I was prepared for his joke this time and let it pass disconcertedly…I was not going to make a fool of myself again. The population of Bishop Auckland could have been no more than 18,000 at that time but there must have been going on for 40,000 supporters for them in the giant stadium. Some had come down on the Thursday, but the majority had travelled down the day before. Firms in the North-East had been encouraged to allow employees time off in order that they could catch the evening trains to King's Cross. The official party of Bishop Auckland Football Club had travelled by train from Darlington but a surprising number of players were missing from that party. Tommy Stewart, Bobby Hardisty, Seamus O'Connell, Derek Lewin and Corbett Creswell had travelled the day before. Tommy Stewart, captain, had appeared on *Sportsview*, chaired by Peter Dimmock, on Thursday night. Jacky Major and Harry Sharratt travelled direct from their homes.

The teams came out on to the pitch and were greeted in the traditional way. From all quarters, the ground erupted with supporters shouting at the tops of their voices. The teams were introduced to Lord Tedder and then the players made their way to their respective sides of the ground for the pre-match kickabout.

The Corinthian Casuals squad included a number of players who had previously played for Pegasus, two of who, Vowels and Alexander, had played in the 1953 Amateur Cup Final when Pegasus demolished Harwich and Parkeston 6-0. Doug Insole, playing at outside-right, played county cricket for Essex and had been chosen for England in Test Matches. Another cricketer on their books was Mickey Stewart, who was on a cricket tour in the West Indies when this game was taking place.

The teams were:

Bishop Auckland (Dark and Light Blue halved shirts, White shorts)
H. Sharratt - R. Fryer, T. Stewart - R. Hardisty, C. Cresswell, J. Nimmins -
F. McKenna, D. Lewin, R. Oliver, S. O'Connell, B. Edwards

Corinthian Casuals (White shirts, Navy Blue shorts)
P. Ahm - F. Alexander, D. Newton - G. Shuttleworth, R. Cowan,
R. Vowels - D. Insole, J. Sanders, J. Laybourne, G. Citron, N. Kerruish

Referee: J. H. Clough of Bolton

There was a comical incident before the game kicked off when Harry Sharratt (who else?) and the referee exchanged a few words. Harry had brought a tracksuit top out on to the pitch with him, which he intended to wear during the game. Referee Jack Clough took exception to the zip-fastener apparel being worn in such a prestigious game and told Harry to wear the more acceptable traditional jersey. Harry relented and changed into his green jersey.

The game got under way with Bishop kicking off. Immediately the Bishop half-back line began to win the territorial advantage. Edwards was put through but his shot was capably saved by Ahm. Play was mainly confined to the Corinthian Casuals' half but the Bishop forwards failed to capitalise. Paul Ahm, 'The Flying Dane', produced a good save from Oliver before pulling off another one from Derek Lewin's angled shot when he dived to divert the ball around the post. Despite those two efforts, though, the forward line of the cup holders was uninspiring and chances went begging. Time after time, when it looked like an opening had been made, the opportunity would be lost by the addition of a further pass with Seamus O'Connell, now welcomed back in to the fold, especially frustrating.

It was nearly thirty minutes before either side constructed a clear-cut opening. Then on the half-hour mark Frank McKenna received the ball on the right wing and cut into the penalty area where he unleashed a fierce right foot shot. The ball zipped along the ground and Ahm was unable to collect the ball cleanly. He went down to his right as Oliver rushed in, but the Bishop forward only managed to strike the ball against Ahm's outstretched body from only three yards out. Agonizingly for Bishop supporters, the ball did a parabola over the crossbar and all that Bishop got out of it was a corner. The corner was taken by Edwards, who sent over a high one that Ahm punched clear. The ball dropped to Hardisty who instantly found Oliver standing unmarked five yards from goal but the usually reliable goalscorer saw his effort rise over the crossbar.

Corinthian Casuals: Not much change

Corinthian Casuals counter-attacked down the right and Sharratt had to be at his best to punch a centre from Vowels over the bar and was then out of position when a Citron header also cleared the bar. Mainly, though, the London side were disappointing and produced little in attack to trouble the cup-holders.

With the first half drawing to a close, the dark and light blue-shirted Bishop forwards mounted another attack, and again it was McKenna who provided the danger. He burst down the right wing and sent over a low cross as Newton challenged. The ball flashed towards the near post and O'Connell lunged for it with an outstretched leg. Much to the frustration of the Bishop supporters, Ahm just gathered the ball before it connected with the inside-forward's foot. Moments later it was Oliver's turn to be thwarted as he saw his effort cleared off the line by full-back Alexander, with Ahm nowhere in sight.

Despite these attacks, it had been a disappointing first half, with Bishop ruing their missed chances. Harry Sharratt had had little to do, other than collect an Alexander free-kick and tip over a Kerruish centre for an unproductive corner, and that versatile dynamo Ron Fryer ably covering for the injured Dave Marshall, and full-back colleague Tommy Stewart, had had a very easy time and the score remained 0-0.

The Massed Band of the Coldstream Guards came out for the half-time entertainment and, without wishing to be unkind, were probably the best players on the field up to that point.

The second half resumed at a much better tempo as far as Corinthian Casuals were concerned. They had decided that there was nothing to fear from this Auckland team, who seemed capable of Jekyll and Hyde performances this season, and that today was the day that the giants could be overturned. The play ebbed and flowed with the Bishop forwards finally realising that to score a goal they would have to shoot. It was their bad luck that when they decided to do so, Ahm was capable of pulling off a good save, or the shooting was off target, O'Connell being particularly guilty when misplacing a header with Ahm, for once, out of his goal. It was Ahm who kept Corinthian Casuals in the game and it was because of him, and Bishop Auckland's previous reluctance to shoot on sight, that with almost on hour gone the score was still 0-0.

Eventually a goal did come, but not to the Bishops.

Fifty-seven minutes had gone when Corinthian Casuals were awarded a corner on their right-flank. Insole took the corner which was cleared for another. The second corner curled away from Harry Sharratt and landed in a crowded goalmouth. There was a flurry of legs and feet but the usually competent Bishop defenders failed to make the clearance. The ball bobbled about and was finally headed goalwards by Kerruish and Citron stuck out a foot to help the ball on its way. Hardisty, standing on the line, cleared but referee Jack Clough was satisfied that the ball had crossed the line and awarded the goal. Citron was credited as the scorer. From where I was standing, behind the goal, it did not look that the ball had crossed the line before being cleared, and many supporters around me voiced their disagreement with Mr Clough's decision to let the goal stand. To their credit, not one of the Bishop Auckland team protested at the decision.

For the first time in the game, Corinthian Casuals were on top. They started to play with the confidence that a goal brings, and for a while had the Bishop players chasing shadows. In particular, Kerruish, the outside-left, began to torment young Ron Fryer with his speed and was able to get in some crosses, but Sharratt ably plucked these out of the air. On the opposite flank, however, captain Tommy Stewart was having a fine game when called upon and was giving little away to winger Doug Insole. But Bishop Auckland had not gained their reputation by capitulating just because they were a goal down and they fought back as only they could. Gradually, the impetus that had been so clearly with Corinthian Casuals died down and Bishop started to play like the good team that they were. The forward line started to link up better than at any stage of the game and yet they still could not get the ball past the commanding figure of Ahm in the Corinthian Casuals goal.

Then, with less than a quarter of an hour to go, Derek Lewin let fly with a shot that Ahm could only parry. In an instant, Frank McKenna, who had been a revelation this season, was on hand to smash the ball into the roof of the net and level the scores. Relief all round in the Bishop Auckland ranks.

The Corinthian Casuals goalmouth area was, thereafter, under siege but the winning goal would not come. Somehow, the white-shirted defenders repelled the blue clad invaders and whenever they were beaten there stood the competent Ahm to punch or kick the ball to safety. Corbett Cresswell went upfield to add support to the Bishop attack but Ahm was brilliant in goal and dived to the foot of his right-hand post to deny the Bishop number five from scoring the winner.

Extra-time was played and during the next thirty minutes the holding Wembley turf took its toll on the players. Tired legs were unable to spray passes with the accuracy demanded and all too often the ball was gifted to opposing players. Both teams did their best to prise out a winning goal but by now defences were well on top and the game petered out for a 1-1 draw.

It was revealed later that Jimmy Nimmins had suffered a broken elbow during the game. Jimmy must have thought that he was jinxed as far as Wembley was concerned, having broken his leg in the final against Crook two seasons ago, and now this. In addition, Ron Fryer had played the latter stages of the game with a sprained ankle and would be doubtful for the replay in seven days' time. To add to Bishop's woes, inspirational figure Bobby Hardisty had come out of the game with a rib injury and his presence in the replay was also in doubt.

Corinthian Casuals: Not much change

Dad and I trooped out of the stadium feeling a bit let down at the result, especially as it was very unlikely that we would be going all the way up to Middlesbrough next week to watch the replay.

We spent the evening with Uncle Dick and Aunty Dora May. I played games with Jeffrey and read his collection of American comics, whilst the adults played cards. Barry slept peacefully in his carrycot, blissfully unaware of the sporting drama that had yet to unfold. The last act would be played out seven days hence.

* * * * *

The drama had begun on the treatment table at the Kingsway ground. On a good note, Dave Marshall would be fit for Saturday and would replace the injured Ron Fryer. Ron Fryer would undergo a fitness test later in the week, but would not recover sufficiently from his sprained ankle. A less happy outcome concerned Jimmy Nimmins, whose fractured elbow was confirmed and therefore meant that he would not play. Bobby Hardisty's rib injury was a major worry and all week there was a question mark over his participation. As late as Friday, the eve of the tie, the Committee were hoping that Bobby's injury would improve but by late afternoon his condition remained the same.

An emergency meeting of the Management Committee was called for that evening and it was decided that John Barnwell, still a schoolboy, would have to take Bobby Hardisty's place.

Ray Oliver says of that night: *'All of the players wanted Bobby to play. We had nothing against young John...he was a brilliant player and was well liked at the club by all of us. But we needed Bobby for his experience. John might have played and had a blinder, but truthfully, the players were apprehensive about playing the young lad in such an important match.'*

A message to the appropriate police station resulted in a constable calling on the Barnwell household that evening. The message that he carried was simple: John was required to deputise for the injured Bobby Hardisty in tomorrow's Amateur Cup Final replay. He was expected to meet up with the rest of the team at Ayresome Park.

The morning edition of *The Evening Gazette* carried the headline, '17-year-old Barnwell gets 11th hour chance to win soccer fame'. The article explained that Bobby Hardisty had not recovered from his injury and that the England Youth international would take his place. With seven internationals, namely Sharratt, Marshall, Stewart, Lewin, Cresswell, O'Connell and Oliver, plus Barnwell, optimism was high and Bishop were expected to win the cup today. The newspaper stated one of their reporters had visited the Barnwell household on the previous evening (Friday) and that John had said; 'It is quite a shock. I did not think that I had much chance to play. I knew there was a slender chance but Bobby Hardisty is not one to miss games if he can possibly help it.'

However, the club doctor, D.T. Prescott, had not given up hope of getting Hardisty fit to play and asked for him to carry out some training on the Saturday morning. He came through the stiff session sore, but no worse than could have been expected. The decision about his fitness had been taken only twelve hours earlier, but could, or indeed should, that decision be reversed? It was decided that no firm decision about Hardisty's participation would be made until as late as possible, even if this meant right up to kick-off time.

The attendance figure for the replay was 29,099 and it is unlikely that any one of them knew of the palaver that had taken place prior to the teams taking the field.

John Barnwell remembers the build up to that weekend and its consequences that rocked the club: '*I always went to the pictures on a Friday night, but Mum and Dad always insisted on me being back home by nine o'clock. I was coming up the road and I wondered what all the people were doing outside our house. As I got closer, cameras started flashing and taking my photograph. They were newspaper reporters come to see me. I asked what was going on and one of them said that I had been picked for tomorrow's Final. A fellow, from the Newcastle Chronicle I think, said that the football club secretary wanted to speak to me. Well, we did not have a telephone so this reporter took me to his offices. It was from the Newcastle Chronicle office that I spoke to the secretary, 'Kit' Rudd, who told me that I was picked for the team and was definitely playing. Whilst he was telling me all the arrangements about getting to Middlesbrough, all I was thinking about was how could I get tickets for my Mum and Dad. He said not to worry and everything would be taken care of.*

'*Living opposite us was Newcastle United's chief scout, Temple Lyle, and it was he who took me to Ayresome Park. Mum and Dad would follow along later, but because I was down to play I had to be there earlier. I went in to the dressing room and someone - I think that it was 'Kit' Rudd - pulled me to one side and told me that I would not be playing, because Bobby Hardisty could play now that the doctor had given him some injections and strapped him up. Bobby was not one hundred per cent fit, but the doctor reckoned that he could see the match through provided that he did not take a blow to the rib-cage. I cannot remember what my feelings were but obviously I was extremely disappointed. I had just returned from playing in the 'Little World Cup' for England Under-17s and everything appeared to be going so well for me.*

'This was my first distasteful experience in football and it left a scar, which I got over but never forgot. I realized that what really hurt was the manner of how they had told me that I was not playing. It was ruthless. It can be said that the decision was vindicated because Bishop won, but what they should have done was tell me that there was a possibility that I would be playing, make sure I was at the ground.

'I watched the game from the bench by the touchline but did not enjoy it. The thing that always sticks in my mind is the assertiveness of my father. He was never a loudmouth, never shouted or anything like that, but he entered the dressing room and demanded to know who had been responsible for treating his son in such a shameful manner. He told 'Kit' Rudd that he may be celebrating now but that what had happened was no way to treat a young lad. He told them in very clear terms that the way it was handled was an absolute disgrace and he went on to say, "You think that you are going to make some money out of this boy, but I am telling you now that he is finished with this club." And then he turned to me and we left the dressing room. A few days later I signed for Arsenal and I have never been back to the club since. Derek Lewin and Warren Bradley are the only two players from that time that I have seen since.'

Two years previously, Seamus O'Connell had been called upon to fill the breach when Jimmy Nimmins broke his leg in the final against Crook and had performed impressively. This afternoon he was to repeat that role as left-half, with Warren Bradley taking over the inside-left spot. Dave Marshall returned to replace Ron Fryer.

Bishop Auckland were not the only team suffering selection problems. Corinthian Casuals were having a bit of a headache too. Mickey Stewart - a future England cricketer and father of England wicket-keeper Alec - had been contacted in the West Indies and made himself available to play in the replay. The club was satisfied that he would arrive in time but from the outset the journey met with setbacks. The first flight from Caracas to New York was delayed due to high winds that resulted in Stewart missing the BOAC connection. As a result he had to fly on a KLM flight to Prestwick instead of to London. That flight was delayed and he did not land in Scotland until 1:30pm, less than ninety minutes to kick-off. He was hustled through customs and ran across the tarmac to a waiting plane, leaving his luggage behind in the airport. The light aircraft touched down at Thornaby Aerodrome at 2:47pm. - thirteen minutes before the teams were due to kick off. A car was on standby for him and raced to the ground. Stewart was in the car changing, partially undressed, ready to don the shirt and shorts as soon as he reached the ground. At 2:57 pm the car pulled up outside the official entrance to the ground, but it was too late as the teams had already been declared and were on the pitch.

Despite his frantic efforts he was unable to play and had to sit in the stands and watch the game.

The teams were:

Bishop Auckland (Dark Blue and Light Blue halved shirts, white shorts)
H. Sharratt - D. Marshall, T. Stewart - R. Hardisty, C. Cresswell,
S. O'Connell - F. McKenna, D. Lewin, R. Oliver, W. Bradley, B. Edwards

Corinthian Casuals (White shirts, Navy Blue shorts)
P. Ahm - F. Alexander, D. Newton - G. Shuttleworth, R. Cowan,
R. Vowels - D. Insole, J. Sanders, J. Laybourne, G. Citron, N. Kerruish

Referee: J. H. Clough of Bolton

The Bishop players produced the best football in the opening period, with Corinthian Casuals having to defend more than they would have liked, left-back Newton being called upon to make a fine goalline clearance from O'Connell's shot.

Corinthian Casuals developed an attack early on but Sharratt easily collected Insole's effort. Mainly, though, play was at the other end of the pitch. Although they were unable to force a breakthrough, the Auckland forwards were playing as a more cohesive unit than they had seven days ago. Seamus O'Connell was having a fine game alongside the commanding figure of Cresswell; so much so that some observers wondered if he was a better half-back than inside-forward.

Seamus O'Connell was an enigmatic player. He could flit in and out of games so easily, much to the annoyance of supporters. When he was on song, there was not a better inside-forward in amateur football. Despite his Irish-sounding name he was in fact English, a native of Carlisle where he ran a cattle business with his father. He had played for several seasons in the Scottish League for Queen's Park, before joining Bishop Auckland in 1953. His partnership with the then recently acquired Ray Oliver paid dividends immediately and they had become the most potent attacking duo in amateur football. Seamus had won international caps for England at amateur level and had even played First Division football for Middlesbrough and Chelsea, winning a League Championship medal for the London side.

This time it was just good defending by Corinthian Casuals that prevented a goal from being scored, not lacklustre efforts. It came as a surprise, therefore when, on thirty-four minutes, the Isthmian League side took the lead. Citron, playing at inside-left, shot from thirty yards. The ball zoomed past Sharratt and hit the far post before going in to the net. Some observers, including Derek Lewin, thought that it had been a fluke, but no matter what, the Bishops were a goal down.

The goal had been scored against the run of play but within three minutes the scores were level. An attack down the Bishops' right flank ended with a fine cross being headed into the penalty area by Hardisty. Before Alexander and Ahm could reach the high ball, Derek Lewin leaped to head it over the goalkeeper's outstretched arms. It was a goal for the scrapbook, as Derek did not get many with his head.

Play was end to end for the closing period of the half, with Sharratt having to produce a good save, punching the ball over the bar. The resultant corner was comfortably dealt with by Marshall, who showed no signs of the injury that had kept him out of the side for the last few games.

The teams came off at half-time with the score 1-1 and both were probably satisfied with the way things had gone. Corinthian Casuals would have been pleased that they were level and that they had coped with the Bishop pressure. On the other hand, Auckland would be content that they had been on top and had not given much away at the back, apart from the goal. In addition, Bobby Hardisty had come through the half unscathed and was helping Bishop to command the midfield. He had not had to endure any blood and thunder tackles, and if all went well then he should prove Dr Prescott's decision correct to complete the full ninety minutes.

The Corinthian Casuals' defence was put under pressure straight from the restart and it was not long before Hardisty, of all people, put the 'Two Blues' ahead. Seamus O'Connell, revelling in the role of attacking wing-half, made a sortie down the left wing. Reaching the bye-line, he sent over a low cross. The Corinthian Casuals' defence could only prod the ball out to the edge of the penalty area. Like a crocodile waiting for a baby deer to come to the waterside, Hardisty was there anticipating the ball to drop. Wham! In a flash, he unleashed a pile-driver that sent the ball above the heads of the defenders into the roof of the net. The Bishop players wanted to hug him, but were afraid of causing further injury to their star player. They made do with a handshake instead and a 'Well done, Bob'.

From then on a third goal always looked likely and it was Lewin who scored it. Seamus O'Connell once again forayed down the left and pushed the ball for Edwards to run onto. The winger centred the ball in to the penalty area. A faulty clearance resulted in the ball falling at Bradley's feet. The pint-sized forward sent in a powerful shot that Ahm could only parry to Lewin. From four yards the inside-forward was dangerous, from three he was absolutely lethal. The ball was instantly flashed past Ahm, high into the net.

To all intents and purposes the game was now over. Corinthian Casuals were unable to score again, although they did create a few scary moments in the Bishop defence. The last act, however, belonged to captain Tommy Stewart, who collected a long clearance upfield and ran hell for leather towards the Corinthian Casuals' goal. From twenty-five yards he delivered a thunderbolt of a shot that screamed into the far corner of the net for a spectacular goal. It was the last kick of the game.

Having triumphed 4-1, it was Bishop Auckland captain Tommy Stewart who was handed the Cup. This would be his last intended season with the Bishops and he deserved to go out on a winning note.

Seamus O'Connell, offering his winners' medal to the unlucky Ron Fryer, illustrated the camaraderie of the Bishop Auckland squad. Seamus already possessed a winners' and losers' medal and was content for Ron to have the latest one. Ron declined the offer, saying that he would have preferred to have won the medal by actually playing. Seamus, however, was very persuasive, and in the end a very grateful Ron Fryer accepted the medal. It came to light afterwards that Dave Marshall and Bobby Hardisty had made similar offers towards Ron.

The decision to play the talismanic Hardisty had been justified in the end, and so had Dr Prescott's faith in his own judgement. It could not have been easy for the Committee to decide on playing Bobby Hardisty, having told John Barnwell that the position was his. On another day, Bobby could have broken down and not been able to carry on; where would the club have been then? Also, who is to say that the young Barnwell would have taken to the occasion? Nerves could have got to him. There is little point speculating. The bottom line was that Bishop won the Amateur Cup and Bobby Hardisty played a great game. That was all that mattered.

Bishop would end the season winning the Northern League Championship with a rather lowly total of 38 points from their twenty-six league games, thereby completing a hat-trick of wins for the League title. And yet, despite winning the FA Amateur Cup and the Northern League Championship, the season ended in near farce for the club. The last game of the season was against Crook at Millfield. Bishop had players missing and fielded ten reserves. Crook were merciless and won the match 12-1. Humiliation for Bishop fans but just as incensed were the Crook supporters who had turned up expecting to see a competitive game, not a 'lie down'.

Crook made an official protest, complaining that Bishop broke the rule that requires a club to play to its full strength or give a satisfactory explanation. It was left to 'Kit' Rudd to defend the club, claiming: 'Cresswell, O'Connell and Lewin were not available because they had gone to the Cup Final. Some players had not turned up, some were injured whilst three others - Hardisty, Lewin and Sharratt - were training for the Great Britain Olympic squad.' He claimed that in the circumstances '..it was the best team available. '

The incident passed and was treated as no more than a storm in a tea-cup by the Bishop Auckland players and officials, who were already looking towards achieving a unique hat-trick of successive Amateur Cup Final wins. The FA Amateur Cup, as always, would remain the number one priority for the Committee. Members of the club, players and officials, and all supporters, could not wait for the next season. Would there be another journey down the A1? Would Wembley Way still be as inviting? Would the ageless Bobby Hardisty have the opportunity of winning a third successive winners' medal? Young Thursby looked as if he could well keep him out of the team. He wasn't getting any younger, was our Bobby.

The next season could not come quick enough.

CHAPTER SIX

Wycombe Wanderers: The Twin Towers

The Liverpool teams of the Seventies and Eighties owed much of their success to the seamlessly smooth transition of players new to the squad. As soon as it was necessary for a player to be replaced, then one of similar quality, or better, was acquired. Changes were almost imperceptible...a new member introduced here, a change of accent there. So it was for the Bishop Auckland teams of the Fifties. When it became necessary to replace the likes of Harry McIlvenny and Tommy Farrer, Ray Oliver and Tommy Stewart were brought in. Bill White followed Jack Washington, and later Harry Sharratt. A forward line of Taylor, Anderson, McIlvenny, Williamson and Edwards (1951 final against Pegasus) had changed to Major, Dixon, Oliver, O'Connell and Watson by the time the 1954 final came around. Five forward positions and all five covered by five different players. Yet the changes had been made so well, that hardly anyone noticed - Bishop just kept on being the club that all others wanted to beat.

Credit for producing a team of the quality that Bishop Auckland had become should go to Les Wilson, Secretary of the club from 1948, when 'Kit' Rudd retired from the post, until 1953. He was a good judge of a player's footballing ability and he was responsible for bringing so many good ones to the club. The 'Glory Days' were a product of his foresight and skill and it was a tragedy that he died when aged only fifty-seven in 1953 and therefore never saw Bishop win any of their Wembley finals. His great friend 'Kit' Rudd, himself a legendary ex-Bishop Auckland player, resumed the post and held it until he retired once again in 1963. He died on Christmas Day, 1969...a fitting day for a gentleman called Christopher.

Christopher Rudd was always 'Kit' to his friends, and that was a lot of people. He had been associated with the club since 1905, as a player and administrator, and was a respected figure in the town. He knew how to deal with people and, most importantly at a football club, knew how to get the best out of them. He was a communicator. Every player at the club could expect a detailed report about their behaviour and performance from 'Kit' after every game as well as instructions on meeting up for the next match, with everything written in longhand.

Another notable member at the club was Ernest Proud. Like 'Kit', he had been with the club since the early 1900s. He did not have far to walk to the ground - his house was 'Delwood', the large house adjoining the ground at the 'bottom end' of the Kingsway pitch. He had played as goalkeeper in the 1900, 1902 and 1906 Amateur Cup Finals. As President of the club he wielded power, but held strong principles in the way that football, and sport in general, should be played. He believed in sportsmanship and the true amateur ideal. Values that, sadly, are rather lacking in today's sporting globe.

Mention should also be made of Jack Sowerby, who had been appointed trainer during this era. He had previously been with Ipswich Town and was able to bring Football League experience to the club. Note that Jack was appointed trainer, not manager. He was the one who would provide the 'magic sponge' when a player went down injured but he played no part in team selection; that remained the domain of the all-powerful Committee.

Derek Lewin recalls: *Jack Sowerby was a lovely man. He was already at the club when I joined. To be fair, I don't think that I played particularly well in those first few games. We were on our way to Ipswich, by train, to play an FA Cup tie when Jack came up to me. 'Derek,' he said, 'I used to play for Ipswich, and it would give me great pleasure if you could play well today.'*

'I looked at him and smiled... that was his way of geeing me up.

'As you know, we drew the game and were unlucky not to win it. Jack came in to the dressing room and headed straight for me. 'Well done, Derek. Thank you.'

'As I said before, he was lovely man.'

Derek goes on: *'We didn't have any team talks or blackboards with dots and circles on. No-one showed us diagrams of where we should be on the field. It just was not done then. Certainly, Jack Sowerby never told us how to play. Everything that we did was off the cuff. Each one of us trusted the others to do their job. I suppose the nearest that we ever came to a team-talk, would be when Charlie Wright, a member of the Committee, would come through to us at half-time and say to us one by one, "Kick 'em. Get stuck in. Kick 'em." We would just look at him and nod our heads, then, when he had returned to the sanctuary of the Committee Room, we would just gaze at the closing door and just shake our heads.'*

With two successive Wembley finals won, it was obvious that Bishop would be installed as favourites to retain the trophy again. Odds as short as 7-4 were called in some quarters, a ridiculous figure considering that the feat had never been attained before and that everyone else would be trying harder than ever to beat them. In the meantime, there was the Northern League Championship to concentrate on, and as defending champions Bishop could be sure of some tough tests ahead. The League Championship was always nice to win, but the truth was that the Amateur Cup was always the club's aim. Crowds were far bigger for those cup games. Mention the crowd figures of those cup matches to today's football followers and they will think that you are telling porkies. They cannot understand that 12,000-plus crowds were the norm. Even league games generated crowds of between 6-8,000.

Early in the season, a friendly match took place at Kingsway, the Icelandic side Valur F C being the visitors. Bishop had no trouble running out 8-1 winners with the in-form Seamus O'Connell getting five of the goals; Ronnie Thompson and Derek Lewin (2) were the other scorers.

Bishop got off to their usual winning ways in the Northern League, but it soon became clear that the challenge from Billingham Synthonia would be a strong one. The Teesside club had shown that they were becoming a useful outfit in the past few seasons and gave notice that they would be challenging for the title. They proved a point when they defeated Bishop 2-0 in their first league encounter. Later in the season they would lose the return game 3-0, but deservedly they would go on to win the title by eight points, only losing four games overall. Bishop would finish third, nine points behind; West Auckland were sandwiched between as runners-up.

The week before Bishop lost to Billingham, they were engaged in an FA Cup first round tie against Football League side Tranmere Rovers. Bishop had been exempted until the first round as a result of their Amateur Cup success the previous season. With the game being held at Kingsway, Tranmere could not discount the non-league side's chances of pulling off yet another cup shock.

Bishop were fielding a weakened side as a result of Harry Sharratt, Derek Lewin and Bobby Hardisty representing the British Olympic football team in Melbourne. With some of their best, and most influential, players missing they faced a stiff task, but in front of 7,000 spectators (slightly disappointing considering that Bishop were playing Football League opposition), the home side started in confident manner. They were first to the ball and got tackles in before the Tranmere players had time to think. The speed of the Bishop players seemed to take the Merseyside team by surprise and often they lost possession of the ball. Bob Thursby, in particular, had a fine game, showing an ability to read the game far beyond his teenage years.

Bob had previously been with Stanley United and it was not long before his outstanding performances for that club came to the attention of the Bishop Auckland Committee. A strong tackling half-back, he would be the ideal replacement for Bobby Hardisty, who was coming to the end of his career.

Bob recalls: *'I lived in Chester-le-Street - still do - and Stanley would organise a taxi for me to get me to the ground. It was a bit of a trek, but the club was paying the fare. Some time during the close season I got an invitation to sign for Bishop Auckland. I can't remember who made the call, but I was pleased to have the opportunity to join the most famous amateur club in the world. I did have some doubts, however. I was quite willing to go to Bishop but I asked them how I would get in the team with Bobby Hardisty there. I was assured that I would get enough games and that is exactly what happened. Bobby was nearing the end of his career anyway, so it was just a matter of time. I was told that I could expect £5 a game. I said, "Hang on...I'm supposed to be joining the best club in amateur football and all that you're offering is £5 a game...I'm on that at Stanley!"*

'Naturally, I signed for them, but I made sure that I got paid 'the going rate'. We were amateurs but all the clubs paid the players to turn out for them - "Expenses, you see,"' he adds, with a twinkle in his eye. *'The Southern lads must have been on really good money with the cost of living being so much higher down there...not that anyone openly talked about such a thing as money, mind.*

'In them days, all that a footballer could look forward to after his career had finished was to look after a pub, or something like that. I made up my mind very early on that I would be better than that. Fortunately, I had something between my ears and was able to put my brain to some good use. I studied for university to become a dental student. Not once did I have to apply for a student loan...my football 'expenses' took care of that!

'In those early years at Bishop I was used as a stand-in, generally for whenever Bobby Hardisty was injured or on international duty. He was nearing the end of his career when I joined the club, but he was still a marvellous player. He had a brilliant footballing brain and his movement was as smooth as silk. Without any shadow of a doubt, he was the greatest. It is ridiculous that I went on to win more caps than him.'

Bob may be right, but this day against Tranmere, he put in a performance that won the praise of all who saw him.

The flame-shirted Auckland players seemed to be everywhere in the opening twenty minutes. The surprise was that it took Bishop that long to open the scoring. Warren Bradley collected the ball on the right wing and as he raced to the bye-line, pulled the ball back and sent over a high ball. From the opposing wing position, Benny Edwards raced in to volley the ball past an astounded Payne, the Tranmere goalkeeper. The goal was a beauty...what a pity that there was no such thing as video then.

Tranmere were rocked by the goal. They had not produced much in the way of goalscoring chances so far, and any confidence that they had before the game was slowly ebbing away. Passes went astray and the amateurs more often than not won fifty-fifty balls. It was a sorry Tranmere Rovers that left the field at half-time.

Auckland continued the second half where they had left off the first. Bradley on the right and Edwards on the left teased a disjointed Tranmere defence. But to the frustration of the home fans, a second goal did not look like coming as scoring opportunities were squandered.

Then, on the hour mark, Bishop got the second goal that their superiority merited. The willing Bradley gained possession of the ball on the right wing. He had been supplying crosses to his inside-forwards most of the match but this time he cut inside his defender and unleashed a shot that headed for the far top corner of the goal. Payne flung himself to his right but the ball was past him and returning from the net before he had touched the ground.

It was time for the Football League side to pull their socks up and show more enterprise and they responded with an immediate attack on the Bishop goal, forcing 'Kit' Hewitt, deputising for Harry Sharratt, to bring off a fine save diving to his left. Three minutes later, Hewitt was picking the ball out of the net when Davies was left unmarked to reduce the deficit. The 2-1 scoreline was not a fair reflection of the game, but the home side had failed to take their chances. Tranmere became a different side after scoring and worked hard to get the equaliser, but Corbett Cresswell had a fine match in the middle of defence and no further goals were added.

There was a sense of dismay when Bishops' opponents for Round Two became known. An away tie to North Wales side Rhyl, playing in the Cheshire League, did not exactly set the heart pumping.

Rhyl was not the dirty seaside town then that it has become nowadays. In the 1950s it was quite an attractive little resort. Summertime would see guesthouses and hotels full with holidaymakers, traditionally mainly from Merseyside and The Potteries. A trip to the seaside might sound nice, but not in the middle of December. Buckets ands spades would clearly not be required.

Given the proximity to Christmas and money therefore being tight, I was surprised that we all went to Rhyl. Mum took Barry for a walk in a pushchair and spent time on the seafront, whilst Dad and I went to the football match.

I seem to remember that it was a reasonable day weather-wise. The sun gave out an autumnal glow as we set out in the morning. 'Little Betsy' was a gem of a car and so far had proved very reliable. We made our way up to Chester and thereafter I pestered Dad every five minutes claiming that I could see the sea and asking how much longer it would be. A lifetime on the coast road ended with us going through such places as Ffynnongroyw and Gwespyr and Prestatyn… 'Are we in Wales yet, Dad?'

Dad and I made our way to the ground. Like many others in similar circumstances who do not know where a football ground is, we did not ask for directions but just followed the crowd. Over 10,000 made their entrance to the little Grange Road ground. Some brave souls climbed the trees that overlooked the ground…they probably had the best view of the game.

Before the game, Dad and I found out that Tommy Stewart was injured and that his place was to be taken by Alan Brown, a decision that surprised us as we thought that Ron Fryer would have been a more suitable selection.

(Bishop were unwittingly responsible for an unsavoury incident that took place one hundred and fifty miles away on the day that they played Rhyl and had an unfortunate consequence for West Auckland centre-half and stalwart Wilf Miller. He had been with the club a number of years and had given fine service. Some supporters, however, decided that he was past his best and that he had played a particularly bad game against Bishop the previous week. They were of the opinion that he should not be considered for future selection. At their next game, against Stanley United, a number of West Auckland supporters waited outside the ground to hear the team selections before paying the entrance money. They had made it clear that if Wilf Miller were to be selected, they would boycott the game. The players took to the field and it was ascertained that the unlucky Miller would not be playing, at which point the supporters proceeded to pay their entrance money and watched the game. West Auckland won 5-1).

For those who had come to see the mighty Bishop Auckland turn on the style, disappointment lay in wait. The Amateur Cup holders never got going and at no stage of the game did they look like winning. The forwards failed to produce any firepower with Ray Oliver and Ron Thompson both having 'off days'; it was only Bishops' defence that kept them in the game with Bob Thursby and Jimmy Nimmins both getting through some sterling work.

In view of Rhyl's superiority in ball possession it was remarkable that the score remained 0-0 to almost half-time. Hewitt, again in goal for the missing Sharratt, was the busier of the two 'keepers, and it was his saves from centre-forward Russell that kept the 'Two Blues' in the game. Russell was proving a handful for the usually competent Cresswell and more than once Thursby and Marshall had to come to the rescue with hasty clearances. The scoreline changed, however, in the last minute of the first half. A high centre was sent over from the Rhyl left and Hewitt jumped for the ball, with Rhyl forward Williams in close attendance. Hewitt was beaten to the ball by the inside-right's head and as he crumpled to the ground, the ball flew deflected in to the net. Hewitt was suffering a gashed lip but worse than that, Bishop were a goal down. Those around us could not help thinking, perhaps rather unkindly, 'Harry would have caught it.'

The surprise of the second half was that Bishop immediately started to string passes together and within two minutes had the opportunity to atone for their first half misgivings. O'Connell broke in to the penalty area and was blatantly tripped. Penalty!

145

Rhyl protested at the decision but it was a definite penalty - I had seen it with my own eyes just a hundred yards away. Up stepped Bob Thursby. He was too young to have any nerves. As smooth as you like he stroked the ball inside the post and the scores were level. Bishop must surely go on from this now. Such teams as Newcastle and Sunderland, Arsenal and Tottenham were waiting for them in the next round.

'Howay, Bishop!'

As usually happens in such circumstances, the goal raised the spirits of the Auckland players and they began to produce their best football of the game. Another attack resulted in a Rhyl defender blatantly handling the ball in the penalty area. 10,000 spectators and twenty-two players saw it. The man in black didn't and waved play on. If Bishop had scored a second at that stage of the game who knows what the final outcome would have been? However, football is full of hard luck stories and this was just one more addition to that list.

The Welsh team became rattled at having to defend as much as they were doing and resorted to some strong-arm tactics. Warren Bradley, four feet nothing and seven stones soaking wet, became the main target. He was beginning to take on the Rhyl defenders who multilaterally decided that he had to be stopped at all costs. The rough treatment meted out to him finally resulted in Griffiths being booked, an action that carried far more shame in the 1950s than it does now.

Then Rhyl got lucky. They had prevented Bishop from adding to their penalty goal and were beginning to muster a few attacks themselves, but their shooting was erratic and wayward. One such effort, however, proved fruitful. Donaldson decided to chance his luck and Hewitt dived to his right, safely covering the ball. To his dismay, the ball struck O'Connell on the leg and was diverted in to the opposite corner of Hewitt's goal. It now looked that the Cheshire League side was going to be in the draw for the third round for the first time since 1926.

And so it proved. From then on Rhyl drove forward, with Irish international Hughes making penetrating runs down the left wing and giving Brown a torrid time. A third goal arrived near the end and it was a dejected Bishop team that left the pitch. It was also a dejected little party that made its way home to Staffordshire as well.

* * * * *

Christmas and New Year were quiet times for us. Mum and Dad always preferred to spend the festive season at home and although we were never a 'party' family, we always enjoyed ourselves. I was allowed to stay up to let in the New Year. There would be sherry and port on the table as well as fruitcake, shortbread and chocolates. At about two minutes to twelve Dad would get up from watching Jimmy Shand on the television, put on his coat and go outside.

Mum and I would be watching the television, waiting for Big Ben to chime in the New Year. A minute or so later, there would be a knock on the door and it would be Dad 'First Footing' with a lump of coal in one hand and a piece of wood in the other. Mum would welcome dad in with a kiss and cross his palm with silver, a sixpenny piece or shilling bit, usually. This signified warmth and happiness to the household for the ensuing twelve months. We would all wish each other 'Happy New Year' and sit down to watch the rest of the television for a while. Then, without fail, there would be another knock on the door and it would be a neighbour 'First Footing'. More often than not, that first visitor would be Gordon, accompanied by his wife Betty.

Gordon was a smashing bloke. He could tell tales - usually tall ones - that would have tears of laughter running from my eyes. Like Dad, he was in the St John's Ambulance Brigade and for some reason believed that this qualified him to become the trainer/medic for the newly-created local football team. The team was made up of lads from the estate and only played friendlies at first, but later on they would join a league. Unfortunately, Gordon developed a reputation for having only one remedy for whatever injury befell any player. Iodine.

You think of any injury that a footballer can incur, whether it be a sprained ankle, gashed shin, bruised knee, toothache, flat feet, anything, Gordon's remedy was that raging lotion, iodine. His reputation became legendary throughout the league and opposing players would deliberately kick hell out of the Coalville team just to get Gordon on to the pitch to see him in action. At the sight of Gordon, immaculately dressed in his St John's uniform, sprinting towards a stricken player, the mere thought of iodine being applied was usually sufficient for him to make a miraculous recovery. I am sure that if any one had suffered decapitation during one of those games, they would have preferred to continue playing while carrying their head in their hands, rather than receive Gordon's remedy.

Sometime in the 1980s Gordon and Betty moved back up to Durham and lived at Roddymoor. Betty died a few years later. Gordon found an opportunity to help the Durham Ladies' Ice Hockey Team...as trainer. I wonder...

The entrance of a new year brought with it the opening round of the Amateur Cup and Yorkshire side Norton Woodseats had been drawn to visit Bishop Auckland.

The game was a poor affair, with the cup favourites showing little of their undoubted ability in front of 6,500 spectators. The performance was indicative of many that the 'Two Blues' had produced during this season and there was concern that another visit to Wembley was beyond the team's reach.

Norton Woodseats had come expecting to be beaten but prepared to put on a good show. All of their players had put in an extra training session on the Sunday morning in an effort to get fitter. And whilst they knew that Bishop had the better players, if they got stuck in, then they were in with a chance. Their plan was to keep the game as tight as possible, challenge for everything and with luck, prevent Bishop from scoring.

As things turned out they had more than a chance - they could have won. Midway through the first half the visitors were awarded a penalty when Bobby Hardisty prevented a certain goal when punching the ball out. Michael Lamb took the penalty and to the relief of the cup holders, Harry Sharratt pulled off one of his specials. Lamb was heart broken. Of all the games in which to miss his first penalty, it had to be this one. A goal up at that stage would have meant such a lot to the underdogs. Equally, it might have gone some way to pulling Bishop out of their lethargy.

The penalty save had the desired effect and just before half-time Ray Oliver rose to head in the ball to give Bishop the lead.

Bishop decided to change their strip for the second half. Some of the players contended that the two-blue strip was not in sufficient contrast to the visitors blue and white. With the referee's permission, Bishop took to the field wearing red shirts for the second half.

A change in shirts did not come with a change in performance and Bishop continued to struggle. Norton became just as bad and the second half saw little to whet the appetite. Bishop won the encounter 1-0 but not many supporters expected to be making a third trip down the A1 to Wembley.

For the second year running, the FA proposed that Round Two of the competition would be on a regional basis - to afford some clubs a degree of financial expediency in cutting travelling costs - and once again Bob Frankland expressed his disapproval, supported by the northern clubs. The opposition to the proposal was soundly based. There were thirty-two clubs in the draw, ten of which were in the north. Of these ten, seven were from the Northern League. Simple logic dictated that if a regional draw were adopted, it would be suicide for the Northern League clubs. The FA stuck to their ruling, officiously pointing out that in accordance with Rule 12 of the competition ...*clubs shall, from time to time, be arranged into geographical groups at the council's discretion until sixteen are left in the competition and these shall be drawn in couples.*

The likes of Joe Hateley, president of Willington, and 'Kit' Rudd, Secretary of Bishop Auckland, voiced their anger at the proposal. They expressed the view, shared by many, that the competition was a national one and that any degree of regionalisation would demerit the competition. Rudd was also charged with saying: 'The trouble is the southern clubs do not like coming north. We are prepared to go south and just get on with it. It is a national competition and if clubs cannot afford to travel as of Round One then they should not enter.'

Objections from the northern division were overruled and the resultant draw saw Willington drawn against Crook, West Auckland against Billingham, Salts (Yorkshire) against Ferryhill Athletic and Evenwood against Whitley Bay.

Southern clubs must have been laughing their heads off.

Derek Lewin says, 'The players weren't bothered about the zoning of the draw. Our attitude was that we could not care less who we met. Okay, it would be nice not to meet someone like Crook, but if we had to we would. We would prefer Crook, or any other Northern League team, to remain in the competition because it was good for the area, but really we were not bothered. It is not meant to sound arrogant, but we knew that we were a good team, and we would let the other clubs do the worrying.'

Bishop were lucky with the draw as they avoided the most dangerous teams, namely Willington, Crook Town and Billingham Synthonia. They were awarded a home tie against Gedling Colliery Welfare, whom they had comfortably defeated 4-1 at the equivalent stage in last season's competition. This time around the game would be held at Kingsway and even though the Nottinghamshire side were carrying all before them this season, having won all of their fourteen games, scoring eighty-three goals in the process and only conceding ten, the Bishop supporters and players were confident of a satisfactory outcome.

The game took place on 26th January and at last Bishop produced the brand of football for which they were renowned. Right from the outset there was an air of authority in the Auckland play and it was no surprise that they took the lead after only six minutes. Seamus O'Connell gathered the ball and back-heeled it to Lewin who stroked it into the net. A good early goal to settle the nerves of supporters and players!

It was Lewin again who grabbed the second following a slick combination between full-back Dave 'Smiler' Marshall and outside-right Warren Bradley. The home side deserved their 2-0 lead, having shown a degree of skill and determination that had been lacking in recent displays. Derek Lewin especially had shown just how good a player he could be and had created all sorts of problems for the Gedling defence. Only a fine one-handed save from Gedling goalkeeper Nichol prevented the Bishop supremo getting his hat-trick.

The second half saw Bishop increase the pace, putting several good moves together, one of which brought about the third goal. Bert Childs, making his cup debut for the 'Two Blues', initiated the move. From the heart of the Bishop defence the ball was passed from one player to the other before a flashing header from O'Connell saw the ball enter the net.

Bert Childs had played for Liverpool and was an English international. This was his first season (and as it turned out, his last) for Bishop Auckland, being acquired to replace Tommy Stewart who had intended to retire but stayed on as a registered player. Only twelve months ago Bert had been a member of the Kingstonian side that had lost 5-1 to the Bishops in the semi-final of the competition.

Bob Thursby once again showed form that would result in him being selected for England come the end of the season, but it was left for Warren Bradley, another England international, to score the remaining goals, the latter five minutes from time.

Surprisingly, Gedling were gifted a consolation goal for Kay following an error by, of all people, Harry Sharratt, but with a 5-1 winning score, no-one could complain. We were back on the rails and the 6,500 supporters could once again think of heading for those Twin Towers.

A third round away tie against Briggs Sports of the Spartan League was played at Romford and although Bishop won 1-0 it was an unconvincing performance. Briggs were a decent team on their day. They had started their season in exemplary fashion, winning their first game 7-3. They won their next seven league games, scoring a further sixteen goals and letting in none. The only blemish during this period had been a 1-0 home defeat in an FA Cup Qualifying Round to the very capable Romford.

Bobby Hardisty suffered a gashed knee in the first half and this led to a staccato performance by the Bishops. Reserve player Dave Robinson, deputising for the injured Benny Edwards, provided the centre that resulted in a Seamus O'Connell header squirming under the body of the Briggs goalkeeper, Mason, for the only goal of the game.

Those Twin Towers looked a bit more distant when the draw for the third round coupled Bishop with an away tie against Crook.

I was hoping that we would get to see the game, but for some reason that I cannot remember we had to make do with waiting for the football results on the wireless. Even then it was only late in the evening that we got to know the result. Unable to get up to Durham to watch the most important game of the day, Dad and I went to the Victoria Ground to see Stoke take on Lincoln City in a Football League Division Two match. We witnessed a bit of history being made as Stoke won 7-0 and Neville 'Tim' Coleman scored all seven goals. He might have made it eight, but the Lincoln goalkeeper saved his other shot.

I seem to remember that it was a neighbour of ours, Jack Hodgson, who came round to the house with news of the Bishop result. He couldn't tell us any details of the match... we would have to wait for 'The Pink' for that.

It appeared from the match report in 'The Pink' that there had been a classic game of football at the Millfield. A crowd of 11,843 had braved the snow to watch these two giant Northern League clubs take each other on.

Bishop had started the stronger and adapted to the conditions sooner than the Crook players. Derek Lewin, in the form of his life, began to tantalise the big Crook defenders who were left floundering with some of his moves. It was Lewin who gave Bishop the lead after fourteen minutes. The goal was a good one with Tommy Stewart (chosen to play at outside-left!) carrying the ball down the left wing and centring for the inside-right to score with his head... another one for the archives!

If that goal had been sublime, then Bishop's second, only five minutes later, was ridiculous. Bert Childs received the ball in the centre-circle and wondered what to do with it. He decided to send a long hopeful punt into the Crook penalty area, where with a bit of luck one of his forwards might create something. Nothing like it! The ball bounced in to the area but no forward or defender took responsibility to claim it. To his disbelief, Fred Jarrie watched the ball enter the net to give Bishop a 2-0 lead. Bert just stood in the centre-circle enjoying the plaudits from his colleagues and the Bishop supporters in the crowd.

Up to this point Bishop had produced the goals to match their football, but the game was about to turn. Crook, despite the disadvantage of being two goals down, began to fight their way back. They started to get more possession of the ball and as the snow began to fall heavier, the Bishop players seemed to weaken. With referee Hedley ready to blow for half-time, Bill Jeffs began a move which resulted in Keith Hopper scoring a confidence-boosting goal for the home side to reduce the arrears.

Crook came out for the second half in determined mood. Bishop came out in equal measure and in the blinding snow both sides strove for dominancy. The weather conditions put paid to the short passing game much preferred by the Auckland players but in the main they coped well with what the Crook side had to offer. That was until the hour mark, when winger Jimmy McMillan was allowed a shot at goal which resulted in the equaliser.

Both sides then had opportunities to score but failed. Ray Oliver appeared to have a simple tap-in but somehow conspired to miss and then Seamus O'Connell sent a shot wide. At the other end, Harry Sharratt was pleased when Coatsworth's effort lacked power and he was able to collect the attempt comfortably.

The game ended 2-2 so both teams had entered the draw for the semi-finals. Two other quarter-finals needed replays, Ilford versus Wycombe

Wanderers and Kingstonian versus Hayes. Only Corinthian Casuals, with a 3-1 win over Tooting and Mitcham United, had got through to the semi-final at the first attempt, and they had been drawn to meet the winners of the Wycombe Wanderers/Ilford game.

Dad and I read the report and I think both of us wished that we had been there. It sounded that we had missed a good game, and as per usual the two rivals had put on a closely-fought game. The replay was scheduled for this coming Saturday and I knew that Dad was working out if it would be possible for us to get up to Durham to watch it.

* * * * *

Well, we did manage to get there, thanks to 'Little Betsy'. Mum stayed indoors at Sunnybrow with Barry whilst Dad and I went to the match.

We arrived at the ground in good time, fully an hour before the scheduled 2:30pm kick-off, and already there were queues lined up to gain entrance. There was an official attendance figure of 12,225 at Kingsway but we heard after the game that the gates had been closed before kick-off with the 'House Full' signs up and that as a result there had been a number of people who had gate-crashed the game. I was lucky and once again a place was found for me on the children's bench, right next to the touchline.

Unbeknown to the crowd, Bishop were faced with a crisis just before kick-off. Dave Marshall arrived at the ground with a groin strain, suffered during a College hockey match earlier that morning. He was pronounced unfit and Tommy Stewart was declared as replacement, but as yet he had not made an appearance. To add to Bishops' woes, Warren Bradley had not arrived at the ground and therefore a replacement was required for his position. Reserve outside-right Rance Richardson was called for and told to put his boots on. Then, at about ten past two, just twenty minutes before kick-off, Bradley arrived and immediately changed to take the field. With Tommy Stewart still not at the ground it was decided that Marshall, despite his injury, would have to play after all.

Bishops' problems didn't end there, either. Ray Oliver was declared unfit and Bobby Hardisty was selected to play at centre-forward.

In the early period of the game, Crook looked the slightly better team. Jeffs looked solid in defence and gave O'Connell little room to shine. For the Bishops, Bob Thursby and Bobby Hardisty were the pick of the bunch, but in general both forward lines lacked cohesion. The skills that had been witnessed seven days earlier, in a snowstorm, were not on show today. Perhaps the best chance of the first-half fell to Ray Wilkie of Crook, but his effort went just wide of Sharratt's right-hand post for a goal-kick.

With half-time looming, it looked for all the world that the score would remain goalless but then Hardisty, standing close to the bye-line betwixt corner flag and goalpost, flicked the ball with his head in to the Crook penalty area. Defenders failed to deal with it and O'Connell sent a powerful header past Fred Jarrie. The deadlock had been broken and I jumped in to the air, as did everyone else around me.

When the second-half got under way, it was Bishop who pressurised, forcing Jarrie to pull off another fine save. Only three minutes had passed when the forceful Thursby won the ball and sent over a cross that centre-forwards would die for. Hardisty met it plum in the centre of his forehead and the ball flew past Jarrie for Bishop's second goal. I tried to defy gravity again as I jumped in the air once more with thousands of other Bishop fans. A 2-0 lead would surely see us through.

The goal made Crook play all the harder and for a while they looked as if they might get back in the game, but it was O'Connell who went closest when his header was cleared off the line by right-back Gardiner. Coatsworth tried hard for Crook but all too often was a lone figure in attack as Crook had to pull players back to help out in defence.

The game ended with both clubs unable to add to the score and naturally I was over the moon. Only one game stood in the way of another trip to Wembley.

That game would be at St James' Park, Newcastle, against Hayes, who had beaten Kingstonian 1-0 with a seventy-sixth minute penalty. In the other replay, Wycombe had overcome Ilford 2-0 and would meet Corinthian Casuals at Highbury.

There was never any real chance of us going up north again to watch the semi-final, but if we were absent in body, we were there in spirit.

To a great extent, the game was overshadowed beforehand with one of the most controversial issues to hit the club.

Ray Oliver had been with the club for almost four years and had served it well. He had scored well over one hundred and twenty goals for the Bishops and his strike partnership with O'Connell was awesome. A cartilage injury the previous season had resulted in him missing a number of games through injury during the current season.

Only four weeks earlier, Bishop had acquired the signature of Billy Russell, the Rhyl centre-forward who had given Corbett Cresswell such a hard time only four months ago in the FA Cup. Russell signed for Bishop on 3rd February.

I think it fair to say at this stage that there was a lot of resentment, both from southern clubs as well as northern clubs, towards Bishop Auckland's policy of searching for the best players, wherever they may be. They did not like players being drafted in from miles away, claiming that it was not within the amateur ethic and was not in keeping with the true spirit of the game. There was even talk that in future clubs would be unable to play anyone that lived beyond a fifty-mile radius of the club's ground. If that had been incorporated in to the rules of the competition, just imagine the huge advantage that the southern clubs, particularly those around London, would have had, given the large population that they would have been able to seek players from.

Bishop, however, were unrepentant. The Committee had always made their annual target the winning of the Amateur Cup...Northern League championships and everything else were secondary. It was true that players like Harry Sharratt and Derek Lewin travelled from Lancashire, Seamus O'Connell from Carlisle and now Billy Russell from Aberystwyth. If these players were prepared to travel and play for Bishop Auckland then that was the club's good fortune. Sentiment played no part in their policy, and if a fine centre-forward like Russell was prepared to sign for them then all the better for the club. Jealousy and sour grapes from other clubs was just ignored.

On the Monday evening prior to the semi-final, the Committee convened to select the team for Saturday's game. According to the press, Ray Oliver had been declared unfit - although the player himself had made it known that in his view he would be fit for the match and that his injury was only minor - and was therefore not considered for a place in the team. Billy Russell was chosen in his place. Only two days before, the 21-year-old Aberystwyth University student had made a brilliant debut in his first senior game for the club in a 5-2 win over Stockton, in Round Two of the Durham Challenge Cup, scoring twice and drawing the acclaim of the Kingsway crowd.

The following day there was news that Ray Oliver had recovered from his injury and was now fit. The Committee said that the team had already been selected and that Oliver would not be required and that Billy Russell was to lead the forward line.

However, Wednesday's edition of *The Northern Echo* carried the bombshell news that Russell was obligated to turn out for the North Wales representative side against a Scottish Junior Eleven at Edinburgh and that the Wales FA were not prepared to release him to play for Bishop Auckland. Despite pleas from the club, the Wales FA would not budge and Billy Russell would not therefore be playing in the forthcoming semi-final against Hayes.

As I understand it, the Committee held a hastily convened meeting that Wednesday and came back to Ray Oliver, asking him to play at centre-forward. He refused.

Ray Oliver is a high-principled man and declined the invitation to play on the basis that he genuinely believed that he should have been selected in the first instance and that the club should not have brought in a complete stranger so late in the season, fine player though Billy Russell was. Ray's record for the club was a proud one and he had always given heart and soul whenever he turned out for the Bishops. He felt deeply hurt that he had been omitted from the original eleven, especially when his fine goal-scoring feats were taken into consideration and in particular his record of goal-scoring in Amateur Cup semi-finals. The story of his alleged injury was just that - a story - put about to disguise any hint of disharmony within the Bishop Auckland camp. There had been no injury. Ray Oliver had just refused to play as a matter of principle.

The Northern Echo sports headline for Friday 15th March heralded 'Ray Oliver "finished" with Bishop Auckland'. The article went on to explain the background of the story and concluded that in the absence of Ray Oliver and Billy Russell, Bobby Hardisty, who had not been selected in the original eleven due to the outstanding form of Bob Thursby, would once again take the centre-forward position. The news was a shock for all Bishop fans who wondered what effect these shenanigans would have on morale at the club.

Bobby Hardisty commented: 'Ray Oliver is one of the best and a grand club man. I wish that I were playing at centre-forward under different circumstances.'

The game itself started with an early setback for Bishop when Seamus O'Connell, captaining the side, suffered a ligament injury to his right knee after only two minutes and for a time was a passenger on the left-wing. Auckland supporters were expecting the worst - such an injury looked indicative of the bad week that the club was having. Prospects did not look any brighter when minutes later, O'Connell had to leave the field and go to the dressing room for further attention.

Like a tiger scenting blood on an injured prey, Hayes threw everything into attack in an attempt to take advantage of the Bishops' misfortune. Speedy wing play on both flanks from Lewis and Reynolds resulted in some desperate defending from Marshall and Childs, but Cresswell was a rock in the heart of defence. Time after time he got his head to high balls and cleared for safety. Despite their frequent attacks, Hayes were a bit disappointing as nervous forwards hurried shots or missed the target altogether. Steadily, Bishop stemmed the tide of attacks and began to gain more shape in their organisation. O'Connell returned, albeit as a passenger, to play on the left-wing with Benny Edwards moving inside and for a while was only of nuisance value. Play became more even, if a lot less pretty, but for the moment that did not bother Bishop. They were showing all of their fighting spirit and so long as Hayes did not get a goal lead, then they would be well satisfied.

Semi-finals are often disappointing affairs. The anticipation and importance of the occasion frequently results in tension among the players who are thus incapable of performing to their best. This results in any hope of supporters watching a classic football encounter being destroyed. Football history of all major competitions, from the Amateur variety to the World Cup, is littered with supposedly mouth-watering semi-final ties that turn out to be best forgotten. The current offering at St James' Park proved to be no exception. Hayes were a capable side but nerves seemed to be getting the better of them, especially in front of goal, where their marksmen hurried any attempts at goal. Bishop had the experience of previous semi-finals but, with the legitimate excuse of O'Connell's injury, were not showing their best. The forward line had become disjointed with Hardisty ploughing a lone furrow up front.

The half-time whistle went with the score 0-0.

When the second half got under way, there was another change to the attacking positions of the Auckland forward line. Edwards reverted to his more natural position at outside-left and O'Connell moved to centre-forward. Bobby Hardisty thus became the third member of the squad to take up the inside-left position...and it worked. The lopsided nature of the attack in the first half became more balanced in the second, with Edwards able to produce his mazy runs and supply decent crosses to Hardisty and the ever-willing O'Connell. Lewis, the Hayes goalkeeper, was increasingly brought in to action and only his fine handling prevented O'Connell from connecting with an Edwards cross to open the scoring. Warren Bradley had the clear beating of Hayes left-back and captain Gadsden and it seemed that if a goal were to come then it would arrive via a flank movement.

Bishop continued to put pressure on the resilient Hayes defence and eventually the goal came, but not from a wing movement. Bobby Hardisty received an O'Connell pass thirty yards out from the Hayes goal and was faced by three defenders. With a sway of the hips he beat one man and then another. His footwork took him past the third and he coolly slotted the ball to the side of Lewis. It had taken sixty-five minutes and a goal of immense artistry to break down the solid Hayes defence, but now the Bishops had their nose in front. If Hayes were to get to Wembley they would need to score and so they would have to attack.

Hayes tried once more pushing men forward with half-backs Long and Gillson trying to add support to the forward line. But, with Sharratt in good form, they were unable to score. But Bishop did.

Only five minutes had gone since Hardisty's gem when Seamus O'Connell collected the ball on the right-wing - he and Bobby Hardisty had played all over the field - and sent a hard centre across the Hayes penalty area. Flying in from the left came Benny Edwards. Whether it was a stoop or a dive, no-one was certain, but his head connected with the ball. Like a rocket it seared towards the far top corner of Lewis's goal, who made a valiant attempt to save, acrobatically diving to his left. He had no chance. The bullet header beat him and Bishop were 2-0 up.

Hayes could see their ambitions of reaching Wembley disappearing over the horizon and put everything into attack. Sharratt brought off a fine save and then Cresswell had to stick out a leg to deflect a strong shot for a corner. From that corner Cresswell, for once, was beaten by Bartholomew who saw his effort headed off the line by the dependable Childs.

Shortly afterwards, the referee blew for full-time and once again the 'Two Blues' were in the Amateur Cup Final. It had been a hard fought match, dour at times, but Bishop had triumphed in the end.

There was a welcome visitor to the Bishop Auckland dressing room after the game...Ray Oliver. He had settled his differences with the club. He said that he had acted on principle when he objected to the inclusion of Billy Russell, a complete stranger to the squad, to lead the attack in such an important game. An approach had been made from the club that he reconsider his threat never to play for the club again, and that he was quite happy for the incident to be put to bed.

* * * * *

With the prospect of paying yet another visit to Wembley, I was the happiest child in the world. As usual, though, the weeks leading up to the game went interminably slow. Time stood still. Patience is a virtue, they say...well, not when you are waiting for a Wembley final it isn't. That period of time, from knowing the result of the semi-final on Saturday 16th March to the final itself on Saturday 13th April, were surely the slowest days that I ever suffered as a child. School helped, of course. I was fortunate in that I liked school, especially playtime. And if, after school, I wasn't playing football with my friends, then I often would take Barry out for a little walk in his pushchair.

Another past-time was jumping the brook. Across the fields that our back door opened onto there was a brook that a few miles downstream joined the River Blythe and eventually ran in to the River Trent. When we first moved down there, the brook was teaming with fish, including some slimy black eel, and trout that the men used to 'tickle'. It was an amazing sight to watch a grown man lying on his stomach at the brook's side with an outstretched arm under the water's surface just waiting for a trout to come along and be tickled. As the tickling progressed, the trout would be drawn in to a false sense of security and in an instant the tickling hand would turn into a vice. The trout would be caught and someone would have a fine supper. Alas, because everybody ended up doing it, the fish vanished and all that there are now are a few bullheads, newts and frogs.

All the lads and lasses would frequently play by jumping from one bank to the other. In some places the bank would be eight-feet higher than the opposite bank but we would still jump it. We must have been mad. It was an innocuous jump that caught me out, just a few days before we were due to go to the match at Wembley. I took off on one bank to make a jump of about four feet. I easily cleared the water but fell awkwardly sideways. I instinctively put out my right hand to break my fall but in doing so fractured my wrist.

The doctor had me sent to North Staffs Hospital and the wrist and arm were put in Plaster of Paris. There would be no more jumping brooks or playing at being Harry Sharratt for a while. What's more, how was I going to get on at school?I was right-handed. I never was lucky…they made me write with my left hand!

* * * * *

Typically, there was a little bit of controversy in the build up to the final. This time it was Seamus O'Connell to feel aggrieved. Seamus was still suffering from the injury received in the semi-final, but was getting better. The Committee, in their infinite wisdom, continued with the immovable policy of selecting Saturday's team on the Monday night. They studied a report from a specialist and concluded that O'Connell would not be fit and therefore could not be selected. Billy Russell would play at centre-forward, his first ever Amateur Cup game, in place of Ray Oliver, and Bobby Hardisty would play at inside-left, the position vacated by Seamus O'Connell. Seamus would, however, travel with the players down to London.

On the Friday afternoon, Bishop carried out their final training session at Stamford Bridge, Chelsea. Seamus stood around but was not allowed to kick a ball. There was also another drawback - Harry Sharratt had not turned up.

Just as the session was coming to an end, Harry arrived, breathless. He had been coming to the ground by car, but the vehicle developed a puncture, hence his late arrival. Harry took to the field as the rest of the squad were leaving. To give him some practise, Seamus decided to take his frustration out on the footballs and rained shots at Harry. Shot after shot, harder and harder, were pounded at the goalkeeper and not once did O'Connell flinch. If there had been any of the Committee watching they may have been impressed. Unfortunately for Seamus, they weren't there.

Harry finished the session and after changing returned to his car. It had a puncture.

Wycombe Wanderers: The Twin Towers

Eventually, Saturday arrived, and once again we were staying for the weekend with Uncle Dick and Aunty Dora May. They would not be going to the match: only Dad and I were going.

And so, three days after Real Madrid had defeated Manchester United 3-1 at the Bernabeu Stadium in the first leg of a European Champions semi-final football match, I sat on the floor, reading the football pages of the Saturday newspaper. I seem to recall that, apart from the Amateur Cup Final, the main item of news concerned two legendary footballers. Hungarian international Ferenc Puskas would be leaving Honved for Inter Milan. He would receive a premium (signing-on fee) of a staggering £64,280 and would receive a monthly salary of £200 per month.

The other bit of interesting news concerned Leeds United and Welsh international John Charles. It was reported that Real Madrid were prepared to pay Leeds United £70,000, and Charles, personally, £30,000. Real Madrid denied that any request to purchase the player had been made, but Italian giants Juventus were interested and publicly declared that they would like the holder of twenty Welsh caps to play for them. With the money that was being offered by these two major clubs, it was no surprise that Charles, surely one of the finest and most versatile footballers ever, was keen to be transferred. With the amount of money on offer, he and his family would be set up for life. Don't forget, this was the time of the maximum wage, something like £14 a week plus bonuses, and perhaps only £12 a week in the close season. Jimmy Hill and his successful fight to get the maximum wage abolished was a long way off.

Bob Thursby comments: '*The maximum wage was the reason why a lot of the lads never turned professional. They could make just as much, probably more, playing amateur football. I was on at least £5 a game when I first started. With a couple of games a week, I had earned nearly as much as a pro...and when I had finished my college, I would have a decent job. A professional footballer was only allowed to earn so much a week. The better ones might be lucky and earn extra from advertising...remember Jack Kelsey of Arsenal and Wales, promoting Brylcreem? Stanley Matthews and a few others may have advertised a certain brand of football boot, but it was only the famous ones that got the chance to advertise. Bobby Charlton, at Manchester United, was only allowed the same as everyone else. Any extras that he may have made would have come from endorsements.*

'*I remember my old mate Ken Chisholm (Sunderland and Leicester City) having a conversation with his pal Len Shackleton after training one day. The talk got around to money and Ken asked Len how much he was on. "£14 plus bonuses during the playing season and £12 in the summer close season," came the reply.*

'"Bloody hell, I'm only on £10," to which Len suggested that Ken should make a call on the Sunderland Secretary the next morning.

'Ken went along and collared the Secretary and demanded to know why 'Shack' was on £12 a week when he was only receiving £10.

'"Simple," said the Secretary, "he's a better player than you."

'"He might be, but not in the close season he isn't!" retorted Ken.'

I read the football news until all of the print was rubbing off on to my hands, from the constant turning of the pages. Thankfully, the time arrived for Dad and I to get going and we more or less repeated the procedure that we had gone through twelve months earlier. We drove to Kilburn and caught the tube to Wembley. The stadium looked regally magnificent with flags flying from the roof of the stand that covered the Royal Box area. The sun was beating down and altogether it was a perfect day for watching a football match…*the* football match.

It was to be the final swansong for two of Bishop Auckland's finest players, namely Jimmy Nimmins and Bobby Hardisty. Wembley may have its twin towers, but Bishop Auckland could boast two as well. Come to think of it, there was a similarity between the two pairs… all four had perfectly shaped bald domes.

Consett is a small town set on the high hills of County Durham (Bob Thursby refers to it as Siberia). It used to be a major steel producer but that industry has long since been allowed to decline into oblivion (Shame! Shame!). Schoolteachers would have you believe that the hardest thing ever to be produced in that town is the steel that used to roll out of the foundry. They would be wrong. That credit belongs to Jimmy Nimmins, the 5' 9" pocket battleship.

Jimmy lived in Consett and worked as an iron-moulder in the foundry. He started his playing days with Consett and had also played for Highfield United and Spennymoor United. He transferred to Bishop Auckland, playing in the finals against Willington, Pegasus, Crook, Hendon and Corinthian Casuals. He had represented Durham County and played in North v South games but for some reason had only been selected for one England trial, for which he had not performed to his ability. Fortune only knocked the once and it is a travesty that he never played for his country. He was a superb ball-winner and was capable of producing teeth-shattering tackles… once an inside-forward had received one of Jimmy's specials, they rarely returned for a second dose. He was a fine passer of the ball and had set up many goals for the forward line. The broken leg that he had suffered in the final against Crook had had no effect on his style of play and his determination to win the ball was undiluted. Wembley would appear not to be a happy hunting ground for Jimmy, for as well as breaking his leg there, don't forget that only twelve months ago he had left the field with a broken arm. All of the Bishop supporters hoped that he would have better luck in this, his sixth Amateur Cup Final. I agree with Chris Foote Wood, author of *Kings Of Amateur Soccer*, which was published in 1985 to mark the centenary of Bishop Auckland Football Club, when he likens Jimmy Nimmins to the Nobby Stiles of the Manchester United and England team of the 1960s.

Nimmins himself said: *'This will be my last season. I have made up my mind and I will not go back on it. I could continue to play for other clubs, but I prefer to finish my career with Bishop. I am thirty-six, three months older than Bobby, and I'm calling it a day, although I may go on tour in the close season.'*

Dave Marshall records; *'All of the players would receive a new pair of boots at the beginning of the season, courtesy of the club. The boots came from Frank Whitwell's, the leading sports shop in Bishop Auckland. Jimmy would get his a couple of sizes too small. He'd take them home and sit with his new boots on in a bathtub of cold water. This, apparently, expanded the leather and the boots formed the shape of Jimmy's feet. Nobody else tried doing it.'*

Bob Thursby says of Jimmy: *'We didn't do any formal training for Bishop. It was not possible for all of the lads to meet at a designated time two or three times a week. Those who lived away would train wherever and with whomever they could. For instance, Derek Lewin would train with Oldham or Manchester United, Seamus would train with Carlisle and Harry would train with Wigan. One or two might get together on a Tuesday and/or Thursday night down at Bishop, but there wouldn't be many.*

'One day, Jimmy suggested that he and I do some training together up where he lived, at Consett. It was bloody freezing so I got well wrapped up in pullovers and two sets of tracksuits, as well as a couple of balaclavas. Out comes Jimmy in a bloody tee-shirt and shorts.

'He was the hardest man that I have ever known. He wasn't particularly tall and was only about 11st 6lbs but by God he was awesome, and not just as a footballer. Because of the amount of body water that he lost working in the foundry, he would have a pint of beer and a whiskey before a game so that he was not dehydrated. One Saturday we were in the changing room and I was getting ready next to Jimmy. As he took off his shirt I noticed a great big gash down his left arm, almost to the bone. I asked him what had happened. He told me that that morning he had been putting in a shift at work and was pouring some molten steel into a tub. Some of the liquid

splashed back and spouted on to Jimmy's arm, burning it. The scar looked terrible. I asked him what he did.

'He just looked at me calmly and made a nonchalant flicking motion with his right hand across his left arm. "I just brushed it off like this." Then I noticed that his right hand was burnt as well, through brushing away the searing liquid. He was the toughest man that I have ever known, and a gentleman.,

On a lighter note, Ron Fryer recalls: *'Me and another player were studying a photograph of Bobby Hardisty and Jimmy together. We decided to have a bit of fun and drew the finest mop of hair on the two bald heads. I was admiring our handywork when a cuff across the head made me smart. Jimmy had sneaked up behind the pair of us and was not amused with what he saw. The memory of that cuff makes me wince even now, some fifty years later.'*

Today Jimmy Nimmins would be captain and lead the team on to the Wembley pitch.

Opponents Wycombe Wanderers were top of the Isthmian League, one of the strongest in amateur football, consisting of such teams as Ilford, Woking, Kingstonian, Romford, Leytonstone, Walthamstow Avenue, and last year's beaten finalists, Corinthian Casuals. Any team that could top that league was worthy of the utmost respect. Wycombe would be a tough nut to crack and despite Bishops' cup record, it was the southern team that had now become the bookies favourites to win the trophy. The week, however, had not got off to a good start for them as the team mascot for the past twenty-five years, a thirty-year-old horse called Epinard (named after a distinguished French sprinter of the 1920s), had collapsed on the Wednesday and was receiving treatment to recover.

Wycombe's cup campaign began with a 4-1 win away from home against St Albans City. In Round Two they had a home tie against Clapton, which they won 4-2. A home tie in the third round saw them win 3-1 against Hounslow, and then came a difficult tie against fellow Isthmians, Ilford. The first game at Ilford was 3-3, but Wycombe won the replay 2-0, on the day that Bishop were putting out Crook Town. The semi-final tie at Highbury against Corinthian Casuals looked a shoe-in for Wycombe. They were flying at the top of the Isthmian League, whilst Corinthian Casuals were, surprisingly, stranded at the basement, holding everyone else up. The semi-final had been a great game of football. At half-time the teams were level at 2-2. Then in the second-half, Wycombe had two players injured, one of whom had to leave the field. Remarkably, they overcame these handicaps and won the match 4-2. Bishop would have to be on their mettle today if they were to beat this outfit.

For the third year running, Dad and I found ourselves standing in the same spot that we had occupied in the previous two finals…was this our reserved place?

After the Community Singing, led as usual by Sir Arthur Caiger, the teams came out of the tunnel on to the pitch and were introduced to the dignitaries for the occasion, principally The Lord Mayor of London Sir G J Cullum Welch. After all the hand-shaking and singing of the National Anthem, the teams broke away for the pre-match kickabout.

The teams were:

Bishop Auckland (White shirts, Black shorts)
H. Sharratt -D. Marshall, A. R. Childs - R. Thursby, C. Cresswell,
J. Nimmins - W. Bradley, D. Lewin, W. Russell, R. Hardisty, B. Edwards

Wycombe Wanderers (Red shirts, White shorts)
D. Syrett - F. Lawson, F. Westley - G. Truett, M. Wicks, J. Truett -
L. Worley, C. Trott, P. Bates, J. Tomlin, F. Smith

Referee: J. W. Topliss of Lincolnshire
(Jack Topliss of Grimsby should have retired from refereeing the previous season, at the age of forty-seven, but was granted an extension by the FA).

Wycombe kicked off, defending the tunnel end, but within less than a minute Bishop could have taken the lead. Bobby Hardisty received the ball and in a moment of exquisite movement brought the ball under control and fired a rasping shot just wide of Syrett's upright.

Wycombe bounced back and created an assault of their own but the white-shirted rearguard stood firm.

Only three minutes gone and already the 95,000 crowd had seen some wonderful action. Wycombe came at Bishop like bees around a honey-pot but they could not gain the advantage. Bishop responded with quick-passing quality football. Fine defensive work was followed up with long raking passes, to make use of the big Wembley pitch, to either Bradley or Edwards who would take on defenders with touchline dribbles. Bishop had found their stride instantly, whereas Wycombe were hurried and lacked any real danger. If they could keep this up, then surely the Cup would be going north again. The Wycombe defence were hurried and ragged in making clearances with long hopeful balls down the middle, which were gratefully accepted by the impeccable Thursby and eager Nimmins.

Nineteen-year-old Thursby, the youngest player on the field, was showing no Wembley nerves and looked a natural footballer. On this evidence, he was the one to take over from the evergreen Hardisty in the right-half berth. Indeed, such was the merit of his performance that he was named in the England squad for the forthcoming European tour immediately after the game. When needed, Cresswell was there also, to keep Bates under guard. With the half-back line of Auckland in control, it was little wonder that Bates and Worley looked helpless at times.

Then, after only fourteen minutes, Bishop were rewarded with the goal that their play deserved. Bobby Hardisty collected a weak clearance by Worley, who appeared to stub his toe in the lush turf as he went to kick the ball near the centre-circle. He moved a couple of paces with the ball at his feet, arms stretched like Blondin over Niagara, to give him balance as he turned. On looking up he saw Billy Russell making a run down the inside-right channel. Hardisty was already aware of the goalscoring ability of the former Rhyl player, as he had scored two goals on his debut for the Bishops just a few weeks ago in his qualifying game. With one slick movement of the hips, he sent an unerring pass that the Welshman anticipated. He was already running whilst Wicks was still in his blocks. Russell let the ball run for a stride and then sent a low right-footed shot past the diving Syrett. The northerners cheered loud and long and all around me was mayhem. 1-0 up after fourteen minutes and playing good football, what more could we want? The answer was, more of the same, please.

Bishop continued to put flowing moves together and the inter-changing of the three inside-forwards had the Wycombe defenders floundering at times. However, for all their efforts, Bishop could not get the second goal. Nimmins was having a solid game in defence and once or twice ventured upfield to start an attack. He was having a fine game and who knows, he might end up actually liking Wembley!

Fittingly, however, the star of the show was turning out to be the artistic Bobby Hardisty playing with a skill and yearning that belied his thirty-six years.

As all Bishop Auckland fans know, Bobby Hardisty shared the same birthday as another football legend, Sir Stanley Matthews. He was born at Chester-le-Street on February 1st 1921. At seventeen years of age he made his debut for Bishop Auckland against Billingham in 1938, on Guy Fawkes' Day. It would be another twenty years (November 15th 1958) before he would play his last game for them, in an FA Cup tie against Tranmere Rovers, after coming out of retirement. There was a brief interlude, in 1946, when he played for Shildon, but he returned the following season. Later in that 1938-39 season, he appeared for Bishop in an Amateur Cup semi-final drawn game against Leytonstone. Bishop went on to win the cup but there was no place for Bobby in that winning team.

The war years saw young Hardisty come into contact with some legendary football names, most notably Matt Busby who would go on to form one, if not two, of the greatest teams at Manchester United ever seen. The friendship between the two players lasted a lifetime. In 1948 Busby played a major role in running the Great Britain Olympic football team and looked towards Bobby to be selected. Not only was he selected but he was also asked to captain the side, a position that he willingly accepted. This was the only time that he had captained a side as he constantly refused to accept the captain's armband elsewhere, believing that it may affect his play, But for the Olympic team he was prepared to make an exception. He won fifteen international caps in all and was selected again for the Helsinki and Melbourne Olympics. He had toured the world with the Bishop Auckland and England teams and was revered wherever he went, such was his stature.

Derek Lewin says of Bobby Hardisty: '*He was a brilliant footballer. If it had not been for the war who is to say that he would not have been an even better and more famous one. Certainly, he would have received countless offers to turn professional. His friend, Matt Busby, would have had him at Manchester United, but by the time the war ended, ideally, he was just that little bit too old. He played for England, of course, and I played with him. The maddening thing was that whenever we were selected we were playing out of position. At Bishop Auckland, Bobby would be at right-half back and I would be at inside-right. We would work in tandem together. Jimmy and Seamus filled a similar role on the left side. Both pairs would work in unison like two pistons of an engine. But when Bobby and I were selected for England, I was usually playing at inside-left and Bobby would be filling my club berth of inside-right. Mind you it just goes to show how good a player he was to adapt so easily.*'

When asked to nominate his favourite football eleven, the BBC commentator, Raymond Glendenning, chose ten well-known Division One internationals but excluded such as Billy Wright and Danny Blanchflower for the right-half berth, opting instead for Hardisty.

The youth of British football lay broken on a Munich airfield in less than twelve months' time and in the aftermath Busby called for his old friend to help Manchester United fulfill their fixtures. Without hesitation, Bobby made his services available to the stricken club, as would Warren Bradley and Derek Lewin. Hardisty became a regular in the reserve side to help them fulfil their fixtures. All three players were good enough to have played for the first team but the assistant manager of Manchester United, Jimmy Murphy, insisted that only professional players would be chosen for the Division One games.

But the Munich Air Disaster was in the unforeseeable future. For today, Bobby was showing the silky skills for which he was renowned. He was a superb passer of the ball and had wonderful vision. He was 'Mr Versatility', being more than capable of playing at half-back, inside-right, inside-left or even centre-forward and could take a decent penalty. For those of us privileged to have seen him, he was completely unflappable and never lost his cool. To a large extent, sportsmanship has gone out of the window in the modern game, but for Bobby Hardisty it was an integral part.

All of the Bishop Auckland players were full of admiration for this tall, elegant footballer and could eulogise about him all night long but perhaps Bob Thursby speaks for everyone when he simply describes Bobby Hardisty as 'The Best'.

He was a master and a gentleman, and for the moment we were witnessing an artist at work.

Hardisty, once again, won the ball and threaded it through to Lewin who combined with Bradley to bamboozle the Wycombe defence and as the little winger sped in to the penalty area he laid on a perfect pass for Russell. The centre-forward's shot was saved by Syrett at point-blank range, as was Edwards' follow-up. Then the mercurial Bradley cracked a shot against a post before Syrett brought off another fine save. Bishop could have been five up but instead only had the one solitary goal to count.

Thirty minutes had gone when Wycombe came dangerously close to grabbing the equalizer. Centre-forward Bates won the ball just outside the Bishop penalty area and, for once, evaded Cresswell. He pulled his right foot back to send in a shot but before he could do so in came Dave Marshall with a trademark sliding tackle. The danger passed and Bishop moved up to forge another attack, but Benny Edwards was unable to provide the finishing touch.

The warning signs, however, were there for Bishop and only five minutes later the southern team drew level. Marshall and Cresswell shadowed Frank Smith, outside-left for Wycombe, as a long ball was played through. Smith appeared to control the ball with his hand and as he did so, Marshall started to pull up, expecting a free kick to be given. To the amazement of the defender, Smith was allowed to carry on and sent a rising shot past Harry Sharratt. Bishop players may have grumbled but they didn't protest. After the game, Smith claimed that the ball hit his chest...Dave Marshall was convinced otherwise.

Wycombe didn't deserve to be on level terms, but sometimes you get more than you deserve.

The Truett brothers had helped shore up an over-stretched defence but they had had little opportunity to help the forwards who were having a tough time against a solid Bishop rearguard. It was they who worked together in a move which saw Bates and Trott bring the ball down the left wing with an ominous looking attack, but Bert Childs showed his skill and retrieved possession for Bishop.

Bishop did not let the goal affect their confidence and came right back. Within two minutes Hardisty sent another defence-splitting pass through to Bradley who evaded Westley's tackle and pulled the ball back from the bye-line for Lewin to ram the ball home from close range. This was the third consecutive year that Derek Lewin had scored in an Amateur Cup Final. As I stated earlier, he had a fine goalscoring record, especially in important matches.

The teams went off to a tremendous ovation at half-time. Both teams had played some good football, but most importantly Bishop were leading and Bobby Hardisty was in scintillating form.

The nerves that Wycombe had occasionally shown in the first half were cast aside for the second. They came out with a determination to grab a goal back and instantly put the 'Two Blues' under pressure. Sharratt, who had had very little to do in the first forty-five minutes, was now in action and was called upon to show all his agility and anticipation to keep the red-shirted forwards from scoring. Bates and Tomlin both saw their efforts saved by the brilliant goalkeeper and inevitably the attacks got less and less as Bishop regained the initiative. Apart from these few minutes on the defensive, Bishop were showing their true form today. The jittery performances of the previous two finals were cast adrift; today they were putting on the style. Another decent chance was created but again it was Edwards who fluffed his lines with a wayward shot when he only had Syrett to beat.

The tempo of the game never slowed and the entertainment value for the fans was immeasurably high. Bishop supporters were happier of course because their team was leading, but they knew that Wycombe were well capable of getting another goal.

Then on seventy-two minutes, Bishop scored a third goal. Bradley saw a centre from the right cleared upfield, but immediately Hardisty returned the ball to him. He took on his defender and gained a corner, which was put behind for a second one. The second corner was better placed and caused a panic clearance by the Wycombe defence. Lurking on the edge of the area was Jimmy Nimmins. He latched on to the ball and flicked it to his right for the incoming Bradley to once again rush past Westley and fire a wicked left-foot shot to Syrett's left. The 'keeper made a fine effort to save but he had no chance.

The goal knocked the stuffing out of the Wycombe players and it was Bishop who came closest to scoring again when Geoff Truett knocked Lewin's header off the line. Bishop finished the game well in command and tried to conjure up a goal for the retiring Bobby Hardisty, but it would not come and at the final whistle Bishop had to be satisfied with a 3-1 win. Satisfied? You bet I was. I was jumping up and down in my excitement for ages. I was delirious… me and the forty-thousand other Bishop supporters.

A very proud Jimmy Nimmins collected the Cup as a tearful ten year-old cried in joy at the tunnel end of the ground. We applauded the Wycombe players as they left the field but our eyes were on the cup winners doing their lap of honour. Slowly but surely my heroes came down to the end of the stadium where Dad and I were standing with the main mass of Bishop Auckland supporters. We had done the same on the last two occasions, but this time we just knew that it was something special.

Bishop Auckland had appeared in eighteen Amateur Cup Finals and had won ten of them. They had appeared in twenty-six semi-finals. Of the last thirteen finals they had appeared in eight of them. There had been nine Wembley Amateur Cup finals and Bishop Auckland had appeared in six. Despite the heartache of losing three Wembley Finals, they had returned to win the trophy for three consecutive years. No team could come even close to such a magnificent record.

As the players stood at the edge of the pitch, acknowledging the shower of praise that was being bestowed on them, Dad stooped down and softly spoke, 'Feast your eyes on that scene, son, for you'll never see their like again.'

We waited for the players to make their exit down the tunnel beneath us. When they had gone from view we smiled at each other and made our way down Wembley Way to the crowded tube station. We would eventually get back to Hendon, but for now all I wanted to do was stay in the sunshine and relive those golden moments.

* * * * *

That night, the Bishop Auckland players and club members attended an official function in their honour at a London hotel, where many speeches took place praising them.

On the following Monday evening, the triumphant team arrived at Bank Top Station, Darlington, carrying the Amateur Cup with them and transferred to an open-top bus to make the now customary victory parade from Darlington, through Heighington, Shildon, South Church and Cabin Gate, at which point the team was met by the Mainsforth Colliery Band that led them down Newgate Street and on to Bishop Auckland Market Place. All the streets were decorated in dark and light blue bunting and flags and streamers.

The team were allowed to make their way to the Town Hall balcony where Committee members made brief speeches. Each player was hailed by the throng as they stepped forward to utter a few words, thanking the supporters, the club and the town.

There was a moment of light relief when it was Harry Sharratt's turn to come forward to the microphone. Prior to the final, Alderman J.R.S. Middlewood, who had praised the team so highly at the function two nights earlier, had promised his new Homburg hat to Harry if the team won the cup. True to his word, he had passed his brand new hat - which must have cost a few bob - over to Harry who was now sporting it on the Town Hall balcony.

When Jimmy Nimmins came to the microphone and later Bobby Hardisty, the place just exploded with everyone cheering even louder than before. All of the players deserved the town's appreciation, but those two were something special.

* * * * *

In recognition of Bishop Auckland's magnificent achievement in winning the Amateur Cup three years in succession, the Football Association presented the club with a full size replica of the trophy, which currently adorns the trophy room at the Supporters' Club.

FULL-TIME

Ringing the Changes

Dad's words rang true. We would never see their like again. Naturally, the team would carry on with new players taking over from those that were leaving. But how do you replace Jimmy Nimmins and Bobby Hardisty? And let's not forget Bert Childs, who had come into the team at the beginning of the season and played such an integral part in upholding a solid defence. He was leaving to live down south and would return to Kingstonian. In the past, whenever players needed replacing, Bishop had simply gone out and found them. They would find it more difficult from now on.

Not everyone was leaving, of course. The 'best goalkeeper ever' would remain for a further seven years before leaving the Bishops to play in a local league in Lancashire, close to where he lived. Dave Marshall and Derek Lewin would carry on for a couple more years. In the 1958-59 season Derek broke his left leg in a freak injury. He caught his leg in between Seamus O'Connell's and the scissor action trapped the leg, causing the break. About the same period, Corbett Creswell would finally decide to turn professional and leave the club that he had served so honourably. Bob Thursby and Seamus O'Connell would be playing for arch-rivals Crook Town...and guess who would become Crook's manager for a while? None other than Bobby Hardisty. Ray Oliver would also leave and Anno Domini would catch up with the ever-youthful looking Benny Edwards. Billy Russell only ever held a short tenancy with the club and after playing just the one Amateur Cup game (the final against Wycombe Wanderers) he left shortly afterwards to join Sheffield United. Russell's appearance in the Final had created a record, as no player before had played in the final without ever competing in an earlier round.

Warren Bradley would join Manchester United the following season, following the Munich Air Disaster. At first his appointment would be a temporary one but such was his skill that he was signed on as a full-time professional. He would go on to become a full international for England. I may have mentioned elsewhere in this book, but it is worth repeating: Warren Bradley remains the only player to win England international caps at both amateur and professional levels, *in the same season.*

Bob Thursby stayed with the club for a few seasons, winning twenty England caps along the way. Fine players like Mike Barker, Billy Roughley,

George Siddle, Ian Read, Laurie Brown and Mike Greenwood would follow in the footsteps of their predecessors but further success became hard to come by.

Dad and I went to see Bishop play Stockport County in an FA Cup tie at Edgeley Park in the 1960-61 season, when Harry Sharratt brought off one of his special saves in a 2-0 loss. Later on in the same season we travelled over to Loughborough to watch them in the second round of the Amateur Cup. There were no grandstands and there was a rope around the ground to separate the spectators from the playing pitch. A few yards away were further football and rugby pitches with games going on. The game attracted about 2,000 spectators and was won by the home team 3-1. Allen Wade coached Loughborough Colleges and playing in goal for them was a certain Bob Wilson.

There were seventeen more Amateur Cup Finals after Bishop's success over Wycombe, but the 'Two Blues' failed to feature in any of them. The nearest that they came to retrieving the trophy was in 1961-62, when they were beaten by Hounslow in a semi-final at Brentford. It would be neighbours Crook Town, by now the best team that the North-East had to offer, who would go on to defeat Hounslow in a replay, to win the trophy.

The Football Association decided that the 1973-74 season would see the cessation of the Amateur Cup competition. The FA thought that the Amateur Cup had outlived its usefulness as a competition and did not truly reflect the modern day attitude towards football and how the game was run...in other words they doubted that any of the clubs entering the competition were truly 'amateur' given the degree of payments that existed within the game and that in future, non-league clubs would fight for the FA Trophy. The last Amateur Cup Final concerned Bishop's Stortford who won the trophy, defeating Ilford 4-1. The game attracted only 30,000 spectators.

In their infinite wisdom, the FA decided to keep the Amateur Cup at their headquarters under lock and key where only the office cleaner has the opportunity to see it. Surely, given the unprecedented record that they had in the competition, it would have been far more fitting to have presented Bishop Auckland with it and then all football fans could witness it on view. Can you imagine what would happen today if FIFA decided to abandon the World Cup competition and that the Cup be placed in storage in one of their cabinets? I think that there would be riots in Rio, given what the Brazilians have achieved in the tournaments. The sooner that the Amateur Cup is delivered to Bishop Auckland Football Club, the better.

Bishop Auckland have failed to make any significant progress in the new competition either as a member of the Northern League, which they finally left after the 1986-87 season, or as a member of the Unibond League, which

171

they currently play in. A degree of success was achieved in winning the Northern League Challenge Cup competition in seasons 1959-60, 1966-67 and 1975-76 and winning the League title in 1966-67 as well as 1984-85.

The club has had a succession of coaches/managers over the years, perhaps the most famous - and successful - being Lawrie McMenemy who took over in 1965. Lawrie was the first manager appointed by the club who had full control of team affairs. Prior to his appointment, team selection and related matters rested with the all-powerful Committee. The Committee chose well in appointing Lawrie as manager, as in his first season with the club they finished a commendable third in the Northern League. The following season saw success on three fronts with the winning of the Northern League Championship by six points from runners-up Whitley Bay, the Northern League Cup in which final they demolished Tow Law Town 4-0, and the Durham County Cup. Unfortunately, Bishop were unable to hold on to their very talented manager, who left the club in 1967 for Sheffield Wednesday where he worked with ex-Sunderland manager Alan Browne. He then became manager of Doncaster Rovers and, in his first season, led them to the Fourth Division Championship; a few seasons later he was to be found at Grimsby where his management skills resulted in The Mariners winning the Third Division title. Southampton were next to appreciate the qualities of this astute manager and under him, although still only a Second Division team, they went on to an unexpected FA Cup Final success over hot favourites Manchester United, defeating them 1-0 at Wembley in 1976.

Regrettably, the fortunes of Bishop Auckland Football Club continued to decline after Lawrie's departure and results on the field once more became disappointing, with the team more often than not finishing the season in the bottom half of the league table and making no impression at all in the Amateur Cup.

The Kingsway ground has failed to meet the required standards set by League authorities and for a while they were forced to play games at Shildon's Dean Road ground. In order to comply with further regulations the club have been forced to play their 'home' games at Spennymoor United's Brewery Ground.

During my research for this project I visited the Kingsway ground. It was such a shame to see the dilapidated stands where once capacity crowds sat and watched their heroes. Thistles and wild foxgloves craned for the sunlight where Dad and I used to stand at Northern League games. A sign nailed to a post in the stand opposite to where the players came out warned of the dangers of a collapsing wall and crumbling concrete steps and terracing. The ghosts of players-past haunted what was left of the decaying structure. I was filled with sadness. A few yards away, a Sunday League cricket match for under thirteens was taking place, the participants oblivious of this middle-aged man, tears welling up inside him, reliving the memories of great games and great players. It is to be hoped that the ongoing efforts by the likes of John Cowey, David Illingworth and current Chairman Terry Jackson to raise money towards the erection of a new stadium are successful and result in Bishop Auckland once again having a football ground of its own (The Kingsway ground was demolished in the summer of 2004).

All Bishop Auckland supporters, past and present, yearn for the return of those halcyon days but it has to be accepted that the clock can never be turned back. And no team has a divine right to always be the best all of the time. The day may come when the good times return, but it won't happen overnight. We will just have to be patient and give everyone involved with the club the support that they deserve. If we don't, then Bishop Auckland Football Club will not survive.

In the meantime, whilst we do not know what the future may bring, there is no harm in reliving the glory of yesteryear. I hope that the foregoing pages of this work have helped revive memories of those remarkable days, when Bishop Auckland ruled supreme and were truly the Kings of Amateur Football. Of days that brought pride and excitement, not only to a small market town in rural County Durham, but to the whole North-East of England. Of days when grown men, and a certain ten-year-old boy, wept at the achievements of their heroes. Of days when it was an honour to watch the footballers who wore the dark and light blue shirts with distinction. Of those marvellous days. Of those wonderful days. But most of all, of those GLORY DAYS.

'THE BROTHERHOOD'

Friday 13th August 2004

At the invitation of Bob Thursby I was requested to attend the annual reunion of Bishop Auckland footballers at the town Golf Club. It was a great honour that was beyond my wildest dreams. Here was I, in the presence of my childhood heroes, and not only with them, but talking and laughing and joking with them.

Some people have said that meeting their heroes was a great disappointment for them. For me, it was one of the most moving and emotional experiences that has ever happened to me. All who were there, as soon as I entered the room, made me welcome.

Bob Thursby was as welcoming as ever, telling his jokes and making me feel at ease. Ray Oliver has had operations to both hips and has lost an eye, but his mind is as sharp and retentive as anyone's. He is the walking encyclopaedia of the players and can recount how, when, where and by whom, goals were scored. Thanks for your help, Ray.

Derek Lewin is the organiser. It is on his shoulders that falls the responsibility of getting all of these ex-players together. He has had heart surgery, in his case a triple by-pass, but that does not stop this workaholic from fulfilling his duties with the Lancashire Football Association. He is also a member of the FA Council.

Len Langford talked to me about his time with the Bishops and Kingstonian. Bobby Watson, who had laid on the pass for Ray Oliver's equalising goal in the 1954 Amateur Cup Final at Wembley against Crook Town was in attendance and looked as lively as ever.

The unassuming Dave Marshall was instantly recognisable and we chatted about the teams of the 1950s and he told me of the £20 bonus that each player had received for winning the cup for the third year in succession in 1957. In his view, Crook were the next best team to Bishop Auckland.

Corbett Cresswell was there, smoking away on his filter-tipped cigarettes. The pair of us chatted about football and other sports, in the process discovering that we shared a similar interest, namely horse racing. Corbett was ex-RAF as was Ron Fryer, who still retains his boyhood looks. Another ex-RAF serviceman was Warren Bradley, who recently underwent a quadruple heart by-pass operation and is now enjoying his retirement after a career in teaching.

174

The Brotherhood

Of the younger brigade, there was Michael Barker and George Siddle, who after playing for Bishop had both played for Queen's Park, Tommy Stewart's old club. Billy Roughley and pipe-smoking Mike Greenwood, an ex-England international, completed the group.

(Les Dixon and Bert Childs were unable to attend. It is believed that Seamus O'Connell now lives in Spain but could not be contacted.)

Passing years have seen their number decrease. Absentees included 'The Twin Towers', Bobby Hardisty and Jimmy Nimmins, as well as Benny Edwards. I would like to think that there is some Elysian Field where they are showing their skills. Also there will be three goalkeepers, Jack Washington, Bill White and Harry Sharratt, all called to play there in 2002. And watching them as a spectator will be Dad, who had died ten years earlier.

It was an honour and a pleasure to have been in such company.

APPENDIX

The following pages give the major achievements of Bishop Auckland Football Club from season 1945-46 to season 1956-57. League tables are given in the traditional style but with the additional end columns showing Bishop Auckland results against each team, home and away, for that season.

1945-46

Northern League Table

	P	W	D	L	F	A	Pts	H	A
Stanley United	22	20	0	2	101	29	40	5-3	1-4
South Bank	22	16	1	5	61	41	33	4-1	1-5
Billingham Synthonia	22	13	0	9	70	57	26	9-3	1-2
Shildon	22	12	2	8	57	48	26	2-0	1-2
Bishop Auckland	**22**	**12**	**1**	**9**	**83**	**46**	**25**	-	-
Evenwood Town	22	9	3	10	45	57	21	2-3	1-2
Tow Law Town	22	8	4	10	55	59	20	5-0	2-3
Willington	22	7	5	10	37	52	19	1-1	2-4
Brandon Welfare	22	7	5	10	42	64	19	5-2	3-4
Crook Col. Welfare	22	7	2	13	54	60	16	4-0	7-3
Ferryhill Athletic	22	5	3	14	44	76	13	8-0	3-2
West Auckland Town	22	2	2	18	29	89	6	11-2	5-0

FA Amateur Cup
R1 Ferguson Pailin (home) 7-1
R2 Stanley United (home) 3-0
R3 South Bank (away) 3-1
R4 Moor Green (home) 4-1
SF Walthamstow Avenue (Darlington) 2-1
F Barnet (Chelsea) 2-3

FA Cup
R1 1st leg Willington (away) 5-0
2nd leg (home) 0-2
R2 1st leg York City (home) 1-2
2nd leg (away) 0-3

Northern Football League Challenge Cup Final
Crook Town 1-2

Other Competitions
Winners: **Durham Benevolent Bowl**
Murton Colliery Welfare 2-1

1946-47

Northern League Table

	P	W	D	L	F	A	Pts	H	A
Bishop Auckland*	26	18	2	6	81	47	38	-	-
Crook Col. Welfare	26	18	2	6	85	50	38	3-5	2-0
Stanley United	26	15	5	6	81	49	35	3-2	1-2
Shildon	26	15	5	6	72	45	35	1-1	1-4
Willington	26	13	5	8	69	53	31	2-0	1-3
Ferryhill Athletic	26	13	3	10	77	66	29	3-0	3-2
Evenwood Town	26	10	6	10	65	72	26	1-3	6-3
Heaton Stannington	26	11	2	13	58	68	24	5-1	3-2
Billingham Synthonia	26	9	3	14	58	60	21	4-1	2-1
Tow Law Town	26	9	3	14	59	68	21	6-2	5-2
West Auckland Town	26	7	5	14	39	62	19	2-1	2-0
South Bank	26	7	4	15	65	61	18	5-4	2-2
Whitby Town	26	7	4	15	46	75	18	2-0	2-5
Brandon Welfare	26	4	3	19	38	117	11	7-1	7-0

*Won title in play-off

FA Amateur Cup

R1 Shildon (away) 1-1
(home) 4-2
R2 Marine Crosby (home) 4-0
R3 Willington (away) 6-1
R4 Bromley (home) 5-1
SF Wimbledon (Dulwich) 2-4

FA Cup

R1 Rochdale (away) 1-6

1947-48

Northern League Table

	P	W	D	L	F	A	Pts	H	A
Ferryhill Athletic	26	20	4	2	90	40	44	1-2	3-2
Bishop Auckland	**26**	**17**	**3**	**6**	**90**	**41**	**37**	-	-
South Bank	26	13	7	6	61	40	33	4-1	0-1
Shildon	26	15	0	11	52	51	30	6-2	0-1
Evenwood Town	26	12	5	9	53	44	29	2-2	1-3
Stanley United	26	10	7	9	60	62	27	3-1	1-2
Tow Law Town	26	12	3	11	58	61	27	3-2	5-1
Crook Col. Welfare	26	12	3	11	53	58	27	4-1	1-5
Willington	26	11	3	12	53	54	25	4-1	3-0
West Auckland Town	26	8	5	13	57	73	21	2-1	5-2
E. Tanfield Col. Welf.	26	7	5	14	52	67	19	6-1	4-1
Whitby Town	26	8	3	15	52	76	19	4-3	9-2
Heaton Stannington	26	4	7	15	47	66	15	1-1	1-1
Billingham Synthonia	26	5	1	20	51	96	11	7-1	10-1

FA Amateur Cup
R1 Penrith (home) 7-3
R2 Ferryhill Athletic (away) 6-0
R3 Norton Woodseats (home) 5-0
R4 Wycombe Wanderers (home) 6-2
SF Leytonstone (Middlesbrough) 0-5

FA Cup
4Q North Shields (home) 3-2
R1 Chester City (away) 1-3

Other Competitions
Finalists: **Durham Benevolent Bowl**
Spennymoor United 1-2

1948-49

Northern League Table

	P	W	D	L	F	A	Pts	H	A
Evenwood Town	26	19	4	3	64	33	42	3-2	0-2
Bishop Auckland	**26**	**19**	**3**	**4**	**79**	**38**	**41**	-	-
Billingham Synthonia	26	16	5	5	69	41	37	3-1	2-1
Ferryhill Athletic	26	14	3	9	53	49	31	3-2	1-2
Willington	26	13	4	9	79	55	30	4-1	2-7
Penrith	26	14	1	11	66	60	29	6-3	1-2
Crook Col. Welfare	26	9	7	10	61	66	25	1-0	3-3
South Bank	26	9	6	11	54	63	24	4-0	2-2
Shildon	26	9	5	12	59	57	23	5-1	1-0
West Auckland Town	26	11	1	14	53	63	23	3-1	2-1
Stanley United	26	7	4	15	47	66	18	3-1	1-1
Whitby Town	26	7	3	16	39	68	17	6-0	3-1
Tow Law Town	26	4	5	17	52	79	13	9-2	4-2
Heaton Stannington	26	3	5	18	41	78	11	4-0	3-0

FA Amateur Cup
R1 Shildon (away) 2-3

FA Cup
4Q Scarborough (away)* 0-3
(home) 0-3

* Game ordered to be replayed at Kingsway following protest by Bishop Auckland.

1949-50

Northern League Table

	P	W	D	L	F	A	Pts	H	A
Bishop Auckland	**26**	**21**	**1**	**4**	**81**	**28**	**43**	-	-
Billingham Synthonia	26	17	3	6	77	46	37	1-1	3-4
Whitby Town	26	16	3	7	67	42	35	2-1	1-0
Willington	26	16	1	9	76	46	33	0-2	2-1
Evenwood Town	26	14	2	10	70	59	30	1-2	2-1
Tow Law Town	26	12	4	10	63	52	28	1-0	0-3
Ferryhill Athletic	26	11	5	10	64	67	27	4-0	4-2
Shildon	26	10	5	11	56	52	25	3-1	3-1
Crook Town	26	10	3	13	61	58	23	4-0	4-0
Penrith	26	9	2	15	54	74	20	6-0	3-2
South Bank	26	8	3	15	46	78	19	5-3	3-1
West Auckland Town	26	8	2	16	45	89	18	4-0	4-0
Stanley United	26	5	6	15	46	74	16	4-1	4-2
Heaton Stannington	26	4	2	20	34	75	10	11-0	2-0

FA Amateur Cup
R1 South Bank (away) 2-0
R2 Ilford (home) . . . . .3-2 aet
R3 Moor Green (home) 3-1
R4 Finchley (away) 3-1
SF Wycombe Wanderers (Brentford) 2-1
F Willington (Wembley) 0-4

FA Cup
4Q Stockton (away) 0-7

Northern Football League Challenge Cup Final
Shildon 3-1

Other Competitions
Winners: **Durham Benevolent Bowl**
Ushaw Moor 3-1
Winners: **Bishop Auckland Hospital Bowl**

1950-51

Northern League Table

	P	W	D	L	F	A	Pts	H	A
Bishop Auckland	**26**	**20**	**2**	**4**	**101**	**34**	**42**	-	-
Billingham Synthonia	26	17	3	6	70	24	37	2-1	0-3
Whitby Town	26	15	6	5	75	42	36	3-1	2-2
Willington	26	14	4	8	81	46	32	0-0	3-2
Evenwood Town*	26	14	3	9	76	58	29	6-3	2-0
Shildon	26	13	3	10	57	49	29	7-1	4-3
Crook Town	26	12	2	12	56	66	26	1-3	3-0
South Bank	26	11	2	13	54	58	24	2-1	2-0
Stanley United	26	9	4	13	60	64	22	6-0	5-1
Ferryhill Athletic	26	9	3	14	53	79	21	2-1	4-1
Penrith	26	7	7	12	43	76	21	8-3	9-0
Heaton Stannington	26	9	2	15	48	68	20	5-2	9-1
Tow Law Town	26	4	4	18	41	95	12	6-0	4-1
West Auckland Town	26	4	3	19	31	87	11	2-3	5-0

*2 points deducted for playing unregistered player

FA Amateur Cup

R1 Evenwood Town (away) 2-0
R2 Shildon (home) 3-1
R3 Whitby Town (home) 7-2
R4 Walton and Hersham (home) 2-2
(away) 4-1
SF Bromley (Leeds) 3-2
F Pegasus (Wembley) 1-2

FA Cup

4Q Horden Colliery Welfare (home) 2-0
R1 York City (home) 2-2
(away) 1-2

Northern Football League Challenge Cup Final

Ferryhill Athletic 6-2

Other Competitions

Finalists: **Durham County Challenge Cup**
Stockton 0-3

1951-52

Northern League Table

	P	W	D	L	F	A	Pts	H	A
Bishop Auckland	**26**	**20**	**5**	**1**	**89**	**26**	**45**	-	-
Billingham Synthonia	26	17	3	6	67	35	37	4-1	4-3
Willington	26	17	2	7	79	49	36	2-1	0-0
Tow Law Town	26	16	1	9	68	45	33	3-2	3-0
Whitby Town	26	12	6	8	71	49	30	4-4	3-0
South Bank	26	12	5	9	64	68	29	7-1	1-0
Evenwood Town	26	10	7	9	53	47	27	2-2	3-2
Ferryhill Athletic	26	10	6	10	60	67	26	4-0	1-1
Crook Town	26	9	6	11	49	59	24	2-2	2-1
Shildon	26	9	3	14	54	62	21	2-0	4-2
West Auckland Town	26	7	4	15	43	61	18	4-1	4-1
Heaton Stannington	26	8	2	16	55	87	18	6-0	4-0
Stanley United	26	7	1	18	38	81	15	9-0	3-0
Penrith	26	1	3	22	32	86	5	6-1	3-0

FA Amateur Cup

R1 Rawmarsh Welfare (away) 5-1
R2 Hendon (away) 1-1
(home) 5-1
R3 Walton and Hersham (home) 1-3

FA Cup

4Q Blyth Spartans (away) 1-2

Other Competitions

Winners: **Durham County Challenge Cup**
West Stanley 2-0
Winners: **Durham Benevolent Bowl**
Willington 4-2
Winners: **Bishop Auckland Nursing Cup**
Winners: **Durham Hospital Cup**
Winners: **Guernsey Victory Cup** (Channel Islands)

1952-53

Northern League Table

	P	W	D	L	F	A	Pts	H	A
Crook Town	26	19	5	2	106	38	43	4-1	7-1
Bishop Auckland	**26**	**14**	**9**	**3**	**79**	**38**	**37**	-	-
Whitby Town	26	15	5	6	71	45	35	1-0	0-2
Shildon	26	12	9	5	60	40	33	1-3	1-1
Tow Law Town	26	13	5	8	56	54	31	10-0	1-1
Ferryhill Athletic	26	11	7	8	51	43	29	3-1	3-3
Billingham Synthonia	26	11	6	9	59	56	28	4-1	2-0
Willington	26	10	6	10	53	57	26	4-3	4-1
Penrith	26	9	7	10	58	64	25	4-1	2-2
Evenwood Town	26	6	8	12	50	56	20	1-1	2-2
Stanley United	26	8	2	16	49	72	18	2-2	1-1
Durham City	26	7	4	15	41	69	18	4-0	2-2
West Auckland Town	26	4	5	17	37	72	13	4-1	3-1
South Bank	26	2	4	20	37	103	8	7-0	8-1

FA Amateur Cup
R1 Shildon (away) 7-2
R2 Southall (away) 0-2

FA Cup
4Q Spennymoor United (away) .1-1
(home) 2-1
R1 Selby Town (away) 5-1
R2 Coventry City (home) 1-4

Other Competitions
Winners: **Durham Benevolent Bowl**
Willington 4-2
Winners: **Bishop Auckland Hospital Cup**
Finalists: **Durham County Amateur Cup**

1953-54

Northern League Table

	P	W	D	L	F	A	Pts	H	A
Bishop Auckland	26	19	4	3	97	34	42	-	-
Crook Town	26	19	2	5	95	38	40	4-1	3-1
Ferryhill Athletic	26	17	5	4	56	27	39	2-2	2-2
Billingham Synthonia	26	15	2	9	61	44	32	6-2	0-2
West Auckland Town	26	15	2	9	58	48	32	2-4	0-1
Durham City	26	15	2	9	62	52	32	1-0	1-0
Whitby Town	26	9	6	11	58	56	24	4-3	2-1
Willington	26	11	1	14	48	51	23	1-0	1-1
Evenwood Town	26	9	3	14	57	65	21	2-0	1-1
Tow Law Town	26	10	0	16	43	64	20	6-1	4-0
Penrith	26	8	1	17	39	81	17	12-0	6-2
Shildon*	26	11	2	13	74	68	16	3-2	6-2
Stanley United	26	3	5	18	33	84	11	6-0	8-3
South Bank	26	3	1	22	36	105	7	5-1	9-2

*8 points deducted for fielding unregistered player.

FA Amateur Cup
R1 ICI (away) 6-0
R2 Ware (home) 6-1
R3 Hallam (home) 5-0
R4 Hounslow Town (home) 4-2
SF Briggs Sports (Newcastle) 5-1
F Crook Town (Wembley) ....2-2 aet
(Newcastle) ....2-2 aet
(Middlesbrough) 0-1

FA Cup
4Q Spennymoor United (away) 1-3

Northern Football League Challenge Cup Final
Shildon 4-1

Other Competitions
Finalists: **Durham Benevolent Bowl**
Ferryhill 0-1

1954-55

Northern League Table

	P	W	D	L	F	A	Pts	H	A
Bishop Auckland	**26**	**19**	**3**	**4**	**87**	**44**	**41**	-	-
Crook Town	26	16	2	8	93	40	34	3-2	4-3
Shildon	26	11	8	7	65	47	30	7-0	3-2
Billingham Synthonia	26	12	6	8	62	49	30	3-2	0-5
Evenwood Town	26	12	6	8	67	59	30	2-3	7-3
Stanley United	26	13	4	9	48	64	30	2-0	10-2
Whitby Town	26	10	7	9	65	58	27	3-1	1-1
Ferryhill Athletic	26	9	8	9	58	57	26	3-1	7-1
Willington	26	11	3	12	42	46	25	2-0	3-0
West Auckland Town	26	8	7	11	58	67	23	6-2	4-0
Tow Law Town	26	8	5	13	45	72	21	1-1	7-2
South Bank	26	5	7	14	36	63	17	0-0	0-1
Penrith	26	5	6	15	38	66	16	3-1	2-1
Durham City	26	4	6	16	47	79	14	7-3	3-1

FA Amateur Cup

R1 Stork (away) 3-1
R2 Erith and Belvedere (home) 5-0
R3 Kingstonian (away) 12-3
R4 Finchley (home) 1-1
(away) 3-1
SF Wycombe Wanderers (Doncaster) .1-0
F Hendon (Wembley) 2-0

FA Cup

R1 Kettering Town (home) 5-1
R2 Crystal Palace (away) 4-2
R3 Ipswich Town (away) 2-2
(home) 3-0
R4 York City Home) 1-3

Northern Football League Challenge Cup Final

Crook Town 6-0

Other Competitions

Winners: **Auckland Nursing Cup**
Finalists: **Durham County Challenge Cup**
Crook Town 0-6

1955-56

Northern League Table

	P	W	D	L	F	A	Pts	H	A
Bishop Auckland	26	18	2	6	85	54	38	-	-
Crook Town	26	17	3	6	92	44	37	2-5	1-12
Durham City	26	17	1	8	82	40	35	2-1	4-3
South Bank	26	12	6	8	51	37	30	1-2	0-3
Evenwood Town	26	12	5	9	58	49	29	5-0	2-1
West Auckland Town	26	13	2	11	66	51	28	5-1	0-3
Billingham Synthonia	26	12	3	11	58	63	27	8-1	4-2
Shildon	26	10	6	10	70	52	26	4-2	1-1
Willington	26	10	4	12	58	71	24	6-2	5-1
Stanley United	26	9	6	11	53	66	24	4-2	3-0
Ferryhill Athletic	26	8	5	13	42	62	21	3-2	1-3
Tow Law Town	26	6	7	13	55	80	19	7-1	3-2
Penrith	26	6	3	17	38	81	15	3-0	5-1
Whitby Town	26	4	3	19	39	97	11	4-1	2-2

FA Amateur Cup
R1 Crook Town (home) 1-1
(away) . . . . .4-3 aet
R2 Gedling Colliery (away) 4-1
R3 Ferryhill Athletic (away) 1-0
R4 Finchley (away) 4-0
SF Kingstonian (Newcastle) 5-1
F Corinthian Casuals (Wembley) . . . . .1-1 aet
(Middlesbrough) 4-1

FA Cup
R1 Durham City (home) 3-1
R2 Scunthorpe United (home) 0-0
(away) 0-2

Northern Football League Challenge Cup Final
South Bank 0-2

Other Competitions
Winners: **Durham County Challenge Cup**
West Auckland 3-2
Winners: **Lord Douglas Bowl** (Isle of Man)

1956-57

Northern League Table

	P	W	D	L	F	A	Pts	H	A
Billingham Synthonia	26	20	2	4	66	37	42	3-0	0-2
West Auckland	26	16	2	8	79	52	34	3-3	1-4
Bishop Auckland	**26**	**13**	**7**	**6**	**76**	**48**	**33**	-	-
Ferryhill Athletic	26	14	4	8	63	48	32	3-1	1-1
Willington	26	13	6	7	60	48	32	2-5	3-0
Crook Town	26	13	5	8	67	62	31	5-1	3-1
Durham City	26	12	5	9	58	50	29	0-0	6-0
Shildon	26	11	3	12	60	56	25	7-2	3-0
Stanley United	26	9	6	11	48	54	24	2-1	1-1
Evenwood Town	26	8	5	13	58	78	21	3-2	4-5
Penrith	26	8	3	15	41	65	19	2-2	3-2
South Bank	26	8	2	16	49	57	18	1-1	1-5
Whitby Town	26	5	4	17	54	84	14	7-2	7-1
Tow Law Town	26	3	4	19	37	77	10	2-2	4-1

FA Amateur Cup

R1 Norton Woodseats (home) 1-0
R2 Gedling Colliery (home) 5-1
R3 Briggs Sports (away) 1-0
R4 Crook Town (away) 2-2
(home) 2-0
SF Hayes (Newcastle) 2-0
F Wycombe Wanderers (Wembley) 3-1

FA Cup

R1 Tranmere Rovers (home) 2-1
R2 Rhyl (away) 1-3

Other Competitions

Winners: **Lord Douglas Bowl** (Isle of Man)
Finalists: **Durham County Challenge Cup**
Hartlepool United Reserves 0-5
Champions: **Auckland and District League**
Winners: **Auckland and District League Cup**

ACKNOWLEDGEMENTS

I would like to thank my wife Jacqueline, and my granddaughter Fuchsia, for the help, support and encouragement that they have given me in producing this work.

I would also like to thank the following people, who have generously provided me with the material that forms the basis of this book, and without whose help this work may never have been completed.

Margaret Adamthwaite
Barry and Eileen Adamthwaite
Mike Amos (*Northern Echo*)
Norman Ayton
BBC
Paul Bailey
Mike Barker (ex-Bishop Auckland Football Club)
John Barnwell (ex-Bishop Auckland)
Keith Belton
Kimberley Bennett (Darlington Library)
Warren Bradley (ex-Bishop Auckland Football Club)
Bert Childs (ex-Bishop Auckland Football Club)
Peter Cororan
John Cowey
Corbett Cresswell (ex-Bishop Auckland Football Club)
Les Dixon (ex-Bishop Auckland Football Club)
Football Club Data Base
Chris Foote Wood
Ron Fryer (ex-Bishop Auckland Football Club)
Joe and Margaret Gelson
Geoff Greetham (Timeform Organization)
Mike Greenwood (ex-Bishop Auckland Football Club)
Margaret Hassell
Jenny Hayball
Gill Holloway
Graham Hughes (Wolverhampton Wanderers Football Club)
Brian Hunt
Sean Hunter

189

Glory Days

David Illingworth
Carol Innes
Terry Jackson (Bishop Auckland Football Club)
Len Langford (ex-Bishop Auckland Football Club)
Derek Lewin (ex-Bishop Auckland Football Club)
Lawrie McMenemy
Dave Marshall (ex-Bishop Auckland Football Club)
Middlesbrough Evening Gazette
Brian Myers (Darlington Library)
Newcastle Journal Newspaper
Northern Echo Newspaper
Ray Oliver (ex-Bishop Auckland Football Club)
Pathe News
Harry Pearson
Chris Pitt
Graham Pratt (*Newcastle Journal*)
Sir Bobby Robson
Christine Roe (Darlington Library)
Julie Roe
Billy Roughley (ex-Bishop Auckland Football Club)
Scunthorpe United Football Club
Kath Sewell
Brenda Sherit (Darlington Library)
George Siddle (ex-Bishop Auckland Football Club)
Jackie Snowdon (ex-Willington Football Club)
Dave Snowdon
Bruce Springsteen Music and Associates
Margaret and Keith Stables
Bob Thursby (ex-Bishop Auckland Football Club)
Nigel Townsend (Timeform Organization)
Brian Turner
Tyne and Wear Archive Service
Unknown Witton Albion supporter who gave me the idea for this work
Neil Walmesley
Bobby Watson (ex-Bishop Auckland Football Club)
Christine Watson (*Northern Echo*)
Katherine Williamson (Darlington Library)
Harry Young (ex-Bishop Auckland Football Club)
Zomba Music Publishers

BIBLIOGRAPHY

The author acknowledges the following publications in the production of this work:

A Bevin Boy Remembers
by Gill Holloway

Association Football Volumes 1-4
edited by A H Fabian and Geoffrey Green

Football: The Amateur Game
by W T D Reed

History of the FA Amateur Cup
by Bob Barton

Kings Of Amateur Soccer
by Chris Foote Wood

Non-League Football
by Bob Barton

Northern Goalfields Revisited
by Brian Hunt

The Bishops
by W T D Reed

The Far Corner
by Harry Pearson

The King
by Denis Law